Magnificat®

PROCLAIMS

Thank you dear priests - your yes brings life to all of us - We love you! We pray for you. With love, Doris, Debbie, Carolyn, Sarah, Diane + Susan

HOLY ORDERS

A Collection of Inspiring Clergy Testimonies

Magnificat is an obedient daughter of the Church and will defer to the judgment of the Holy See regarding private revelations, apparitions, and other such matters. Until then, the Second Vatican Council urges us to discern the Spirit in the case of such extraordinary graces [*Lumen Gentium* 12], which means being neither gullible or incredulous, but subjecting them to all relevant theological and human tests of credibility. Some of these experiences may help one have a closer walk with the Lord, providing they are not contrary to the faith and morals of the Church.

Magnificat®

PROCLAIMS

HOLY ORDERS

A Collection of Inspiring Clergy Testimonies

Magnificat® Central Service Team, Inc.
Metairie, LA

DEDICATION

This book is dedicated to St. Joseph and Our Blessed Mother Mary, who were entrusted with raising Jesus. We would also like to recognize the parents (living and deceased) of the Magnificat Central Service Team and the contributing authors of this book:

Adlai and Dolores Barber

Michael and Julia O'Flynn Barry

John and Elma DiBacco DePrisco (Bates)

Donald R. and LaChita G. Calloway

Giuseppe and Lavinia Giovannini Cantalamessa

Joseph Anthony and Rina Lucia Marino Cerulli

Harold "Babe" and Sarah Brown Cohen

Leon and Mary Cordileone

Patrick and Lena Crowley

Arthur and Anne Doktorczyk

Joseph and Helen Barrett Clark (Ford)

Oswald Harold and Sarah Elizabeth Gore Hampsch

Galip and Adele Jacobs

Alex C. and Margaret V. Jones Sr.

Francis and Caroline Weeks (MacInnis)

Frank and Ouida Montague

Joseph Sau Van Nguyen and Teresa Kim Anh Thi Nguyen

Joseph Nhuan Van Vu and Hai Thi Le

Ken Burmeister and Janice Brogna (Rodriguez-Torres)

Gilbert and Evelyn Jones Scarnecchia (Ross)

John James and Catherine Scallon

Casmer and Monica Zimmerman Skonezny

Carlo and Anna Struzzo

Thái Văn Minh and Nguyễn Thi Kim Anh

Leon and Lynn Toups

Clarence and Myrtle Kelly (Wilson)

Holy Orders is the sacrament through which the mission entrusted by Christ to His apostles continues to be exercised in the Church until the end of time: thus, it is the sacrament of apostolic ministry. It includes three degrees: episcopate [bishops], presbyterate [priests], and diaconate [deacons]. *Catechism of the Catholic Church* (CCC 1536)

Clergy is the group or body of ordained persons in a religion, as distinguished from the laity.

CONTENTS

FOREWORD

The Ministry of Magnificat to Catholic Women is indeed a blessing to our church. Members of Magnificat have offered spiritual support to so many and have touched the heart of God's people. We are indeed richly blessed by this special ministry to women.

The following pages are filled with testimonies of clergy from around the world who have experienced God's grace in their lives. We are grateful for those who have given support to Magnificat and participate in their ministry. Furthermore, many clergy have been personally blessed by this ministry.

May God continue to help us, like Mary, to give a whole-hearted "yes" to all He asks of us.

Wishing you God's blessings, I am
Sincerely in Christ,

Most Reverend Gregory M. Aymond
Archbishop of New Orleans

FOREWORD

Mary said, *"My soul proclaims the greatness of the Lord"* (Luke 1:46).

From the beginning of Magnificat, A Ministry to Catholic Women, October 7, 1981, the women of Magnificat have had a reverential love and appreciation for the Holy Eucharist and therefore the priesthood. This is true because we believe this ministry was begun and formed by Mary, Mother of Jesus, the High Priest! Over the years we have continued to love and pray for the priesthood and the deacons, priests, and bishops who have remained close to us, especially the Spiritual Advisor of each of our Chapters.

In earlier years, I have been blessed to travel to visit many of our Chapters, and to meet their Spiritual Advisor and on behalf of the ministry to thank him for his dedication and service to the Chapter. One after another responded with appreciation in words of gratitude for what they had received from their commitment to Magnificat. Many said that their priesthood had been nurtured and enriched through the women in Magnificat.

It has been my joy, as well as an honor and privilege, to preview the testimonies of the men in this book who heard the voice of the Lord say, "Come, follow Me." In obedience to that call, they left everything and followed Him in the many and varied paths the Holy Spirit led them. My heart burned as I read their anointed testimonies!

It is my strong belief that this book will be used as an instrument of grace to inspire, encourage, and bless all of us, lay men and women, those who are preparing for the priesthood, and all those who are serving in the Church today.

We fervently pray that this book will serve to honor the priesthood as well as inspire others to follow in their path. May we all echo Our Lady's words in proclaiming the greatness of the Lord!

Marilyn Quirk
Magnificat, Founding Coordinator

PREFACE

 has been proclaiming the greatness of the Lord since 1981. This international apostolate started from humble beginnings in New Orleans, LA. On October 7, Feast of the Holy Rosary, the first Magnificat Meal was held.

The *Magnificat* (Luke 1:46–55) is the great hymn of praise that Mary prayed while visiting Elizabeth. Both women had been deeply touched by God. Elizabeth was bearing a long-awaited child; Mary was carrying within her womb the very Son of God. They came together to help one another, to speak of God's action in their lives, to sing, to pray, to share a common table, and to be strengthened for all that was to come.

Magnificat came into being out of a desire to share with all Catholic women the fruit we have experienced through the Catholic Charismatic Renewal. We describe this fruit as:

- a deeper knowledge and love of Jesus Christ
- an experience of the release of the power of the Holy Spirit
- an appreciation and love for Mary, our Mother and Model
- an appreciation and love for the Catholic Church

Magnificat Meals are hosted by local Chapters worldwide about every three months on or around a feast day of Mary, to whom we consecrate this ministry in a special way. We call our Meals "Magnificat" because, like Mary and Elizabeth, we want to come together in God's presence. May we too recognize what God has already done in us and call forth in each other a new openness to the power of His Spirit in our lives.

Magnificat® Central Service Team, Inc.
1629 Metairie Road—Suite 3, Metairie, LA 70005-3926
Tel: (504) 828-MARY [6279]
magnificatcst@aol.com ❖ www.magnificat-ministry.org

Like us on Facebook at: MagnificatMinistry

Follow us on Twitter at: MagnificatCST

ACKNOWLEDGMENTS

We want to thank everyone for your prayers to bring this second book in the Magnificat Proclaims series to fruition! In addition to all of our wonderful contributing authors, there have been many who have played a role in this endeavor. A number of generous souls have contributed their time, talent, and/or treasure. We would like to begin by thanking our media angel, Felice Gerwitz, for her guidance throughout the self-publishing process and the countless hours she spent transforming these oral presentations into a prose format. Many of the testimonies were transcribed from the recorded Chapter Meal CDs primarily by the amazing Virginia Shaffer with an assist from Peggy Forlenza. Marilyn Quirk was a tremendous help with the review process, while Lenora Grimaud and Paulette Renaudin contributed their writing skills. Marge Sinicropi offered her assistance with numerous clerical projects. We were blessed to have Susan Marlow professionally edit the work, and Susan Spann provided legal counsel. It is said a picture is worth a thousand words, so we are very grateful to Fr. Omar for offering us his helpful hands and graphic designer, Cathy Behrens, who created the beautiful book cover and layout.

Although it will be difficult to mention everyone who had a part in bringing *Magnificat Proclaims—Holy Orders* to reality, we do want you to know how much your support has meant to us. We also want to express our gratitude to the Magnificat Chapters worldwide for their commitment to magnify the Lord, the Magnificat Central Service Team for their confidence in this undertaking, and the Communications Ministry for their role in spearheading this anointed mission. To God be the glory!

INTRODUCTION

This second book in our Magnificat Proclaims series features clergy who have shared their testimony at a Magnificat Meal. You will read how some of the Magnificat Spiritual Advisors and others received their call to the priesthood. God has used them in many ways to bless this ministry. These are their stories—honest and real.

The paths to a priestly vocation are as varied as the stars in the sky. Some of them received their call as children and "played Mass" during their youth. Some men went on pilgrimage and heard their call from Jesus and/or Mary. Some men started the seminary, quit to get married, and then, after their wife passed away, completed their studies to become priests. Others heard the call but were unable to respond right away due to life's circumstances. Every vocation entails a journey of faith, which moves a man away from his own will and moves him toward God's will in his life.

The journey to ordination is never easy. The "scenic routes" are full of mystery, from times of darkness to light, with unexpected hardships to mountain-top experiences. Each situation gives them the "green light" to move toward ordination. These stories are being shared with us by courageous men who chose to answer the call. Scripture tells us how powerful and life changing testimonies are in Revelations 12:11: "They conquered him [devil] by the blood of the Lamb and by the word of their testimony."

The Magnificat Ministry, dedicated to Our Lady, has realized the need to intercede for and support all priests and most especially our Chapter's Spiritual Advisors. Therefore, Magnificat's 5th objective is to imitate Mary through spiritual adoption of priests and seminarians. We hope you will enjoy reading how the Holy Spirit has worked in their lives and you will begin to join us in prayer for our beloved priests.

We thank all of our contributing authors for sharing their stories of what God has done. Each testimony continues to tell the "Good News" of our hope and faith in Jesus Christ, Our Lord. As you read *Magnificat Proclaims—Holy Orders*, we trust you will sense the heavenly anointing on this book and be blessed!

Magnificat Central Service Team
Kathy MacInnis, Diane Bates, Sara Ford,
Kim Rodriguez-Torres, Donna Ross, Mary Wilson

Bishop Michael C. Barber, S.J.

───────◇◇◇◇◇───────

This is not about me.

My vocation is all about God. To see what happens when a ministry is built around a person and not around God, one need only look at Mars Hill Church in Seattle, Washington. It was a famous church with a famous pastor, also called "the cussing pastor." He was rough and tough, and his church grew massively. This pastor had so many people attending his church that they opened branch churches in other areas and erected screens to beam his sermon to all the churches at the same time.

Mars Hill has since collapsed. An article in *The Wall Street Journal* stated, "That's what happens when you build a ministry around yourself and not around God." That is why this scripture sums up my journey: "Not to us, Lord, not to us but to your name give the glory" (Psalms 115:1).

St. John the Baptist said, "He must increase and I must decrease" (John 3:30). In this context I share my vocation, the marvels the Lord has worked for me, and the things God has done in my life. Perhaps my story will help you reflect on your own life and see how God has worked. If you didn't see God present before—know He was there.

Three Bible verses have helped me throughout my life. The first is from the Old Testament. "Cast your cares upon the Lord and He will support you" (Psalms 55:22). During some of the most difficult times in my life I opened the Bible to this verse, and it spoke to me.

The second verse reads like this: "Unless you take up your cross and follow me, you cannot be my disciple" (Matthew 16:24). People ask, "What is that necklace you are wearing?" It is not a necklace. It is my cross, the pectoral cross. Our Lord said, "Take up your cross and follow Me." A bishop is supposed to wear it at all times.

The third verse contains the last words Jesus spoke before He ascended. "Lo, I am with you all days, even until the end of the world" (Matt. 28:20). It's okay, "I am with you all days." These verses are woven into my story.

My family was typical. My mother was from San Francisco, and my father came from Oakland. All the members of my family were born in San Francisco or Oakland except me. Mom and Dad were living in San

Francisco. My dad, an insurance salesman, was asked to take a special assignment in Salt Lake City for one year during the early 1950s. As Mom prepared to give birth, she applied to the Catholic hospital, but it was full of Mormons because this hospital was air conditioned. So I was born in Latter Day Saints Hospital. God has a great sense of humor! It is only one block from the temple in Temple Square.

We moved back to San Francisco within a few months of my birth, and I was baptized in Mission Dolores. The old mission still stands, but beside it is a new church. All the baptisms were performed in the old mission using the same font that Fr. Junipero Serra used when he baptized the Indians. The young priest who baptized me was Fr. John Cummins. He is now a bishop.

When I was consecrated as bishop, Bishop Cummins was in attendance. Many of the other bishops asked, "Do you remember him?"

I thought, *Really? How could he possibly remember me with the hundreds of babies he baptized?*

He simply said, "No."

Attending Mass at Mission Dolores as a toddler, looking up at the altar and the curtains behind the altar, and sitting on the kneeler are all cherished first memories for me. The kneeler made a nice chair for a toddler. Often I'd stand up on the pew. These memories are filled with awe, mystery, reverence, and attraction for the Mass, the church, and the altar. It was a wonderful and mysterious place. Everything there was attractive to me.

We moved to Novato in Marin County, as many people did in the '50s, and I was enrolled in Our Lady of Loreto School. The church was under construction, and I made my first Holy Communion in the parish hall, which was being used as the church. I made my first Confession there as well.

I remember school as a time of fun and wonderment. I enjoyed the nuns who taught me about the Catholic faith. They were Ursulines from Santa Rosa and very attractive, like magnets. In those days the nuns wore full habits, and the Mass was in Latin. There was an attraction to the faith. An air of mystery surrounded it.

Much later I learned the vocabulary associated to this feeling: *Domus Dei, et Porta Coeli.* "This is the House of God. This is the Gate of Heaven." The altar and the sanctuary are a place where earth and heaven meet. Like the top of the mountain when Moses climbed up and the clouds came down, earth and heaven meet.

When it was time for me to attend high school, we moved to Sacramento. It was there that we faced difficulty, our first "crosses" as a family. My father lost his job, we defaulted on the loan for our house, and our house was repossessed. We had to move out and find someplace else to live.

This was a time of great trial, especially for my mother. Mom and Dad were not especially religious. Dad only went to Mass on Christmas and Easter, but he sent us to Catholic school. Mom took us to Mass every Sunday, but she wasn't involved as a volunteer. However, her interior faith was strong. She had an Irish faith, cultural in origin and inherited from her mother. Coming from a large family and living through the Depression, she knew in her gut that God was going to help.

It was that kind of raw faith that came into play when we lost our house and my dad lost his job. I remember Mom saying, "We have to pray for your dad to get a job." To help out, Mother went to work so she could pay our tuition to keep us in Catholic school. She worked in a public school cafeteria washing pots and pans. Then she found another job, which she kept for ten or fifteen years, working in the men's section of a department store. She made minimum wage, but it was enough to keep my two brothers and me in Catholic school.

We had a fantastic pastor at St. John Vianney parish in Sacramento. His name was Monsignor Richard C. Dwyer. In a diocese where seventy-five percent of the priests were Irish, he was one of the few local boys who had been born and raised in Sacramento. He also came from a wealthy family. They owned the Delta shipping lines. We would see trucks on the road with the Delta shipping insignia. If Monsignor Dwyer had not become a priest, he would have become a millionaire and inherited a fortune.

I served Mass for him as an altar boy and learned that his mother was not Catholic. He always prayed for his mother's conversion. I was only eleven or twelve years old, but I will never forget the Mass when I was serving. It was a weekday. During the Mass one of the assistant priests came into the church, right up on the altar where Monsignor Dwyer was preaching. He whispered into the monsignor's ear and left. The monsignor stopped his sermon and started crying at the altar. The priest had whispered, "Your mother has been baptized into the Catholic faith."

That was fantastic news, and it made an impact on my life. Monsignor Dwyer was really tough, so crying was out of the ordinary for him. When he smoked his unfiltered Camel cigarettes, he stepped outside the sacristy. He was big and strong. He owned a ranch in the Sierra foothills, where he raised horses and cattle. He visited the ranch and helped take care of the livestock and split wood.

Every year he took a long horseback ride through the Sierra Nevada with his friends. He slept out, just like the cowboys on TV shows like *Rawhide* or *Bonanza*. He went on a safari to Africa. When he returned, he gave each of us altar boys rings made from the tail of the elephant he had shot on the safari. He had a footstool made from one of the elephant's feet.

Monsignor Dwyer was big in our eyes, and you didn't fool around in the church or make mistakes when serving Mass. He wanted everything done just right. We looked up to him, and he took an interest in my brothers and me. He encouraged us to serve. He invited us to serve funerals. This always allowed us to get out of class. He invited us to come and work on the grounds doing gardening to make some extra money. He was always very encouraging.

In the eighth grade, I was elected president of the altar boys. Monsignor Dwyer gave me the keys to the church so that I could open the church in the mornings at six o'clock before Mass. I set my alarm and rode off in the dark to open the church and turn on the lights before the priest arrived. As an eighth grader, he trusted me. Two years later he trusted my younger brother with the same responsibility.

Monsignor Dwyer had a big influence on me. However, he never pushed. He didn't say things like, "You have got to become a priest." All he did was invite us into the life of the Church and lead by example.

Four years later when I was a senior in high school, it was difficult to tell him that I wanted to become a Jesuit. We laugh about it now, but he wanted me to be a diocesan priest and follow in his footsteps.

I didn't attend the Jesuit high school in Sacramento like my younger brothers. I went to a school run by the Salvatorian fathers. It was a small but good school. I made a lot of friends, acted in plays, and was on the track team. I participated in student government and went to Mass every day. I wanted to go. It was something I felt I had to do, so I got up early. I believed if I attended daily Mass everything would go okay in my life. It was a time to pray for Mom and Dad as well.

I always wanted to be a priest, from the time I was a little boy and even more so when I was in high school. The desire never left me. People ask, "Did you have a conversion experience? When did you know?"

I didn't have a conversion. I always loved God and knew I wanted to be a priest—although I didn't know what kind of priest. I visited the diocesan seminary in Mountain View in the early '70s, and I graduated from high school in 1972. However, I couldn't join because things were in disarray. At that time, some seminarians were smoking pot and not everybody was going to Mass. I said, "I don't want any part of that behavior."

When I was sixteen or seventeen, I sent postcards and letters to all the religious orders I could find: Franciscan, Dominican, Marist, Salesian. I wanted to look at the literature and see if that was someplace I should pursue. Each of the orders wrote back and said, "We got your postcard.

This is a clear sign God is calling you to be a Dominican, Franciscan, etc." Some of the vocation directors showed up at my high school. I got called out of class, and the principal would say, "There is a priest here ready to sign you up."

The Jesuits wrote back and said, "Here is some reading material. Before you write us again, talk to your parish priest and get guidance from him." Their hesitant response made them appear more attractive. I read all the materials the Jesuits sent and felt an inner attraction to the ideals of St. Ignatius, *ad majorem Dei gloriam*, "to the greater glory of God."

I liked the stories of St. Ignatius and St. Francis Xavier going to India and China. I liked the fact that the Jesuits had a long training, twelve years, from the time someone joined until the time he became a priest. I liked the fact that the Jesuits ran high schools. I thought I would like to teach high school—to pass on the faith in that way and coach sports. I liked that the Jesuits were not restricted to any one ministry. Some were in high schools, others in parishes, universities, foreign missions, and retreat houses.

Jesuits said, "Whatever gifts God has given you, we will try and develop those for the service of the Church." The more I looked at the Jesuit literature, the more I liked it. I wrote back and asked, "What more do I need to do?"

"Go talk to Father Joseph King," they told me. "He is a Jesuit priest at Jesuit High School, and he will be your spiritual director and confessor." He was a kind, old priest in his seventies. I visited him regularly.

I was invited to go on a retreat for high school boys who were thinking about joining the Jesuits. It was held in Los Gatos, where the mother house was then and still stands today. A winery next door to the mother house, built in 1888, overlooks the hills and San Jose.

We all gathered while the priest explained the concept of a retreat. This one was silence . . . absolute silence. He said, "I will give you things to mediate upon, and you have your Bible. Go to your room and meditate for an hour. Afterwards, I'll give you a talk."

We did as directed. I took notes on the talk, returned to my room, and slept for an hour. Then the priest said, "Go for another hour and pray." I went back and fell asleep. There were three hours of this a day, and then each of us met with the priest.

"How is your prayer going?" he asked.

"Oh, just fine," I said.

I was embarrassed because I kept falling asleep. However, I was attracted to the teachings. Walking around the grounds I saw the place where so many Jesuits made their novitiate. I visited the chapel where they said their vows. There was—and still is—an austerity to this place. Some of the older Jesuits had retired and were saying Masses or eating in the refectory. I observed all of this and liked every aspect. I enjoyed saying the Rosary while walking around the grounds.

I was elated when I realized God was calling me while I was still in high school. "This is it! Join this one." After I made my decision, I felt at peace. I went to Fr. King, my spiritual director. "I feel God is calling me to be a Jesuit. I would like to apply."

Back then I could apply as a senior in high school to enter the Jesuit novitiate. I went through a long application, was interviewed by five priests, and received a psychological profile and letters of recommendation from school and from my pastor. I prayed and waited for the decision.

A letter arrived some weeks later. I was not accepted. My first reaction was, *Oh, no!* However, the letter was not a "no, never," but instead a "no, not now." They suggested I needed more time to discern, and they recommended college—Loyola University of Los Angeles. A spiritual director would be assigned.

I couldn't afford to go to college, but they knew something about our financial background. God gave me a scholarship through this school that paid the tuition, and God provided a job on campus that covered my room and board. It was unbelievable. I spoke to my spiritual director, the priests, and I made many friends. This school is now called Loyola Marymount. I met many young Jesuit scholastic seminarians at the college. They had just taken their vows and were involved in their first studies, completing their college degrees.

I attended Loyola for a year, but I still felt anxious. I had been directed to attend college for two years before reapplying, but I asked my spiritual director, "Can I apply again? I really want to do this."

He said, "Let's give it a try."

I went through the entire application process again, and this time I was accepted. I remember my joy. I received the letter while I was at home in Sacramento with Mom and Dad. I sat down on the living room carpet, looked at the letter, and realized my whole life had just changed.

I get to join the order of Ignatius and Francis Xavier. Wow!

It was an overwhelming experience. My parents asked, "What does that mean?" After I explained, they said, "Great! Whatever you want to do in life, go do it." I then explained the steps in entering the novitiate, and the finality of entering the Jesuits. I would leave home and be told exactly what to bring, down to the pairs of clothing.

My mother cried the day I left. It is similar to when children get married. Dad told me the night before, "It is going to be real hard on your mom." I didn't realize what it meant for a parent to lose a son or daughter to a convent, or to a novitiate monastery or—for that matter—one who gets married.

I couldn't understand. I was *so* excited. I had waited for this moment for years.

The novitiate was in Santa Barbara, and I wanted to arrive in a way that others might consider strange. I wanted to go on my own to the Greyhound bus depot and walk from the depot up into the hills to the monastery. So that's what I did. I walked up to the front door, and it was really great! On September 7, 1973, I entered the Jesuits. I have been a member ever since.

I talk a lot about "take up your cross and follow Me." When I entered the Jesuits, I was attracted to this kind of discipline, the silence, and the ideals. After I entered, though, a lot of it fell apart. The 1970s was a time of great tension throughout the Church, with ramifications from the Second Vatican Council.

After Vatican II, some people thought we should throw out everything that had come before—you can even see that in Church architecture today. In some churches, statues were removed, or the ceiling painted over that once showed paintings of the Blessed Mother.

Instead of wearing the cassock or even the Roman collar, we wore secular clothes in our novitiate. A few guys hid cassocks in a closet. We were ordered to turn them in, and they were burned. It was a time of interior confusion for me. "God, why did You call me here? You put a carrot in front of me, Lord. Yet, You are taking away all of the things I desire. What does this mean?"

Little by little, Our Lord said, "This is where you are to stay. Don't just trust what you see. Go by your heart."

This really helped my prayer life. Sometimes Mass was said without using the missal. The priest just made up prayers. Sometimes we had Mass outside under a tree with a wine glass and a loaf of bread. This illustrates the turmoil we saw in the Church. Young guys today find it hard to believe the chaos when I share my experiences. Unfortunately, it was not just with the Jesuits but in many other orders and places as well.

I said, "Lord, this is not what I signed up for, but what do You want me to do?" By no means was I a St. Stanislaus guy. I was not the perfect religious. I was lazy and had a mouth. I kept saying, "Lord, what do You want?"

Our Lord told me to stay. "This is it. Trust Me."

I requested and was granted permission to take my perpetual vows in the Jesuits, which I did.

My twelve years of training were rather turbulent—a kind of a spiritual boot camp. It had its ups and downs. Some of the ups—the happiest part of my training—was teaching high school. This is part of the Jesuits training before someone is ordained. They feel if we can survive a classroom of high school boys, we can survive *anything*. I taught sophomores and seniors, and most of the seniors were taller than I was. I had barely started shaving, and there I was saying, "Sit down, you!"

In return, they tested me. High school boys can be difficult, trying to get away with whatever possible. However, it was a wonderful time. When the boys were taking their final exams, I walked up and down the aisle, saying the Rosary to keep them from cheating. I was watching them. "Keep an eye, keep an eye, the radar must be on," I said to myself. Yet, I sensed this was where I needed to be—this was where I was needed. I felt that these were my sheep, and I was the shepherd that our Lord spoke about in the Scriptures.

In addition to teaching, I loved to coach swimming and water polo. We had Mass and prayed before the start of each game, before every water polo match. I gathered the guys off to the side after their warm-up. We put the yellow polo ball in the center, laid hands on the ball, and said the Hail Mary.

At the end of the Hail Mary, I said, "Mary, queen of victory."

"Pray for us!" they responded.

Then I would say, "Queen of defeat."

"Pray for *them!*"

Those were wonderful times.

Thirty other Jesuits taught at the Loyola School in Los Angeles. I was learning to trust God more and more. At the end of the prerequisite three years of teaching—which is typical in diocesan training—a seminarian received one year of pastoral training. As Jesuits we had a three-year minimum requirement, and afterwards I could apply to go to theology. Then there would be a new reevaluation before I received permission for theology.

I was held back and received a letter saying, "You are not approved for theology." I was upset, but I said, "Okay, Lord!" I asked the superior, "Does this mean you want me to leave the order?" I had already taken perpetual vows of poverty, chastity, and obedience.

"No," he said. "We are just not sure about your readiness." He read a list of objections.

"What do you want me to do?" I asked.

"We don't know," he replied. "Do you want to teach here another year?"

"No. If I can't get approved here, I need to go someplace else to receive another chance at another school."

He asked, "Do you have any suggestions?"

"I want to go to a foreign mission's school," I told him. "Somewhere outside the USA to have a fresh start."

The superior agreed and sent me to Xavier High School on Truk Island, part of the Caroline Islands of Micronesia. When the Japanese returned these islands after World War II, they became a United Nations "trust territory," which the U.S. administered.

Truk was a marvelous place—a small island situated near Guam, which was about an hour away. We jokingly called Air Micronesia airlines "Air Maybe." We landed on a gravel runway, but beforehand the pilot said, "We will now pass over the runway to drive away any livestock that may be there, and then we will land."

I arrived at the mission school and was met with a hot climate nearly on the equator. I could barely cover up with a sheet at night, and I sweat all the time. This was the norm. I rode in the back of a pickup truck through the jungle, and up and down the hills. When we arrived at the school on top of a hill, every student lined up to shake my hand. I was touched.

I joined the other Jesuits, who were from New York. I lived and taught there for a year. The students came from Truk, Pohnpei (formally known as Ponape), Marshall Islands, Yap, and Palau. The islands were beautiful, and I had a wonderful experience that year.

I finally received approval to study theology. My first choice of seminary in which to study was Rome. The second choice was Berkeley, and my third choice was Boston.

They sent me to Toronto.

This turned out to be good for me. I now see the pieces and how neatly God arranged things this way and that in my life. Sometimes you figure out why He put you in a specific place or allowed a specific event to happen in your life. Sometimes you only find out when you get to heaven.

God placed me in Toronto because a kind superior was in residence there. When I appeared for my first interview, I said, "Well, I kind of failed, and I was held back. Then I went over to teach in the Islands. I don't know if I'm ever going to be ordained."

He looked at me and said, "I'm here to make you the best priest I possibly can make you."

I thought, *Really? Okay!* I was excited about the possibility.

He supported me throughout my entire three years of training. Happily, I was ordained in San Francisco.

They say ordination day is the happiest day of a mother's life. Mine was fantastic. My brothers made it special by purchasing not only a new dress but also two embroidered hankies for Mom—one for the ordination and one for the first Mass. Sadly, my dad was very sick and could not come to my ordination. He was in the hospital in Sacramento.

I was ordained with six other Jesuits by Archbishop Quinn. After the Mass, the archbishop asked me about my father. I explained he was in the hospital. He said, "Would you like to come into my office and call him?" I did!

The next day, I said my first Mass in Sacramento. Dad was permitted to come to the Mass, but then he went right back to the hospital. He died about a month after I was ordained. I was happy he lived to see me ordained, and I was blessed to say his funeral Mass.

The one thing I had learned in my life—up until the time I was ordained—was that I never got anything I asked for. Everything was always "no." You want to go to Rome? No. How about Toronto? All I could do was be obedient.

Things changed after I was ordained. I asked, "Do you think I could be a missionary in Samoa?" The request was sent to the cardinal. He accepted me, and I was the only Jesuit. The Jesuits were considering opening a mission, and I was sent to see if this was a possibility.

So, my first assignment as a priest was back in the Pacific, in Western Samoa. The trip was incredibly long—five hours from San Francisco to Hawaii, then south for five more hours to the Samoa Islands chain.

Again, the experience was fantastic. I learned the Samoan language. *"Ia fa'atasi le Ali'i ma outou. Ia fa'atasi fo'i ma 'oi"* means "The Lord be with you. And with your spirit." This is a most beautiful language. It sounds like flowers. All the vowels the Poles threw away, the Samoans picked up!

I lived on the farthest island in Samoa, Savai'i, and cared for twelve villages. In the village of Falealupo, I collected rainwater for drinking and boiled it before using. The living conditions were primitive—no running water or electricity. We burned kerosene lanterns at night.

The people did not use money. A different family would bring me food every day in a procession through the village. I celebrated Mass every morning at dawn. Everybody was Catholic, and it was a tremendous experience. I worked under Cardinal Pio Taofinu'u, who was the first Polynesian archbishop and cardinal. He is now deceased, but he was like a father to me during my stay. He was a Samoan chief.

He brought me a gift for Christmas. I was surprised when I saw his truck drive up to my rectory. When he got out he was accompanied by men who carried boxes. Inside were three cases of Franco American canned spaghetti. "You are looking thin," he told me. "Our food doesn't agree with you." What a caring man!

I worked on the island for two years, and then furthered my education through graduate studies. My plan was to return to the Pacific and teach in the seminary in order to encourage local vocations.

From Samoa I was sent to Rome. This was a dream come true! I studied at the Gregorian University. While there, I saved money and paid for my mother to fly to Rome. She stayed inexpensively with the nuns at a nearby convent. Curfew was 10:00 a.m., at which time they locked and bolted the door.

I said a novena to St. Thérèse, the Little Flower, because one of my lifelong dreams was to meet Pope John Paul II, to attend his morning Mass, and to have my mother with me. I didn't know anyone there to make this happen, but I knew St. Thérèse. So I wrote a letter.

The night before my mother left for home, I received a phone call. "Please be at the Vatican tomorrow morning with your mother and your passports." And they told me the hour. We were brought upstairs to the pope's private chapel. My mother and I met him and had Mass with him. He also gave us rosaries.

I have a picture of that event, which is a treasured memory. The pope was so sweet. His secretary ushered him around to meet the guests. When he walked up to me, the secretary introduced me. "This is Father Michael Barber. He is a Jesuit."

Pope John Paul II looked at me. "You, a Jesuit? But … you are so friendly!" He had a wonderful sense of humor.

At that time my brother Steve, who is two years younger than I, also visited me in Rome. We attended midnight Mass in the Vatican with the pope. It was another fantastic experience. A few months later my brother wrote to me. "I am applying to enter the Jesuits." He was accepted and was ordained about eight years later. I once asked him, "What made you apply to the Jesuits?"

He said, "It was midnight Mass when I saw the whole world there in St. Peter's. Every country was represented. The scene was so spectacular that it moved me." He was the chaplain at San Quentin state prison for many years. Currently he teaches at Loyola High School in Los Angeles.

I spent five years in Rome, taught at the Gregorian all five of those years, and was then sent to Oxford University in England for research and teaching. I was also administrator of the Jesuit College at Oxford. One of my happiest memories is of the time I spent as one of the chaplains to the Oxford students. We had a chaplaincy at the Newman Center. They held Mass in the morning, which included guitar playing, but I was told to do something for the graduate students.

I decided to begin a Mass at 8:30 p.m. on Sunday nights. We used candles for lighting and sang the Gregorian chant. I wanted the service to be a contemplative experience to encourage interior participation. I didn't know if any students would attend and was surprised when they came … and came … and came! The outpouring of fruit from this experience was the many students who went to confession and then later brought their non-practicing Catholic friends to Mass.

From those students came a young woman who later became a nun, a young man who is now a Dominican priest and professor in Washington, and another student who is now the governor of Louisiana.

I believe we must focus on the sacred, which centers on God, and this will attract the kids.

After five years in England, the California Jesuits said, "We want you home." I took a good assignment at Menlo Park, teaching at the seminary.

I believe the future of the Church will turn for the better if we have good parishes. Good priests make good parishes and encourage the Catholic life. They provide opportunities for us to encounter Christ. Bring Christ to the people, and the people to Christ.

The first Gulf War broke out during my time in Rome. In August 1990, Saddam Hussein invaded Kuwait. At that time many American naval ships stopped in Italy on their way to the Middle East. They needed Catholic priests at the port in Naples to say Mass for the American sailors. There were very few priests in Naples, so I volunteered.

I was saying Mass one day on a guided-missile cruiser in the harbor while the ship moved back and forth across the bay. It was quite an experience. The captain gave me a tour of his entire ship, which I really enjoyed. The captain was Catholic, and many Catholic sailors were not practicing their faith. Others were converting to other religions because there were not enough priests in the Navy to take care of them spiritually.

When I left the ship, the captain eyed my black suit and said, "We need to get you some gold stripes to put around that suit next time."

One morning as I was praying, I felt a strong call to sign up as a navy chaplain. The thought kept coming back and became stronger. I knew it was not coming from me. I asked permission from the Jesuits and they said, "As long as it doesn't interfere with your normal duties." I explained it was for the Navy Reserve. I became commissioned in Naples and flew to the USA for boot camp over two summers at the Naval Officer's School. I have served in this capacity since 1991.

In the early 2000s I was back in the USA and teaching at the Menlo Park seminary. The second Gulf War was about to start. Priests and doctors are the first to be called up during a conflict. While at Menlo Park during

Christmas vacation I received a phone call and then a written order: "You must report in twelve days with your sea bag for active duty."

I went to the rector of the seminary, Fr. Gerald Coleman, and said, "I have to go."

He agreed. "We will find someone to cover your classes."

For the first time in my life I was scared. I didn't know the seriousness of the war, or if I would die. We were required to fill out our last will and testament and say good-bye to everybody.

My mother's health deteriorated during this time. She was in the hospital and could no longer live on her own. She needed to go to a rest home. *Oh, my gosh!* I thought. *I have these orders to report, but I can't let her go to a rest home.* My other brother was married and living in Kentucky, so he couldn't help. I stormed heaven. "Lord, help me! What do I do?"

I went to St. Anne's Home in San Francisco, to the Little Sisters of the Poor. I knew they were full, with a long waiting list. I prayed a novena to St. Joseph. "Help me! Help me take care of my mother." St. Joseph took care of his family, and I needed to take care of my mom. Before I went in to see Reverend Mother Superior, I promised, "Lord, if you get Mom in, I'll do anything for these nuns for the rest of my life."

I entered and told Mother Superior who I was and my request for my mother. I had never met her, yet she said, "Well, we have one room open." They sent two nuns to Sacramento to interview my mother, and Mother Superior told me they would take her.

"Oh, God! Thank you! Thank you!" God listened to my prayers when I was in need. I needed that prayer answered more than anything else in my life.

I brought my mom to St. Anne's Home. I said a Mass for the nuns and then pushed the wheelchair with Mom into the garden. I said a Hail Mary in thanksgiving near the Lourdes shrine in the back. Then I said good-bye to my mother. I didn't know if this was the last time I would see her or not. I was going to war, and she was in a rest home.

I reported for duty and was sent with the Marine Corps. We flew to the Middle East, and the war began shortly thereafter, when the U.S. invaded Iraq in March 2003. It was one of the best times of my life as a priest. I was needed!

A convert or a revert came to see me daily. The dialogue always went something like this: "Father, I haven't been to Mass in a long time. What do I do?" "Father, I want to become a Catholic." "Father, my wife is a Catholic and I want to go to Communion when I go home with her. How do I do that?" "Father, help me."

The best experience was being sent around in my own armored convoy. We were on the Kuwait side of the Iraq border. I had my own convoy to attend to the soldiers who were dug in along the border preparing to invade. When I arrived, the men stopped their war plans. The colonel gathered everyone together.

"I am a Catholic priest," I said, "and I have been sent here. The battle will begin soon, and I would like to say Mass."

Everyone attended.

"If it is not your time to die no bullet will find you," I told them. "If it is your turn to die there is only one thing that will keep you from getting into heaven, and that is mortal sin. But we have the sacrament of Confession that can wash away any sin—any mortal sin. I will not leave this camp until everyone who wants to confess can."

There was a huge line. All the Marines—even the Protestants—came up and said, "I'm not Catholic, but I have got to get this off my chest."

I gave them a holy card of St. Michael. We pasted it inside our body armor and our flap jackets for protection. It was extremely satisfying to me, and I think beneficial to them. I was there month after month.

We didn't have cell phones. We didn't have the email options we now have, and I was desperate for word about my mother. I tried to write letters, but we were way out in the desert. There were a couple of phones, but with over 3,000 Marines in my unit, we had to wait anywhere from three to six hours in a line. When I stood in line, someone would invariably come up and say, "Chaplain, you are needed over here. There is a unit leaving, and they won't leave until you bless them." So naturally, I lost my place in line.

One Sunday afternoon I was finally able to call my mother. She was watching the war action on television. She was worried, thinking all the guns were aimed at me. "Are you all right?" she asked. "Are you all right?"

"Yes, Mom. I have 3,000 Marines guarding me."

She said, "I am so grateful!"

"Mom, I'm praying for you."

She replied, "I'm praying for you every day as I watch the war televised."

We had a very nice talk. Two days later my mother died.

Our Lord allowed me to talk to her beforehand. I said, "Lord, your ways are so mysterious." I later learned that the nuns surrounded her bed and sang the Salve Regina.

A Red Cross message was sent, but it took a couple days to find me. The head chaplain for whom I worked called me in and did what I had done for many others. "Sorry to give you this news. Your mother has passed away." Then he read the official telegram.

I was sorry to be so far away from my mother. I think every child wants to be near their mother's bedside when she passes. I didn't think I had a chance to bury her, but the colonel somehow worked it out. He called two days later. "Get your bag and get to the Jeep. I am sending you home. You only have one mother, so I want you to go home."

I traveled through the desert, got in a plane, got to another place, and got to Bahrain. It was a long journey home, but they hadn't buried Mom yet. So I was able to say her funeral Mass.

When I was ordained, I had asked Archbishop Quinn if I could revive an old custom called *Manutergium*. It involves pouring the holy Chrism oil on the priest's hands during the ordination rite and rubbing it in. Then a long purificator is used to wrap and bind the hands. "Would you mind doing that for me?" I asked Archbishop Quinn.

"Yes, I will," he said. "There is nothing that prevents it."

When I went up and knelt before him, I produced the cloth. He bound and wrapped my hands. The cloth soaked up the holy Chrism oil, which smells like perfume.

When a priest's mother dies, this cloth is wrapped around her hands and it is placed with her inside the casket. I saved my cloth for that purpose. My mother received two because my brother, Father Stephen, also received one at his ordination.

Life in this world is a cross and a resurrection, up and down. Our Lord is always there for us, but there will be some type of struggle, times of trial, and even suffering. That has been the case in my life. But the Lord is always there for us—always! You may not see it at the time, but you must trust in Him. That is the life lesson that has served me well and taken me to the place where I am today.

This reading from St. Augustine has consoled me for many years. Perhaps it might touch and console you as well. It speaks to my heart about the true meaning of life.

"There is only one thing you can be sure of: that you will die; everything else in this life, good or bad, is uncertain except death. Wherever you turn there is uncertainty; only death is sure, but even the day of your death is uncertain.

We are wanderers with no permanent home on earth; that is in heaven, and we do not know when we shall hear, 'Come, set out for heaven.' Only let us be ready. We shall be, if we long now for our true fatherland.

And yet only with difficulty, because of our weakness, can we unceasingly direct our hearts and works to God. We try to find something in this world to rest in, to pause and lie down. I do not mean the resting places lovers of evil seek: foul amusements, cheating others, a life of luxury.

No—look at the good man: he seeks his whole refreshment in his family, in a humble life, in the house he has built for himself; these are the satisfactions of the innocent.

But our all-embracing love must be for eternal life, and so God allows bitterness to be mixed with these things. Don't be upset when these innocent pleasures have their trials; the man journeying to his own country must not mistake the present world for his home."

This last thought is from St. Theresa of Avila. "Let nothing disturb you. Let nothing frighten you. All things are passing away. God never changes. Patience obtains all things. Whoever has God lacks nothing. God alone suffices."

Bio–

Bishop Barber was born in 1954 in Salt Lake City, Utah, during a temporary job assignment for his father. He lived in San Francisco, Novato, and Sacramento as a child, graduating from St. Pius X Preparatory School in Galt. Bishop Barber entered the seminary of the Society of Jesus (Jesuits) in 1973. He received his undergraduate degree from Gonzaga University in Washington, and graduate degrees in theology from Regis College at the University of Toronto and the Gregorian University in Rome. After being ordained a priest in San Francisco in 1985, Bishop Barber continued his studies in Rome and at Oxford University. In 1991, he became a commissioned officer in the United States Naval Reserve and achieved the rank of captain in 2012. He served as group chaplain for the 3rd Marine Aircraft Wing, as deputy division chaplain for the 4th Marine Division, and deputy force chaplain for reserve affairs for Marine Forces Pacific, among many other assignments. He was director of the School of Pastoral Leadership in the Archdiocese of San Francisco. From 2002–10 he taught at St. Patrick's Seminary in Menlo Park and was director of spiritual formation. Immediately prior to his appointment as Bishop of Oakland, he served as director of spiritual formation at St. John's Seminary in the Archdiocese of Boston. In addition to his native English, Bishop Barber speaks Italian, French, Samoan, and liturgical Spanish.

Rev. Fr. Michael Barry, SS.CC.

T here is a lot to be learned when we reflect upon our lives. The principal thing is that God has a plan. It is easy to say that when we think back, but almost impossible to agree with it when we are going through hardships in our daily lives.

I was born into a small family of two girls and one boy. I was that boy. Our family was Catholic to the core. I received my sacraments, and I can still remember my First Communion. My grandfather insisted that I have a navy suit with short pants.

We were a poor family but enjoyed a good life even though we did not have much materially. I remember one time tearing up the wooden floor to burn for heat. Nevertheless, we got on with what we had.

My father was a house painter and worked hard for us. My mother, because we couldn't make ends meet, was a waitress. She went out to special events and served, and then she came home. She didn't work constantly, but she brought in much needed finances that helped the family.

At Christmas, we each received one toy and a lump of coal. Growing up we didn't expect much. We knew this was all our family could afford. If you didn't get the lump of coal, you cried. How silly, right? A lump of coal was a sign of "good luck."

My maternal grandparents lived with us. My grandmother was bedridden. She taught me my prayers and served as my banker to save the few pennies I received for my allowance. My grandfather was a stone mason. He tried to teach me about the quality of stone in public buildings. Our good life came in terms of love and affirmation.

I went to school at the local elementary school. It was there that I had a teacher named Mrs. Lillis. She told me I had a vocation at the early age of eight. I was her favorite.

I progressed and went on to secondary school, which was called high school. Our high school was five years instead of the typical four years one is used to seeing in the States. We had to get our BA to graduate. In my second to the last year, the "Fourth Year," I decided to quit school. That was it! I talked to my folks, and my father said, "No. No son of mine will climb ladders. I don't want my son climbing ladders."

So I decided to become an electrician. I was determined to drop out of school.

My mother said, "Are you sure?"

"Yes."

"Tomorrow morning you are going to get up a half hour earlier than going to school," she told me. "You will take your lunch and your overalls with you."

The next morning as I walked onto the landing, there at the bottom of the stairs were my overalls. Wrapped inside was a hammer, a screwdriver, and my lunch. *Wow, this is it!* I thought.

When I got down to the bottom of the stairs, I said, "Mom, I'm going back to school."

I have avoided work ever since.

The second to the last year in high school is difficult. The last year a student takes the state exam and has two years to prepare. God knew what He was doing, or maybe it was my mother, but I came close to leaving school.

During my last year of high school, I became interested in a girl named Margaret. At the top of the street there was a shop where we purchased groceries, and she was a shop assistant. Needless to say, I spent a lot of time in her shop.

We were attracted to each other. She was a very pretty girl, and I was a handsome guy at the time. (When you got it, you got it!) Before entering the shop, I always stopped and held the door open for the people coming in and out. I stood there saying, "You go ahead. You go ahead."

The neighbors complimented my mom. "You have a very polite son. He is very polite."

My motivation for being polite was to stand there for as long as I could, so I could see Margaret and stare at her without looking obvious.

Finally, Margaret and I decided we would meet. This had to be done "undercover," undercover like the CIA, FBI, and KGB all rolled into one. No one could learn about this meeting. She had a bike, and I had a bike, so we decided to meet at a place fifteen miles away. This meant fifteen miles there and fifteen miles back. That was thirty miles, but love knows no bounds! So, off I went. We had a great Sunday afternoon. We talked and rode our bikes around. I came back a very happy camper.

I went to school the next day, and when I came home my mother said, "You have a girlfriend."

"No, I don't."

"You are thinking about being a priest, and you have a girlfriend?"

"No, I don't!" I insisted.

She was relentless. "Yes, you do."

"No, I don't *really*." I could be stubborn, as well.

"Well, then, who is she?"

"She's the girl up at the shop," I explained, hoping that would satisfy her.

"Oh."

God knows everything, but mothers do too. "How did you learn about the girl?" I asked.

"You were seen in Monkstown yesterday."

You know, a man can't even have his freedom without everyone telling on him! That is small town living.

At this time, two priests were encouraging me to join their orders. One was from the Holy Ghost Order; the other was from the Sacred Heart Order. Both were in my home constantly. Yet I was upset, especially after figuring out that Margaret and I had genuine feelings for one another. One night I cried. I was sixteen years old, I knew I wanted to try the priesthood, yet I knew I wanted to marry Margaret.

Which was the right choice?

Only one choice could come first. I decided I would try the priesthood. If that didn't work out, I could come back. I finished school and got my degree. The Holy Ghost priest was very controlling, while the Sacred Heart priest seemed more at ease with me. Therefore, I choose the Sacred Heart.

In August of 1958, I asked my mother to sign the documents giving me permission to enter the novitiate. She knew what they were, yet she asked, "What are they for?"

"I'm going away to study for the priesthood."

"I'm not signing them," she said. "You are too young. You don't know your own mind." She refused to sign, believing I was too young to make the choice.

I was upset. I *did* know my own mind! In my frustration, I broke down crying.

At that moment, my father came in and asked what was going on. I explained that Mom refused to sign the papers. My father had dropped out of school after the fourth grade. He was not an educated man, but he was a wise man. He had tremendous wisdom I realize now.

"What papers?" he asked.

"The papers to discern if I have a vocation to be a priest."

"Come with me," he said. We went to the front door of our home. "Open the door."

I opened it.

"Now close it." Then he repeated, "Open it, close it. Open it, close it."
I was puzzled. "Dad, what are you doing?"

"As long as I am in this house, this door will always be open for you,"
he said. "You go try it. If it doesn't work out, if it doesn't suit you, then
come back. This door will be open. I'll sign the papers."

We went inside, and he signed them.

Mom, in a sarcastic voice, said, "Well, then, I'll sign them too. You'll
be home in a week."

I would have been too, except that she'd said that. I decided, *I'm not
coming home in a week. I'm going to give it a month, at least a month!*

When I arrived, I didn't know anyone, and the food was bad. We went
to bed at 9:00. Why would anyone go to bed at 9:00? Because we had to
get up at 5:30.

I was professed on the Feast of the Assumption, along with eleven
others. My mother came up to me and said, "At first I was against this, but
now I am on board."

We had a month's vacation and then the seminarians were assigned to
continue their studies in the United States. We were traveling on an ocean
liner, so I had to leave my house at three in the morning to get to the boat.

I was ready to say good-bye to my mother and father at the house, but
my mother insisted on coming. My dad stayed home. He had to go to work.
My mother and I took a taxi to the boat. It was September and raining. It's
always raining in Ireland. I got to the end of the street and turned around.
My father was at the door waving.

That was one of the toughest times in my life, to leave my family, and
to leave my father that way. A cold shiver overcame me, and I heard a voice
in my head. *You will never see him alive again.* I dismissed it. My father was
only forty-eight, and in six years I would be back for my ordination.

When we arrived at the docks, my mother wanted to see inside the boat.
All the other parents stayed on the shore, but no—not my mom. She had to
see the boat! "How big is it?" she asked. "Where are you going to sleep?"

Upon entering the ship, the conversation went something like this:
"Now, where will you sleep?"

"I'll sleep here."

"Oh, no, you won't. You need to sleep on top."

Even though I was leaving to travel far away, my mother still insisted
she knew best. And she did.

There were thirteen newly professed seminarians sent to the United
States for further study. We arrived in the States and took philosophy classes.

At the end of philosophy class, it was decided that three seminarians would attend the Catholic University of America, and I was one of them.

On St. Stephen's Day, December 27, 1961, while studying at Catholic University, the superior called me into his office and told me, "Your father died."

I said, "It can't be. I got a card that said Dad is doing fine. Everybody is fine."

"No. Here is the telegram."

I was in denial. "No, that can't be. Somebody is playing a joke."

"No," he said. "No, they are not."

"He can't. He can't." I broke down and cried. "How can this be?" When I could talk, I said, "I would like to go home for the funeral."

The superior said, "No, you can't go."

"Why not?"

"You would be setting a precedent."

"A precedent?"

"Yes," he said. "There are 100 other seminarians, you know."

"But it is my dad. I only have one dad."

"No, I'm sorry. We will send our condolences."

I thought, *It's so unfair, so unfair!*

I began thinking that the one responsible for this was God. It was His fault. My father was young. Many other guys were older. They were in their sixties and seventies. Why didn't He zap one of them? Why *my* dad?

I was upset with God. Why would God take my father? He was one of the younger fathers of all my classmates. I was giving my life to God, and He took my father? I became intent on proving God wrong. It took about thirteen years before I was healed of the loss and that wound.

I finished my studies and returned home to Ireland for ordination. It was a glorious day on June 14, 1964, when I was ordained a priest of Jesus Christ in Cootehill, County Cavan, Ireland. All of my family was in attendance.

When I arrived home I went upstairs to my father's bedroom in the back of the house. I was overcome with deep sorrow. Here was someone who had longed for this day but never saw it. Why would God let this happen? It was beyond me and any rational explanation.

After the ordination, we stopped at a little café to get something to eat. I was sitting next to my mother. I had a white shirt on, and I didn't wear my collar. I had taken it off. The waitress was paying a lot of attention to me. My mother picked up on this and said, "Honey, you are three hours too late."

In 1964, I returned to the States for my first assignment as a teacher at Bishop Amat High School in La Puente, California. I taught school five days a week and then filled in at a local parish to say Mass on the weekends. It was a hectic schedule. I was also enrolled at California State University, Los Angeles to pursue a master's degree.

When vacation time came, I didn't go home. Other priests went home, and I took over their work at the parish and helped with whatever needed to be accomplished. I worked in hospital ministry visiting and praying for the sick and anything else that needed to be done because I felt that God had made a mistake. God made a mistake in taking my father.

I was working for the Lord, but like any typical worker, I was mad at the boss. All God had to do was apologize and say, "Mike, I zapped the wrong guy." I was going to prove to God that He had made a mistake. There was bitterness. There was anger and bitterness. Then it hit me. *Why didn't they let me go home?* I felt the injustice of the entire situation. It took years to finally let go of the injustice.

I remember asking my mom, "Why didn't you tell me Dad was sick? Why didn't you tell me something was going on?"

She said, "When you came home the first time from the novitiate, he was painting the maternity ward in the hospital and had a heart attack. He was the first patient in the maternity ward."

"Why didn't you tell me?"

"Because he didn't want you to know. Your father said, 'If Mike is going to make up his mind, I am not going to be the one who influenced him. He has to be the one to decide, independent of anything else. He has to make up his own mind, and not because of my sickness or my health.' His last words were, 'I won't see my boy ordained.'"

I thought, *What a wise man.* He thought I had to make my own decision. You talk about a vocation to be a father—he really was a great father. He wasn't educated in the sense of the world, but he was such a wise man. He only wrote me two letters in his whole life, which I treasured.

I continued to serve God as a young priest, but I was arrogant. Those who know me now may not imagine me as ever being arrogant, but I was. I felt people didn't have enough questions that I could not answer. Only *I* had the answers. I began making changes, such as cutting back on my "religious stuff," such as the Rosary, which I felt was a repetitious prayer.

My priesthood began a downward spiral pattern. I found myself exploring all sorts of different activities. One time I was filling in for another priest, and we had our retreat in Malibu. This was some years after ordination. I registered for the retreat and went. After attending, I returned home to find another priest in residence who was a lifelong friend. He looked at me and said, "You need a drink."

"You are right," I agreed. "I do need a drink." I had never had a drink until that day.

"There is nothing there but vodka," he said. "There is no soda or tonic." I never drank, so I didn't know the difference. "That's fine. I'll take that."

"Nobody drinks vodka straight. We need to mix it with something."

"No," I insisted. "Vodka is fine."

He filled up about four shots of vodka, and I took it straight.

"What's wrong with you?" my friend asked.

"There is nothing wrong with me. Why?"

"That should have hit you."

It didn't hit me at all. Unfortunately, this started me drinking. I found I liked Scotch better, and I drank a lot of Scotch. So much so that I even knew the different types of Scotch, which is the good and which is the bad.

I enjoyed school and took an opportunity to get another degree. I already had a degree in theology, but I decided to go back to California State University, Los Angeles. I made sure I always had a full schedule. I would say Mass in the morning at the convent, teach school all day, go to class in the afternoon, go home, study, and then prepare for class. On the weekends, I went down to the parish and heard confessions. On Sunday, I would say two Masses and then prepare for school on Monday morning.

There was always a full schedule, but what suffered most was prayer time. Constantly in the back of my mind was this swirling whirlpool of thought which reminded me, *God messed you up, didn't He? God messed you up.* I was tormented by these thoughts, and they kept coming.

I even had dreams. I was at my father's grave. They would throw dirt on his face and he would go down. Then he would come back up and he was smiling again. He wouldn't die. He wouldn't go. I remember waking with tears streaming down my face.

I was driving home from school one night with another priest and he said, "I'm going to leave the priesthood."

I was shocked. "What?"

"Yes, I'm going to leave."

"What are you going to do?" I asked.

"I'm going to get married."

"To whom?"

He told me the name of the girl. "I met her at school."

I thought, *How could I have missed that? He has a girlfriend, and I didn't know. Wow! What a shock. How did he meet this girl? What went on?*

He did leave the priesthood. And then another priest left. Another friend of mine left.

I began thinking, *Maybe they are right. Maybe that is what I am supposed to do. Maybe I am supposed to get married. All I have to do is find the right girl.*

So I asked them, "How did you meet these girls?"

They said, "You can't go out with your white shirt and black pants. You can't go out with your suit of armor. There is another suit that you must get."

At that time, the height of fashion was something called a leisure suit. Some readers may remember these leisure suits. I thought they were very cool. I purchased a brown leisure suit, and I thought I looked good, but then I had to have a shirt to go with it.

At that time, I was very limited in regards to income. I think my income was about ten dollars a month, and the shirt I liked was fifteen dollars. It was burnt orange. I thought I had good taste. I purchased the burnt-orange shirt and wore it with my leisure suit. You were supposed to leave the jacket open a few buttons. That was to be macho, but I didn't know it.

I began to go out. At the same time, I was struggling within the Community, as the Community wasn't "going anywhere." So, the search began, and I soon found someone. I decided that I would stay in the priesthood one more year. I knew that any intimacy was out of the question until I was out of the priesthood. I was now job-hunting, planning for when I left.

With about six months to go before I left, the young lady stopped seeing me. I asked her why. She said that I was not exciting enough for her.

I began to look at my life and the decision I was about to make. First, I realized that I basically had no real prayer life. I didn't pray the Rosary. I had no spiritual director. There were many missing elements in my life. I thought about what I had given up to become a priest. I had left my home, my girlfriend back home, I was away from my native land, and I had no real friends. The friends I had were all leaving.

I did a lot of soul searching. It was a crisis time in my life. What was God doing? I had God, but God apparently didn't have me.

I decided to get a spiritual director. I don't know why, because I wasn't going in that direction. But he was very good. I told him I wasn't going to attend any more Community meetings.

He said, "No, you should go there."

"When I go, I get so upset. I get angry."

He said, "Go there and keep your mouth shut, and don't say anything."

I agreed and kept attending the meetings. At the same time, our Community moved from one school to another. This was a hard thing for me. I loved the school where I was teaching. I got along well with the kids.

This new school was a rival in football. They suspected anybody coming in from their rival school. Add this to all the turmoil I was still going through over the death of my dad and thoughts of leaving the priesthood.

I remember coming to an awareness during my downward spiral. Francis Thompson wrote a poem called "The Hound of Heaven." *He pursues me down the highways and the byways of my life.* The Lord never leaves us.

"Even though you are unfaithful, I am still faithful," says the Lord. God is always there. That's where wisdom comes from. The Lord was there all the time. There were many good people around me, but I was just now seeing the truth.

One night I got the image that if I loved God, which I did, and I loved my father, it is one and the same love. It is one and the same love—they have to come together. And I had to let go of the hurt.

I pray with many people suffering from hurt and brokenness in their hearts. Divorced people, people who have lost children, and people with cancer and terrible, terrible tragedies. There is much hurt, and I teach them that they must let go.

I decided I would release my dad. I would let him go. I would bury him. I would give him into the fullness of God's love. This decision didn't happen overnight. It took a long while, but when it did, a lot of peace came into my life. There was consolation, but once I received consolation—that grace—there came another challenge. God was moving within me.

I decided that there was not a good woman out there for me. It dawned on me why there wasn't and that was because I wasn't a good man. That was the real reason. Here I was strutting around in this leisure suit, and this was not who I was. This was not what I wanted. This was not the reason my father died without telling me he was ill—so I could make this decision without pressure to become a priest. This search for another life outside the priesthood was not why I left home. The reason was not any of these things.

I decided to stay a priest.

Meanwhile, I was moved to a parish school. Besides being principal of the school, I was the third assistant for the parish. I was assigned to begin a prayer group, a Charismatic prayer group. I approached it with an authoritative demeanor. In the first meeting, we had over 120 eager people. I told them what to do and what to expect.

The next week we had sixty. Then it dwindled to four people. A man named Ed came to see me for six consecutive days to pray with me. Finally, on the seventh day he said, "I've been coming here to pray with you for six days, taking an hour off from work, and we haven't prayed."

I said that we had prayed. He said that we talked about prayer but definitely did not pray. He told me to kneel down and he would pray for me.

He has it all wrong, I thought. This guy was arrogant for sure.

He was a tall guy—much taller than I—so I knelt. I was a little bit angry with him.

As he came toward me, I realized in a split second that he had something I didn't have despite all of my education, degrees, and even ordination. He prayed that I would accept Jesus into my life as my Lord and Savior. That is what I wanted, and he prayed over me for the Baptism in the Holy Spirit. I received the Baptism in the Holy Spirit at that time, but he had something else I wanted.

Then he said, "Now, I will pray with you in tongues and pray for the gift of tongues."

I thought, *That will be easy. I know some Irish, some Latin, and Greek and German.* I was ready for that.

"It cannot be any language you know," he said.

That's not fair, I thought. *I didn't get the gift of tongues.*

Things changed in my life rapidly. I learned that with Jesus it is never *this*, it is always *that*. I began to pray more and had a desire to pray with others. I returned to praying the Divine Office. I was hungry for more. I learned that God was not finished with me yet.

Soon the prayer group numbers increased, and I looked forward to the prayer meeting. I traveled to attend Charismatic conferences and discovered a whole community of people who were on fire for Jesus. I experienced a whole new life in Christ. *This* was the reason I had left my family, my native land, etc. I had arrived. Life was good only with Jesus. There was a newness coming into my life.

Then it happened. I hit the wall again. As I said, God was not finished with me yet. I encountered problems at the school, mostly financial having to do with salaries. I disagreed with the administrator, and I lost. I was fired. Another setback. Why was God doing this to me? I realized that you never ask God "why." You always ask "what." *Why* shows that you are in charge. *What* means that God is in charge.

I ended up as the Charismatic director for the Diocese of San Bernardino, a position that I quickly realized had no salary, car, or residence. *Thanks a lot, God!* I had to generate my own income and find my own car.

If that wasn't bad enough, the people were saying that I was not like my predecessor. I was not exciting enough. Where had I heard that before? Still, I served as director for nineteen years and began to build up the Charismatic community, including an annual Charismatic Conference that drew over 1,000 people.

God still wasn't finished with me. I went to my spiritual director and once again told him I couldn't go to any more of my Community meetings because I always left angry. He told me to keep going, but to keep my mouth shut. So I went.

One year later I was elected provincial. Go figure! That's God's hand at work.

Earlier, we'd had a Charismatic conference entitled "Blessed Are the Poor." The late Fr. Rick Thomas was there on Sunday morning. He challenged the people to reach out and help the poor. He put two baskets on the floor and told the people to fill them, not with a dollar or even five dollars, but with what was in their wallets and purses. Of the 500 people present, we collected $6,000. Then he told them that we would go into the streets of Riverside and give the money to the poor and homeless.

When I came upon the scene, my staff of four were in tears. They said, "You have got to stop him."

"Why me? Why didn't you stop him before he got started?" I was going up the side of the arena to stop him when a voice told me, *"What he is doing is right, but the way he is going about it is wrong."*

I took what I heard seriously and told Fr. Rick what I'd heard. We prayed for discernment, and he agreed. You see, it is more important to see the *what* of God rather than the *why* of ourselves.

Many miracles happened that day. We had $1,100 left of the $6,000 that had been given away indiscriminately and decided to feed the poor in San Bernardino for the month of September, 1987. We only had enough money for that month, but it was the beginning of Mary's Table and eventually of the tax-free Mary's Mercy Center.

Now I had a dilemma. I was elected provincial and had three ministries: the provincial (a very big job), Mary's Table, and the Charismatic directorship. One had to go, so I gave up the directorship.

It was also during this time that the sex scandal arose in the Church. I was constantly attending meetings and programs and praying for healing. We had only two cases, but it was devastating nevertheless.

Mary's Mercy Center continued to prosper. I had dreams of opening a drug rehabilitation center and had two recovering addicts who volunteered to help with this ministry. Everything was set except the two men relapsed.

That finished my dream for the drug rehab center.

God had something else in mind. Within months we opened a center for unwed mothers as an alternative to abortion. That grew, and with the four lots we purchased, we began to build a state-of-the-art home for unwed mothers. The shell was built, but we were still 1.1 million dollars shy of what we needed to finish the home. We could not raise the money because of the recession. I looked at the shell and told God that He could have it. In fact, I said, "If you want me to, I can get some gang members to burn it down."

That was on April 13. On May 13 the San Manuel Band of Mission Indians gave us $500,000, and the Economic Development Association (government) gave us $600,000. We had exactly the right amount of money to finish the construction and opened on the Feast of the Immaculate Conception that year, 1995.

We had three basic rules: Don't judge them. Serve them. Find Christ in them.

Other things started to happen. I became familiar with other ministry groups, such as Magnificat, and the importance of praying the Rosary kicked in big-time. I can't get through my day without the Rosary. I didn't know why I couldn't do it back when I was struggling. Now it is very important for me to have the presence of Mary in my day.

We are a congregation devoted to both hearts—the heart of Jesus and the heart of Mary. The love of Jesus modeled by Mary. We have a vocation to minister to our modern society. But it is trying to live a life honoring God, to manifest it. That is the challenge. I was reading the other day about St. Benedict's teaching on the Eucharist. Believe it, celebrate it, and live it. Those were the three points he was making.

When I look back on my life, that period of doubt, I ask myself why I didn't leave the priesthood. I now know why—because I wasn't meant to leave. When I think about my vocation, I think about my family back home. My mother loved me dearly, and yet she would say during my tumultuous priestly years in the 70s, "He is not a priest at all." She would never tell me directly, because to her I represented the Messiah.

My brother-in-law would say, "As soon as you put your foot through the door, everything is like heaven. It is like paradise. When you leave, all hell breaks loose."

Mom would say, "Why don't you go up to see Mrs. So-and-So? She was asking about you."

I answered, "Okay, I'll go visit."

Then she would say, "Put on your collar when you go."

"Mom, she knows I'm a priest. I'm not going to do that."

"She'll feel good if you do."

"But I won't feel good if I do."

As soon as I became part of the Charismatic Renewal, Mom would say, "The priest is back. The priest is back." She could tell the difference when I couldn't.

I was going through the motions, doing the work—the priestly duties. What is necessary, however, is the love of Jesus Christ to shine through. Christ has to be there in the center. We cannot as priests get through our prayer life without the Eucharist.

I was the love of my mother's life. When it came time for her to die, she was living with my sister and her family. My brother-in-law called me. "She is not going to make it. You better come home."

"Okay, I'll come home." I got on the plane. It is a long trip, a ten-hour trip. I was praying she would be alive when I arrived. If I had to pray, I probably would pray, "The Lord is my shepherd."

And she would say, "That is not our prayer."

I got home and bought a paper right away. Her death would be in the paper, and it wasn't there. I was so relieved, but I felt that was typical of my mother. She was hanging on. I asked, "Lord, why didn't You take her?"

I got to her bedside, and my sister was there. "You can go now," I told her. "You can go see Dad and John (my uncle—her brother). You can go home. You can go home now."

My sister was upset. "No, no. Don't say that." She is a heavy-set woman, and she threw herself across the bed. "Mom, don't go. Don't go."

I'm thinking, *She killed our mother!*

My brother-in-law walked in. "You've had a long night. You go to bed, and I'll call you at 12:30, and then you can come back."

I said, "No, Henry. I'll stay here and you go to bed."

Henry is a good man. He left, and I stayed there and held Mom's hand. I talked to her through the night. I talked about the past, when I was young. Every Saturday, my two sisters would get on the bus and go shopping. They loved to go downtown shopping. But I wouldn't. I always stayed at home with my mom. After my sisters had left, I went down to the shop with money my mom gave me to buy "snowballs"—pastries with cream inside and powder on top.

I would buy four—two for Mom and two for me. We'd talk about school and things happening in our lives. Then she would say, "You better wash your hands. If the girls come back and see the powder on your face, they are going to know." It was our little secret.

As I was sitting beside Mom all night, I was thinking. *This is the woman who gave me life. And here so close to death, she is still giving me life.* I knew she loved me so much, and it was so special that I could sit with her holding her hand.

What a gift this woman was to me. She wanted to hold on to me because, as she later explained, "I didn't want you to go. I had lost a husband and I didn't want to lose a son."

And yet, when people came in she was so proud of her son.

On my parents' 25th wedding anniversary, my mother was doubled over with osteoarthritis, but when they came in to take her picture, she straightened up. She came to visit me in the United States when she was seventy-eight or seventy-nine. We were in one of those "luxury diners" called Denny's, ready to order dinner.

The waitress asked, "And what does the old lady want?"

"There is no old lady here," Mom said. "Who are you talking to?"

The waitress got it. "Madame, what would you like?"

I remembered all this while I held her hand. *Yes, I am going to miss her.* She was always there, no matter what. I thought about her losing her husband at such a young age. She didn't have money and she worked, and worked, and worked. It was a saintly life in a sense.

At six o'clock in the morning, I went to wake my brother-in-law.

"Did she die?" he asked.

"No, she is still here."

He said, "You must be exhausted."

"No, I am not tired at all."

I thought how tough it must have been to have a son away. I was the light of her life when I came home. She might have been sick, but to her I was the best antibiotic in the world. She would snap back to life. I could see God's love.

While we go through tough times, there is always consolation, and then comes the challenge. One of the things I have learned is that when God moves, we are pulled along. Because I expected my mother to be dead, the Lord spared her so I could spend time with her. Here was a great gift, a gift I couldn't imagine when I got off the plane. A gift that I didn't have with my dad, but I had with my mom.

When we talk about a vocation, there is always going to be a challenge. There is going to be a challenge with personal issues, with church, with rejection, within marriages, with those who are single, and with life in general.

I learned what makes us strong is "letting go." Let go of the problems, the hurt, and the rejection. Try and see through the mist of tears what God is doing, and what God is doing in your life. God is doing a lot more.

Two scriptures that I rely on are 1 John 4:19—"We love because he first loved us." God first loved me. God first loved us. No matter who we are or what we have done, no matter what we have gone through, God's love is there. He loves us no matter what.

The other one is Philippians 1:6. "I am confident of this, that the one who began a good work in you will continue to complete it until the day of Christ Jesus." He who has begun this good work in you will see it through to completion but you must see it through with Him. You must make the journey through it with Him.

When I look at my life, there is so much I see of God's hand. Back in 1999, the Community had an election for provincial. I was vice provincial at the time. My term was finished, and then I was elected provincial. Unanimously, not one vote against me. Wow, what a surprise, given the circumstances that at one point I had wanted to leave the priesthood. I wanted to leave this group. There is balance all the time and in all things if God is in the midst.

Through all of this, I learned four important principles: 1) What got you *here* won't get you *there*. 2) It is never *this*. It is always *that*. 3) God isn't finished with me yet. 4) God speaks to us every day because He loves us.

Lord, I thank You for those reading this, and I ask Your blessing upon them now. I ask for the outpouring of Your Spirit, and Lord Jesus, especially that these words will be received as You intend. I pray this through Christ, our Lord. Amen.

Bio –

Using his Irish wit and wisdom, Fr. Mike Barry brings hope to many. Born in Cork, Ireland, where his sisters and their families reside, he was ordained a priest of the Sacred Hearts of Jesus and Mary in June 1964. He was elected their provincial for the Western Province from 1999 to 2005.

He was the director of the Charismatic Renewal Center and the Evangelization Office for the Diocese of San Bernardino in Southern California for almost twenty years. Fr. Barry founded Mary's Mercy Center, Inc., in 1992, to meet the needs of hungry and homeless women and children in the area. Recognized for his contributions to the Universal Church, in 2005 he received the *Pro Ecclesia Et Pontifice Cross Award*, a pontifical honor.

Answering the call of God to the healing ministry, Fr. Barry has authored many publications. He uses retreats, workshops, conferences, and his weekday radio program on KPRO, *Time for Hope*, to educate others on the charisms of the Holy Spirit.

Rev. Fr. Donald H. Calloway, MIC

It is my joy to share the story of how I became a Catholic and then a Roman Catholic priest. I literally went from having waist-length hair to wearing a Roman collar. Divine Mercy, Our Lady, and the truths of Catholicism totally changed my life.

A lot of people no doubt look at me now and think, "Nah, come on. You are a halfway good-looking guy. You probably grew up Catholic. You became a priest. No, you didn't really do all those things you said you did."

But it's all true. Some aspects of my story may shock the daylights out of readers. Looking back on my former life, they continue to shock *me*. I still cannot believe I'm alive and that I'm a Roman Catholic priest. By sharing bits and pieces of my earlier life, you will see where I came from. The full story will magnify the mercy of God.

I was born in 1972 to young parents who were somewhat redneck—more or less hillbillies from the backwoods of West Virginia. My mother was seventeen when I was conceived. She was inexperienced in life and didn't have much exposure to a lot of things. She married a man a few years older. They moved to Michigan soon after I was conceived, where my dad got a job at Ford Motor Company. Neither one of my parents was a practicing Christian.

I grew up with absolutely no religious training whatsoever. After I was born in Dearborn, Michigan, Dad began drinking a lot. He also got involved in a whole bunch of crazy stuff—riding motorcycles, womanizing, and spending all the money on himself. My mother couldn't stand it, and they separated when I was only a few years old. I don't remember any of those early years.

I wouldn't see my biological father again until I was eighteen. A lot would happen between those years.

After the divorce, my mother and I moved back to West Virginia. We lived on my grandfather's farm in the woods. It took about thirty minutes of driving on dirt roads to reach the nearest town. We lived a simple life way out in the sticks. At some point in my life, my mother met another man and they married. He wasn't a practicing Christian either. Unfortunately, he also turned out to be a drunkard and a womanizer.

It was from these examples of flawed manhood that I developed an understanding of what it meant to be a man. Basically, it meant drink beer and chase women. I thought this was the essence of what it meant to be a man and what it means to be a father, and I wanted to be like that. I had no one to correct me or to tell me it wasn't good.

My second father was so bad that Mom had to seek employment. She ended up joining the Navy. When she went to boot camp in Florida, she left me with my stepfather for what felt like an eternity. The example he gave me was horrible. He constantly went out womanizing and drinking. I was basically on my own, and I imitated what I saw.

When my mother returned from boot camp she was assigned her first duty station in Norfolk, Virginia. Almost as soon as we arrived, Mom's second marriage fell apart. It didn't take long for her to meet a military officer, and they started dating.

At first, I didn't like him at all. *This guy is different from the other guys. He's like an officer and a gentleman,* I thought. *That's not the kind of dad I want.* With my two previous fathers, I was able to do whatever I wanted. And I liked that.

Well, they fell in love and got married. He became my third father and adopted me. That is why my last name is Calloway.

Less than a year later, my half-brother Matthew was born. When he was born it was decided that Matthew and I should be baptized. It wasn't really my parents' idea. My new dad's parents in North Carolina kept nagging my parents to have it done. So, my parents surrendered to it. They were Episcopalians, and my parents found an Episcopalian church where I could get baptized.

All I remember from my baptism was that some dude poured cold water over my head and then we went outside and ate donuts. That's it. No family were invited; no friends either. Nobody took pictures. My parents wanted the certificate to silence the grandparents. We never went to church again. I never saw the inside of a church even at Christmas or Easter. Religion meant nothing to my family.

As a military family, we moved around a lot—every two years or so. Our first move took us to San Pedro in Los Angeles County, California. It was awesome. Then we moved to Santee in San Diego County.

My life took a serious turn for the worse in California. I was now of the age where girls were no longer icky and yucky. They smelled amazing and looked delicious. MTV had also just launched. I really got into music, and Southern California was paradise to me. I started smoking marijuana, drinking, used foul language, and dressed like a freak. I wanted to do everything I saw on MTV. I was thirteen years old.

Then one day my life radically changed. My dad came home and said, "Guess what? We are going to move again."

Where could we move that would be better than San Diego?

"We're moving to Japan," he told us.

"No, we're not," I said. "You can go, but I'm not going."

I was extremely upset and wondered how this could happen to me. My friends were in San Diego. Everything I loved was in San Diego. I was so alarmed I even thought, *Do they have girls in Japan? I'm going to have to eat fish and ride a bike.* Everything I loved would be taken away.

So I rebelled.

I tried to find a way to go back to West Virginia and live with relatives; or go to Asheville, North Carolina, and live with other family. I did not want to go to Japan.

You watch what is going to happen when we get to Japan, I thought. *You want to see a fallen angel? You are going to taste it. You are going to feel it. I will make every day of your stinking life miserable.*

That is exactly what I did.

When we arrived in Japan I started rebelling. I didn't go to school the first day. Instead, I took off and went looking for trouble. I looked for Japanese kids wearing Ozzie Osborn and Iron Maiden shirts. I wanted to party.

I was tired of my parents changing my life and making me lose my friends. I figured if this was all there was to life, I wanted my piece of the pie. I wanted it now, and I didn't care when or how I died. *Give me pleasure!*

I got involved with Japanese girls and lived a lustful life. I drank heavily and drank hard liquor. This was easy to do in Japan. It's difficult for someone underage to obtain alcohol in the United States, but in Japan many alcohol machines are outside. You put your money in the machine, and you get your beverage. Japan breeds alcoholism.

I was also introduced to hard drugs. I started doing heroin and anything else I could get my hands on. All I wanted out of life was to satisfy my senses. Eventually, I didn't see the need to return home, so I ran away. I was fifteen years old.

I ran away with another military kid. Neither of us spoke Japanese or wanted to get a legitimate job. We had no money, but we did have Japanese friends. In order to sustain our lifestyle, we turned to a life of crime. We stole cars, motorcycles, guitars, surfboards, and huge amounts of money left in store registers overnight.

We constantly stayed on the move. If you were Caucasian and didn't have black hair, you were suspect. At this time, my mom and dad were completely dead to me. I never wanted to see them again.

One day we were approached by a criminal organization known as the Yakuza. They introduced us to beautiful Japanese girls and offered us a proposition to work for them. We started doing little jobs in casinos and gambling parlors, and I was close to being initiated into the organization.

The Japanese mafia is a serious outfit. When you are initiated, the top half of your pinky is cut off, and your back gets tattooed all over. They never initiated American boys, but we got all the other benefits.

My friend and I ended up causing an international incident. The United States and the Japanese government were tracking us down. On the military base where my parents lived, the U.S. government talked to my friends and secretly listened to my phone conversations. I occasionally called my friends on the base and offered them guitars, motorcycles, girls, and money.

During this time, my mom was going through a major crisis. Her mother's heart was crushed. She didn't know if I was alive or dead or what was happening to me. She only learned I was alive when she heard a report of another robbery by the American kids on the run.

My mother is almost full-blooded Italian. LaChita Bianco is her maiden name. For some reason, though, she wasn't Catholic. When my great-grandparents came to the United States from southern Italy, they didn't pass on the Italian language or the Catholic faith.

I didn't know that Mom had a Filipino friend in Japan who was super Catholic. At this woman's suggestion, Mom talked to a Catholic military chaplain. She had tried everything to find peace, meaning, and hope. The priest told Mom about the wonder and truths of the Catholic Church. He talked to her about the sacraments, St. Augustine and St. Monica, Our Lady, the Eucharist and Confession.

Mom loved it! Catholicism was in her Italian blood. It had lain dormant, but now it was awakening.

Sadly, before Mom could continue exploring Catholicism, she had to leave Japan. The authorities told her that when the U.S. government eventually apprehended me, they would need a member of my family in the States who could receive me back. Thus, with much pain in her heart, she left Japan while my dad stayed behind to continue to search for me. She left crushed and broken but with the hope that she could continue her journey to Catholicism back in the USA.

I had no idea my mother no longer lived in Japan. To be honest, I would not have cared even if I had known. She was stone-cold dead to me. Eventually, I was apprehended and kicked out of the country. When they deported me, they handcuffed my ankles and my hands together. I was placed on a military cargo plane and accompanied by two MPs (military police).

When we landed in Los Angeles they took off the handcuffs and released me into the custody of my father, who had been on the same flight. Since I hadn't done anything on American soil and I was not of the age for prosecution, they let me go.

I was tempted to thank them for the free ride back to California and bolt out the door. I didn't run, though. I wasn't sure if my old friends in San Diego would still be there. Many of them were also military kids. So I reluctantly went with my dad to the east coast, where Mom was now living.

We flew to Philadelphia. When we landed, I saw my mom and my brother. She ran toward me and started to pour motherliness all over me, telling me how much she loved me. To my great shame, I pushed her away, looked her in the eye, and said, "I hate your guts! I hate you!"

She cried uncontrollably. It didn't faze me at all. I was dead inside.

Unknown to me, Japan and the U.S. had an arrangement. Upon returning to the United States I had to enter a rehabilitation facility. My first rehab was in Altoona, Pennsylvania, at a place called New Beginnings at Cove Forge.

My experience there didn't help at all. I ran away while I was there and even learned how to do more drugs in the rehab. The silly team-building exercises did nothing to help me either. Unfortunately, like all secular rehab programs, they offered nothing more than a band-aid to a spiritual problem.

When I got out, I continued the same cycle of death I had left … and worse. I started doing drugs I hadn't been exposed to in Japan. I got involved with crack cocaine, LSD, and mushrooms. Basically, if I could smoke it, snort it, or drink it, I did. I was high every single day, all day. I lost my identity. I was fried.

During my time in rehab, my mom, dad, and brother became Catholic. When Mom told me, I couldn't believe it. I thought being Catholic meant you were in a medieval cult or something. I wanted absolutely nothing to do with it. My mom invited me to church, but I told her she was crazy for being suckered into being a Catholic. They were so religious that it made me sick. I couldn't even stay in their house.

This is when I became a Deadhead.

I left my parents' house. I had nowhere to go, so I hitchhiked around. A dude in a VW bus picked me up. He told me he was going to a show. I had no idea what he meant, but I soon learned he was going to a Grateful Dead concert.

I wasn't into the Dead at that point, but I went along. That first Dead show was unlike anything I had ever experienced. I became a total fan and found myself traveling all over the east coast attending show after show. I became a hippie. I mocked my parents' new-found religion, but I found myself practically worshiping Jerry Garcia.

I eventually ended up homeless, so I went back to my parents' house in Pennsylvania. They had totally changed. They were loving, merciful, and kind. I never chalked these changes up to religion. I did find it strange, though, when Mom put religious stuff under my pillow or in my pants pocket. I had no idea what the stuff was—usually some kind of medal, or a card with something called "St. Michael the Archangel" on it. I tore it up or threw it away. It meant nothing to me.

During this time, I was doing inhuman amounts of crack cocaine and LSD. At one point I woke up in another rehab—the Charter Fairmont Institute—because I overdosed and was found on a street in Philadelphia. This rehab was different, however. It was also a psychiatric institute, a locked-down, padded facility. I couldn't escape this place. But nothing changed, even though I was there for several months. When I left, I picked up right where I had left off.

I was only eighteen years old.

I agreed to go to Louisiana with a friend. We had no money, so we stole a car, stole the gas by filling up and speeding away, and doing other criminal activity to eat.

We decided to stay in Louisiana. I got a job working on the Mississippi River on a tugboat tying up barges. It was a crazy situation. The tugboat captain was doing cocaine upstairs while I smoked weed below. I tied up massive barges with huge cables using the only knot system I knew—a shoe knot. To this day, I'm thankful nobody was killed because of my stupidity.

I ended up getting fired from the tugboat job. Now I had no money at all.

I needed to eat, so I began shoplifting food items. This led to being thrown in jail and charged with a misdemeanor for stealing a case of beer and a bag of chips from Piggly Wiggly, a southern food-chain store. My friend bailed me out and we fled the state. I was now wanted for failure to appear in court.

I didn't know where to go at this point, so I thought it would be a good idea to find my hillbilly relatives in West Virginia. I'd heard they lived off the grid and were hard to find. I found my biological father, but we didn't get along at all. He was a total redneck. I was a stoner hippie.

I told my father the situation and how I was running from the law. He agreed to let me live on his property but not in his house. So I moved out to his property, way back in the hollows of the woods. I took along an ax, a shotgun, matches, a tarp, a tent, and a car battery and cassette deck (to listen to music). I also had a ton of macaroni and cheese and a big bag of marijuana. I lived out there for almost two months.

When my supplies ran out, my biological father still didn't want me in his house, so I went back to Mom's place in Pennsylvania. I learned my parents were moving to Norfolk, Virginia. They asked if I wanted to move with them. My answer was a quick "yes." At this point, my hair was down to my waist and I had a Grateful Dead tattoo on my back. Sadly, I don't remember when or where I got it.

It was 1992, and I hit rock bottom. I saw no purpose to life and wanted to die. I contemplated taking my own life.

One night while I sat bored in my parents' house, I decided to go out into the hallway and pick up a *National Geographic* magazine to occupy my mind. My parents subscribed to *National Geographic*, but for some odd reason, I found none on the bookshelf. However, there was a book with a yellow binding titled *The Queen of Peace Visits Medjugorje*.

"What the heck is that?" I wondered. I wasn't even sure how to pronounce it.

I pulled it out and looked at it. I had no clue what it was. I figured it might have something to do with the Catholicism "cult" my parents were into. Something about that Jesus fellow, Christianity, and lots of dos and don'ts, rules and regulations.

"And people call *me* weird? I'm going to check this out and see what kind of freaks and weirdos my parents have become." I seriously believed my parents were waiting for the mother ship from planet Juju to come take them away. I was *that* ignorant about Christianity.

I returned to my room with the book. I didn't really want to read it, but there was a picture section. I cracked it open and saw young kids kneeling down with their hands folded. I didn't know what to make of it. The picture's caption read, "The children are now seeing the Blessed Virgin Mary."

Since when is it a blessed thing to be a virgin? I thought. Stupid weirdos! *Who the heck is a virgin nowadays anyway?* I didn't have a clue who those kids were talking about.

I started to read the book, and I couldn't believe it! These little kids were seeing an exquisitely beautiful woman who came from a place called "heaven." They said she smelled like roses and came in a clap of thunder. She was so beautiful that they had been forced to their knees and cried tears of joy because of her beauty.

"What is this?" I asked myself. "A beautiful woman who smells like roses? Count me in!"

I dug in and devoured that book.

The God I did not know had baited me with beauty. He knew I wouldn't read a book about Jesus. I thought Jesus was the great dork-maker in the sky. But what about a book that talked about a beautiful virgin that smells like roses? I was all ears.

I was a wounded and messed-up man. God was well aware of that. He knew exactly how to grab me—and it worked.

I stayed up all night consuming that book. It totally blew me away. I had never heard anything like it before. I didn't understand most of it. The book was very Catholic and used a lot of Catholic lingo. But in my heart and soul I knew it was true. This woman was for real, and her message was for someone like me. She said Jesus was God and the Catholic Church was the Church He founded and where we could be healed. She told the children to fast and pray. The world needed to turn to God while there was still time.

It rocked my world.

I closed the book in the wee hours of the morning and knew my life would never be the same. That woman, the Virgin Mary, had floored me with her words. I had sought the perfect feminine beauty since I was twelve years old. All along I had been seeking perfection and beauty—but in all the wrong ways. Everyone told me, "Do whatever makes you happy. Do whatever makes you feel good." However, I had come to the end of my rope from living that kind of life. I knew there must be something more, and it had just been revealed to me. Jesus wasn't the "thing" I thought He was. He was real. Christianity was real. God was real. I was convinced of it.

When Mom got up at about 5:30 that morning, I met her at the bottom of the staircase. As she walked down the steps, sleepy-eyed and barely awake, I tried to express my need. "Mom, I've got to talk to a Cath—"

I couldn't force myself to say it. I tried again, but the words wouldn't come out. To formulate a spiritual need aloud to my mom was like the ultimate death. I continued to try to speak but with the same result.

Mom looked a little frustrated. "Donnie, what are you trying to tell me?"

I finally blurted out the words loud and fast. "Mom, I need to talk to a Catholic priest, okay?"

She thought I was kidding. "Yeah, right."

"I'm not kidding." I told her about the book I'd stayed up all night reading.

"What book?'

I told her.

Without a word she ran right to the phone and punched in digits at mach speed. "Father, good morning," she said to the person on the other end. "It's LaChita Calloway. You've got to talk to my son. How about eight or eight-thirty?"

Apparently, the priest told her he had to wake up first.

Mom's response was to try another priest. That didn't work either. They all said she should call back later and make an appointment.

I blurted out that I knew how to find a priest. There was a military chapel inside the main gate of the naval base.

"Run, Donnie, run!" Mom said.

I ran like lightning—long hair flowing in the wind, funky clothes, and bound for freedom. That's how I felt as I sprinted past military units doing their morning marches. When I finally arrived at the chapel I couldn't believe it was called "Our Lady of Victory Chapel."

I couldn't quite force myself to go inside. I didn't feel worthy to enter a church. Instead, I looked around until I saw a sign that read "Chaplain's Office." There were all kinds of military personnel inside. To their eyes, I'm sure I looked like I had jumped the fence—totally out of place for a military installation. I saw the confusion on their faces. Not knowing what else to do, I screamed, "Catholic priest!"

Eventually, someone came over and introduced himself as Father John. I had no idea what that meant. "Are you a preacher?" I asked.

He clearly didn't know how to respond but eventually said he was similar to a preacher.

That was all I needed to hear. I had a man of God before me, and I begged him to help me. I started to tell him about all of my wickedness, things I thought would be called sins. He interrupted me at this point and said he had to go celebrate Mass.

I had no idea what he meant by that.

He could see I was confused and told me to go inside the church. After he was done, we could meet back in his office and talk.

It took everything I had within me to touch the chapel's doorknob and go inside. *Me, in a church? It must be the end of the world!*

I slowly made my way through that door. Stepping into that church was like getting into a burning hot bath. When I entered, I saw five Filipino women in the front row. *Oh, no,* I thought. *These people are hardcore Catholics.*

I went to the back pew as fast as I could. After several minutes, the women began doing something very strange. I had never heard or seen anything like it in my life. They seemed to be doing some kind of incantation using a necklace. I could understand only a few words.

Then one of the women turned to me at the back of the chapel and held up her necklace. She asked me to pray the next decade.

What the heck? I thought.

"The Second Sorrowful Mystery," she said.

I had no idea what she was trying to communicate and said nothing. I didn't know they were praying the Rosary.

What seemed like an eternity later, the priest finally entered the chapel. I recognized his face, but he was dressed like a hippie in a robe. He started reading from a book and doing things I didn't understand. I found most of what he was saying to be unintelligible, but then something happened. The priest bent over and picked up a little white circle. "Take this, all of you, and eat it. This is My Body," he said. Then he raised the little white circle.

That was when I heard a voice speak to me. Not an audible voice in my ear but one spoken to my soul: "*Worship!*"

I thought I was losing my mind, but I felt a rush of knowledge come over me. All my being was focused on the little white circle the priest was holding. I absolutely knew that little white circle was God.

The priest then picked up a chalice and said, "Take this, all of you, and drink from it. This is My Blood. The Blood of the new and everlasting covenant." He elevated the chalice.

Once again, I heard the voice telling me to worship. A rush of knowledge came over me that made me acknowledge that what the priest held in that chalice was the blood of God. I was absolutely certain.

Every cell in my body focused on what the priest was doing. The next event completely blew my mind. The Filipino ladies approached the priest. He came from behind the altar and approached them. He had God (the little white circle) with him. The priest gave God to each of those women and said, "The Body of Christ." Then he did the same thing with the chalice, saying, "The Blood of Christ."

I was freaking out. What that voice had told me was true!

After Mass, I went to the priest and told him what I had just experienced. I totally overwhelmed that poor priest! I told him I wanted to become a Catholic today.

The priest had no idea what was going on and told me to slow down and relax. He had a full day ahead of him. He gave me three things—a crucifix, a painting of Jesus, and a large picture of his grandpa—and sent me home saying we would talk the following day.

I had no idea why he was giving me a picture of his grandpa, but I took it and ran home. In the days ahead I would learn his "grandpa" was really a picture of St. John Paul II. I would fall totally in love with that pope.

When I returned home, I threw away almost everything in my room. I tossed out my dirty magazines, drug paraphernalia, and even my clothes into a few black, Hefty garbage bags. Mom didn't say a thing, nor did she try to stop me. I hung up the items the priest had given me—the crucifix, Jesus, and "grandpa."

Now what? I thought. Not knowing what else to do, I picked up the book I had read the night before and did what the kids were doing. I prayed.

I knelt down on my knees, rested my hands on the dresser drawer, and tried to talk to someone I couldn't see. It felt totally weird. I was either losing my mind or about to "get religion."

I didn't know how to pray. I couldn't remember ever having said a prayer in my life. I didn't realize I had hung the image with the heart of Jesus right above my dresser. As I looked at that picture, trying to pray, all of a sudden I snapped. I realized that Jesus was truly God and that *He wanted me.* I looked at His heart, and it was on fire. His hands were in a gesture of invitation. I began to cry uncontrollably.

I can't explain how intensely I was crying. I cried like a little baby. It was pure contrition and repentance. I was so sorry for all of my sinfulness, all of my perversions, all of my wretchedness—all of the wrong things I had done in my life. My tears flowed so profusely that the small amount of clothes in the dresser drawer were soaking wet. You could have drained those clothes in a bucket and filled it.

I knelt there all day unmoving and crying my eyes out. I was being given a second chance at life. I was experiencing a divine detox from all my filthiness and shame.

When I got up off my knees, it was evening! I felt so refreshed from the experience that I just wanted to lie down, sleep, and wake up the next morning and go back to the priest. Once I lay down, however, something happened. A presence entered the room that was so evil, so frightening, that I became paralyzed with fear. I couldn't move. It was Satan.

I wanted to scream and get out of the room, but I couldn't. The presence was trying to take me … trying to carry me off. What could I do to put up a fight against a fallen angel? Nothing physically. I'm made of dust. Spiritually, though, I did the only thing I could. With all the power of my soul, I screamed from my heart to the heavens, *"Mary!"*

Satan fled the room. He was completely gone. In his place I heard the most amazing female voice I've ever heard. The voice was sweet, tender, and beautiful. It was like liquid love pouring over my soul and emotions. "Donnie," the voice said, "I'm so happy!"

Since no one calls me Donnie but my mom, I immediately knew who it was—the mother of Jesus. By calling me Donnie she was telling me that she was *my* mother too. I drifted off into the most amazing sleep I've ever had in my life. That night I slept like a little child tucked against his mother's breast—safe, secure, and tightly wrapped in her mantle. Satan could not touch me. I was in the arms of Mary.

When I woke up the next morning, everything was different. I went to the priest and began the process of learning. Almost everything I had previously learned about life was wrong. I signed up for RCIA classes and practically lived in church. I went to church all day, every day. I sat there, knelt there, prayed there, slept there, and read there. I made the Stations of the Cross until I wore myself out. I learned how to pray the Rosary from the Filipino women. I eventually got a job and spent a lot of money buying roses for Jesus, Our Lady, and St. Joseph. I prayed about what God wanted me to do in life now that I knew He was real.

I had no idea what God wanted me to do other than become Catholic. So, while I was in the process of becoming Catholic, I prayed to know the will of God for my future. I found no peace in any other vocation than becoming a priest. I was surrounded by beautiful Catholic women, but I could not get away from my desire to do what Father was doing at the altar and in the confessional. I wanted to save souls. A lot of souls.

I began to contact vocation directors even before I became Catholic. Our Lady led me to the religious community I was to join. I learned about the Congregation of Marians of the Immaculate Conception. When I found out they promote devotion to Our Lady and spread the Divine Mercy message and devotion, I knew it was a perfect fit. I wanted to be an apostle of mercy and draw others to Jesus through Our Lady.

Due to my past, the Community was reluctant at first to discern with me. However, they prayed about it and believed that giving me a shot was a chance worth taking. They showed me so much mercy and kindness. After going through a long application process, they accepted me. I had only been Catholic for about a year!

I studied ten years to become a priest. Since I had dropped out of high school, I had to relearn almost everything. But God spoiled me with a phenomenal education. The Community opened up a house in Steubenville, Ohio, and I was part of the first group of men from the Community to attend Franciscan University. It is in my opinion the best Catholic university in the world.

I studied under Scott Hahn, Mark Miravalle, and many other incredible professors. I soaked it up and couldn't get enough. Then I went on to seminary. I studied at the Dominican House of Studies in Washington,

D.C. and loved it. I learned the incredible theology of St. Thomas Aquinas and learned so much about the human person and God's plan for us. At the end of it all, I was ordained a priest at the National Shrine of Divine Mercy in Stockbridge, Massachusetts, on May 31, 2003.

And my mom? Well, she's a saint in my opinion. I call her my St. Monica. She is like my best friend now. There is absolutely nothing like being able to give Mom Holy Communion and pray a Rosary with her. We travel on pilgrimages all over the world and give thanks and praise to Jesus and Mary for what they have done for our family.

My message for you—especially for mothers—is that you can have hope. You probably have someone in your family—a husband, a son, a daughter, a grandchild, a brother or sister—who is far from the truth. God will bless your prayers and your sacrifices. Cling to hope. My mom held out hope when there was no hope left, and look what happened! She became Catholic, her husband became Catholic, and her delinquent son became a priest.

Never give up. Never stop praying. Trust Jesus at all times. He is faithful.

Bio –

Fr. Donald Calloway, MIC is a convert to the Catholic faith and was ordained to the priesthood in 2003. Fr. Calloway was raised without any religion or father figure to model. Although baptized as a Protestant at the age of ten, he never received any formal Christian instruction. Moving often, he slipped into a lifestyle of sex, drugs, and rock music. The rebellion of his early teen years intensified when his family relocated to Japan, and he ran away from home. His life degraded to delinquency and crime.

Today, Fr. Calloway is the Director of Vocations for the Marians of the Immaculate Conception in Steubenville, Ohio, and the author of the most comprehensive book ever written on the Rosary, *Champions of the Rosary: The History and Heroes of a Spiritual Weapon.* His amazing journey to the Catholic faith and the sacrament of Holy Orders is a powerful witness to Our Lady's loving intervention and God's abundant mercy.

Rev. Fr. Raniero Cantalamessa, O.F.M. Cap.

———◇◇◇◇———

The audience of the Papal Household is certainly more important but not as beautiful as this audience. In his first letter to the Corinthians Saint Paul mentions an apparition of the risen Jesus to more than 500 people at one time. So, if the Lord was able to reveal Himself to more than 500 people at one time, He certainly can do it again spiritually today.

Not only *can* He do this but He *most certainly does.* He is present among us in this huge Cenacle. "Wherever two or three are gathered in my name, I am there" (Matthew 18:20). We should be aware that He is present not only sacramentally in the Eucharist. He is present in another, more personal, more intimate way to each one of us. Let us welcome this special Guest among us.

I share my personal testimony with pleasure. It has to do with religious life because I am a religious priest. It also has to do with the Charismatic Renewal. I don't necessarily intend to convince you to join the Charismatic Renewal, only that this is the way the Lord has led me to a new life and a new understanding of my ministry.

If my testimony challenges you, then decide if the Lord is calling you also. The important part is not so much to join one particular movement or spiritual experience. The important thing for everybody in the Church is a new Pentecost. This is the grace, the special grace the Lord asks for during this difficult time in the Church. John XXIII asked God for a new Pentecost, and God has answered his prayer. There is a new Pentecost going on in the Church. Everyone is invited to enter into the Cenacle. Maybe for some of you, today is the day of Pentecost.

Let us pass to my personal testimony. I was born in the middle of Italy, in the city of Ascoli Piceno, on July 22, 1934. I entered into the college seminary in the Capuchin order but had not yet decided what to do with my life: whether to study and then go out, or if I should continue in this line. Three months after entering the seminary, we had our first retreat. For the first time, I listened to the beautiful truth about our religion, the love of God, eternal life, and the Gospels.

Listening to these meditations, I perceived that the Lord was calling me to become a Franciscan religious priest. It was with such clarity that I could never doubt my calling after that. The Lord called me to be His disciple full-time, full-heart in the Franciscan style. "This is the biggest grace the Lord could afford me after baptism," I told my companions.

I started my formation, which lasted about fifteen years. I was ordained a priest in 1958, and what a joy to celebrate my 50th priestly anniversary with so many Magnificat women! See how powerful Our Lady is to pick me out of Italy at this time in my life. After my ordination, I was sent to Switzerland to graduate in theology. I specialized in the New Testament and the Fathers of the Church. My superiors then sent me to the University of Milan to specialize in classical literature and in Greek and Latin, in order to deepen my knowledge of the Bible and of the Church fathers.

After graduating with a degree in literature, they asked me to remain at the university. I became a professor at the large Catholic University of Milan. I was very happy there. My superiors were very proud of a fellow Capuchin in this position. I even became head of a department at that university.

In 1975 a lady whom I had accompanied in her spiritual journey returned from a retreat in Milan. "I met some very strange people in that house," she said. "They pray with clapping and raising their hands. They even speak about miracles happening among them."

Being a wise spiritual director, I said, "You never go again to this spiritual house."

She obeyed. But as women do, she didn't give up easily. She began inviting me to know these people. One time she invited me to Rome for a prayer meeting. I was skeptical because I was a very traditional Catholic priest formed before the Council. I was afraid of every novelty. I went to the meeting but looked at the assembly rather critically.

The leaders of the group were aware of my hesitation. They told the others, "Don't go to this particular priest. He is an enemy, so be careful."

But seeing a priest among them, some would come and ask for confession. Hearing their confessions was the first strike in my life. It was as if the Lord was shaking me up. I had never met such deep and true repentance! Sins seemed to fall from the souls of these people like stones, and at the end they had great joy—grateful tears of joy. I had to say to myself that this was truly the work of the Holy Spirit.

For the first time I understood what Jesus meant when He said, "The Paraclete, when He comes, He will convince the world of sin" (John 16:8). These people were really conscious of sin, convinced interiorly, and I started to reflect on this phenomenon I witnessed. There was something that attracted me to their conversion experience.

As a teacher of history of ancient Christianity, I saw that what was happening among these people was very similar to what had happened in the early Church, in Corinth for instance. I was fascinated. At the same time, however, I was taken aback. I gave a course at the university on the first charismatic and prophetic movements in the early Church, trying to understand something about this time. While I was in this position, the people of the renewal kept inviting me to give some teachings.

Thanks be to God for those beautiful ladies in my life! In 1977, another lady in Milan offered me a ticket to attend a Charismatic ecumenical rally in the United States, in Kansas City, Missouri. I had to start learning English. This opportunity to visit America was a good one, so I accepted.

I planned to visit my Franciscan friary in Washington, D.C. and study English. Then after a week, I thought it would all be over. I attended this Charismatic event of over 40,000 people. I was astounded by the sheer numbers and the impact of the rally. Praise the Lord! It was a phenomenal event. Half the people in attendance were Catholics. The other half came from various other denominations. Something attracted me, something I was unprepared to receive.

I remember one evening during the event. A leader took the microphone and started saying—in my opinion at that time—some very strange words. "You bishops, you pastors, you people, mourn and weep because the body of My Son is broken." Again and again he said, "You laypeople, men and women, mourn and weep because the body of My Son is broken."

Little by little, I began to see people falling on their knees all around me. As a single assembly, this huge crowd sobbed and repented because of the divisions in the body of Christ. During all this, above the stadium a huge sign proclaimed, "Jesus is Lord!" For me it was a prophetic vision. I said to myself, "If one day all the Christians are united in one body, it will look like this, when we are all on our knees, repenting under the Lordship of Christ."

This was the moment when I conceived the book *Life in the Lordship of Christ*, now on the market with the title *Life in Christ*, by Liturgical Press of Collegeville. It was the beginning of a discovery of the Lordship of Christ. My prayer for you right now is that the Holy Spirit will lead many of you to this new world, the world of the Lordship of Christ.

Why is the title "Lord" so important? St. Paul says, "No one can say 'Jesus is Lord' unless he or she is under the influence of the Holy Spirit" (1 Corinthians 12:3). In another passage, Paul says, "If you proclaim him with your lips that Jesus is Lord and in your heart you believe that God raised him from the dead, you are saved" (Romans 10:9).

You have already entered into the world of salvation. Do you want this beautiful proclamation to resound? Then learn these two short phrases. The first phrase: "Jesus is Lord." The second phrase: "God raised Him from the dead." It is a *kerygma*, which literally means "a cry, a shout." Not *any* shout, but the shout that proclaims the central mystery of our faith—the death and resurrection of Christ. Oh, the Lordship of Christ!

This title is so important because when you say "Jesus is Lord" you are first of all proclaiming the whole paschal mystery. You proclaim that He died for our sins and rose again for our justification. Secondly, when you say "Jesus is Lord," you are making a decision. Not just offering a toast, but making a decision for your life. It means that we receive You, Jesus, as our Lord. We surrender to You. We submit to You. We proclaim You as our leader, the meaning of my life. You are the One who has rights upon me.

So really, you are choosing your destination. According to St. Paul, when a person proclaims "Jesus is Lord" from the bottom of his or her heart, this moment divides his life into two parts: before and after.

In the life of any person there is a moment, an event which divides life into two parts. For married people, this is usually life before marriage and then being married. For priests, it is life before ordination and after ordination.

For any person, there is an event which really divides life into two parts: before knowing Jesus as personal Lord and after knowing Him. Read Philippians, chapter three, where St. Paul describes what he used to be before: a Pharisee, born of the tribe of Benjamin. Then read what Paul was after he discovered the supreme advantage of knowing Jesus as his Lord.

When we speak about the Lordship of God, we should always define this. It is not a word that is supportive or sympathetic, so we immediately think of dominion or oppression. No, the Lordship of Christ is something very different. He died for us. Usually, people in power send their servants to die for *them*. Jesus died for *us*. We should always remember this and honor Him. He is our Lord and our Friend.

This was the moment, in Kansas City, when I started discovering the beautiful, liberating world of the Lordship of Christ. But, I am ashamed to admit, I was still very critical about the people in the Charismatic Renewal. When the crowd sang a beautiful song about the story of Jericho, "Lift high the banner of love, Jericho must fall," it had a special meaning for me. The group that came with me from Italy nudged me and said, "Listen carefully, because 'Jericho, it is you.'"

Jericho fell, but not immediately. After the rally we attended a retreat at a convent house in New Jersey. I decided to leave and join my Franciscan friars, but an Irish priest, Fr. Brendan Murray—to whom I am very much indebted—invited me to stay and join a Life in the Spirit seminar, which had been planned for the week.

Why was I wary? After all, this wasn't a house of prostitution. If I decided to stay it wouldn't do me any harm. So I told the Lord I would stay. "Lord," I prayed, "I will give You one more chance to convince me that this is really Your work."

I began attending the sessions. One detail I still recall was the day we were in a prayer meeting in the hall. I was still struggling with objections. "I am a Franciscan, a religious priest. What am I waiting for? What can these people give me that I don't possess? I already have St. Francis of Assisi as my spiritual father."

At that moment, a lady opened her Bible and—not knowing anything about my thoughts—began reading a passage. It was the passage where St. John the Baptist says to the Pharisees, "Don't say in your hearts, 'we have Abraham as our Father.'" I understood the Lord was answering my thoughts.

I stood up. I spoke no English. I spoke Italian, but it seemed everybody understood. "Lord," I said, "I will never again say that I am a son of St. Francis of Assisi, because I realize I am not. If it is necessary to receive this grace of the Baptism in the Holy Spirit to become a real, true son of St. Francis, I accept."

I prepared myself to receive this Baptism in the Spirit, which is very simple. People pray over you for a renewal of your baptism, your religious profession, and your entire spiritual being. Later on, I tried to deepen my understanding of the Baptism in the Holy Spirit, but it truly is simple. After all, the expression wasn't invented by the Charismatic Renewal.

Who invented the expression "Baptism in the Holy Spirit"? Jesus did. Speaking to His disciples before leaving them, He said, "You shall be baptized in the Holy Spirit in a few days" (Acts 1:5). And what happened in a few days? Pentecost. So it is quite clear. It is not baptism in water. It is the release of the gifts of the Holy Spirit, this coming of the Spirit.

Let me share another detail of my preparation for the Baptism in the Holy Spirit. One evening during the retreat, while I was walking in the park, the Lord spoke to me through an image. I saw myself as a man upon a chariot holding the reins of the horses. I immediately understood this was an image of my life as a person who wanted to be in control of his life and decide what to do, where to go.

At the same time, it was as if Jesus stood beside me and gently said to me, "Do you want to give Me the reins of your life?"

There was a moment of panic. I understood this was serious. But at the same time I immediately realized that no one can be in control of his or her life. We cannot decide where we will be tomorrow, so I said, "Yes, Lord, take the reins of my life." I must also confess that later on sometimes I tried to get back control of the reins. This is why we have such a merciful Lord, always ready to forgive us.

The day came when the retreat leaders prayed over us and spoke prophetic words over me. They spoke of a mission of evangelization or preaching, that I was being set apart to bring the Word to kings and nations. One person prophesied, "You will experience a new joy in proclaiming My Word."

I am not a joyful person by nature; quite the contrary. But whenever I proclaim the Word of God, people say there is a joy flowing outward. This is a fulfillment of this prophecy. In my program on Italian television my best tool is my smile.

During the prayers at the time of asking for an infilling of the Holy Spirit, there is often a moment when we are asked, "Do you choose Jesus as your personal Lord?" This is part of the experience, choosing Jesus again as our personal Lord and Savior in a free, conscious way, to confirm our Baptism by saying a willing "yes" to the Lord.

At the moment I said this, I lifted my eyes and met the crucifix that hung up on the altar. In a flash, the Lord spoke to me. The meaning was clear: "Be careful. Jesus, whom you are choosing as your personal Lord, is not an 'easy' Jesus. It is I, the crucifix."

Those praying for me knew I still harbored some doubts about the Charismatic Renewal as being much too emotional and superficial. But in that moment, I understood that the work of the Spirit leads you straight to the core of the gospel, which is the cross of Jesus. This dispelled every last doubt.

I received the grace of the Spirit, but nothing dramatic happened during the prayer of the Baptism in the Spirit. The day afterward, I took a plane from Newark to Washington. During the flight I started to realize that something had happened. A change. When I opened my breviary and started reading the Psalms, it seemed to be written the day before, and specifically for me. The words came alive!

I realized the fruit of the Baptism of the Holy Spirit is that the Bible becomes a living book that speaks to you. It is the channel for the voice of God. I had confirmation of this many times later on that only the Holy Spirit can explain the Bible. Only the Holy Spirit allows you to hear the voice of God in the words of the Bible.

One year it was the Year of the Word of God. I gave my meditation on the Word of God to the Papal Household during Advent and Lent. I stressed the importance of the spiritual reading of the Bible. Otherwise, the Bible becomes just a book and people studying the Bible can lose their faith.

The following testimony illustrates how the Holy Spirit can lead simple people to understand the voice of God. One day when I was preaching a mission in Australia, a man came to me and said, "Father, I have a big problem in my family. We have an eleven-year-old boy who has not yet been baptized. The problem is that my wife has become a Jehovah's Witness and doesn't want the baptism to be mentioned. If I baptize the boy, there will be a conflict. However, if I do not baptize the boy, there will be a conflict with my conscience. When we married, we were both Catholics and promised to raise our children in the Catholic Church."

"Let me pray tonight," I said. "Come tomorrow, and we will see what can be done about the situation."

The next day, this man came to me. I could see he was very relaxed. "Father," he said, "I have found the solution." I was relieved because I hadn't found a solution yet.

"Going home yesterday," the man continued, "I prayed for a while and then I opened the Bible. I happened to read the passage where Abraham takes his son Isaac to be killed as a sacrifice. And I saw that when Abraham takes his son Isaac to the immolation he doesn't mention anything to his wife."

The Word of God had led this man to select the best solution for him and his son. Since he had reasoned that Abraham didn't mention anything to his wife, he believed he could do the same. Nothing now prevented him from baptizing the boy. I complied by baptizing the boy myself. It was a great joy!

The Holy Spirit can open your eyes to the real meaning, not just the historical events, which are important but just the first step. The goal of the Bible is not to provide us with a beautiful document of ancient or current culture. God revealed the Bible to strengthen and share His life and to convince people of His love.

When I finally reached my friary in Washington, I had further confirmation about the strength and importance of prayer. In fact, I had a new desire to pray. Praying was a struggle in my life, but now I was attracted to the chapel and to prayer at almost every hour.

The prayer acquired a Trinitarian dimension, which should be a structure to all Christian prayer. This means that the Father spoke to me about the Son, and Jesus spoke to me about the Father. Each Person of the Trinity seemed to be eager to reveal the other. I learned more about this Trinitarian life, which is something beautiful and unique.

Christian prayer is something special. It is found in no other faith. While you can learn a technique, the essence of Christian life is something different. It is not just a creature speaking to his God on the other side of the line. It is God praying in you. Praying in the Spirit means that God is praying within. It is God praying to God. It is a Divine way to pray. We have in ourselves the very source of prayer, the Holy Spirit. Yet we go around learning how to pray. We should dig deeper and find the fountain of prayer, which is the Holy Spirit living within.

After three months I returned to Italy. It had been my three months of honeymoon, growing deeper in God's presence and love. People who knew me in Italy, as you can imagine, were very, very surprised at the transformation. Some said, "Look at the miracle. We sent Saul to America, and they have sent us back Paul!" I began joining these laypeople and sharing their prayers.

During a special prayer meeting, I was inspired by the Holy Spirit to speak aloud, "Lord, do not allow me to die as a retired university professor." At the time I didn't understand the meaning of the words. However, a few weeks later I had my answer. I was praying in my room at the friary, and the Lord spoke to me again through an image.

This was nothing supernatural, no outward vision, but the way God communicated with His creature, which I believe is deeper and much stronger than the exterior communication. It was as if the Lord Jesus passed in front of me. I saw precisely the same Jesus as when He returned from the Jordan and began to preach about the kingdom of God.

As the Lord passed before me, He said in this interior way, "If you want to help Me in proclaiming the kingdom of God, leave everything and follow Me."

As a Franciscan, I was already supposed to have left everything. But in reality I had not. I was not poor. I was very rich indeed. I was honored and respected by the students, especially a few days before the examinations. I understood that God was saying to me, "If you want to help me in proclaiming the kingdom of God, leave your teaching position, leave your academic position, leave everything and become an itinerant preacher of the gospel in the style of your father, Francis of Assisi."

As a religious, I couldn't act just on this interior inspiration. I went to my General Superior in Rome, a man of God, and said, "I think the Lord is telling me to completely change my life."

He said, "Let us wait one year." This is the classic answer all superiors give, and a very wise answer indeed. So, I continued teaching for one year. This was a lesson in the discovery of the gift of obedience. Not the *duty* of obedience but the *gift* of obedience.

It was obedience that saved my calling. During that year, everything became a blur and obscured. I became afraid and wondered what I should do. During my entire priestly life I had only preached sermons on Sunday. I discovered the importance of having authority within the Catholic Church, whether it was the bishop, my confessor, or my spiritual director. In fact, anyone who represented objectivity in discerning the will of God regarding my calling. This also applies to anyone. It is the way you can be assured that your personal inspiration comes from the Lord.

After a year, I returned to my superior, and we prayed together. "Yes, it is the will of God," he said, and gave me permission to resign my position. I went to the rector at the university and resigned my teaching position. I went on a retreat to prepare myself for this new ministry and prayerfully seek God's will.

There I discovered something precious, which I could call a "new" Jesus. Christology—which means the doctrine about Jesus—had always been my main focus, my area of specialization. I had written my thesis on the Christology of Tertullian and had given courses on the Christology of John, of Paul and the Fathers of the Church.

However, during the retreat I discovered another Jesus, a living Jesus, a Jesus in flesh and bones. Not just a compilation of doctrines and dogmas, not a historical person of the past that we can remember or sacramentally make present. Of course, He is the *same* Jesus, but I discovered Him in a deeper and different way than in the past. I found the Jesus that is close to me. And He is in you, as well.

What especially helped me was a passage in the letter to the Philippians, where St. Paul tells of his own experience. He explains what he was before and what he became. He ends by saying, "I have done all this. I have left behind all of my assets that I may know Him." Reading this Scripture in Greek, I was struck by the pronoun *eauton*. This is a personal pronoun. At that moment it meant more to me than all the books I had written or read. When St. Paul says "that I may know Him," he means a real person. Someone with whom you can speak. Someone with whom you can share everything. I received a great desire to know this Jesus as St. Paul knew Him.

Even today, any time I comment on the account of the Pentecost, I am impressed by the way the Holy Spirit makes Jesus alive to the apostles. When the apostles received the Holy Spirit, they were all together. A strong wind blew, and wind is symbolic of the Holy Spirit. The apostles began preparing for something special to happen due to this external sign. The wind was a call of interior grace that the Lord prepared for them at this time.

Wind shares the same name as the Spirit in the Hebrew and Greek languages. There was even a sign for their eyes. They witnessed something extraordinary: tongues of fire. This is meaningful because fire and the Holy Spirit were always associated together. Next came the reality of Pentecost, where they were filled with the Holy Spirit.

What does being filled with the Holy Spirit actually mean? For them it was life-changing. This was not just a new idea, a new insight into the Holy Spirit. It was more like an earthquake that shook them to the core. Afterward, these people were completely changed. So something astounding must have happened. Unfortunately, when we read the words "filled with the Holy Spirit," we disregard the significance without realizing there is an abyss beneath these words.

The Holy Spirit is the furnace of love burning between the Father and the Son in the Trinity and uniting them. A love so strong as to be a person. Think about how excited we are about love in general. How many experiences of love have you enjoyed? The Holy Spirit is the furnace. All the love we know and have experienced in life are just sparks of this furnace.

To say the disciples were filled with the Holy Spirit means they were filled with the love of God. They had an overwhelming experience of being loved by God. Imagine a young person who discovers the girl he loves and desires, loves him. Now imagine the disciples filled with the love of God, and that love comes from the very Source of all love. There is a much more faithful representation of what truly happened at that moment than the traditional representations of Pentecost. The typical portrayal of twelve apostles around the table, quietly observing a phenomenon with closed hands and looking into a void is not what I believe captures the essence.

A representation of Pentecost hangs in a young church in Africa, which I think is much closer to reality. Some of the apostles are covering their eyes because of the excessive light. Some are raising their hands, and others are embracing. Only one person sits quietly, and that is Mary, because for her this outpouring of Divine love is not a surprise. She has already had a Pentecost experience. For the apostles, however, it was earth-shattering. Today, when a person experiences a "new Pentecost," the most enduring feeling is the love of God.

I attended the 40th anniversary conference of the Charismatic Renewal in the Catholic Church in England. Beforehand, a survey was distributed to people attending from England, Scotland, Wales, and Ireland. The survey asked, "What do you think has been the greatest blessing you have received from the Holy Spirit?"

The answers revealed a simple truth: "It was the first time I understood what it meant to be loved by God, and experience the tenderness of God's love." A lady I knew answered, "I had lived all my life with this bitter feeling of not being truly loved by anyone, and not being able to be loved by anyone. But this feeling disappeared and never returned." This is incredible, this experience of the love of God.

St. Paul explained Pentecost this way: "The love of God has been poured into our hearts through the Holy Spirit which has been given to us" (Romans 5:5). This is a shorter, not a narrative description, but this too explains Pentecost. Pentecost is the love of God, which means the love God has for *us*, not our love for God. This comes later as an effect, not as the cause. The immense, Divine love of God has been poured into our hearts.

This is what Jesus meant when He said, "You will be baptized in the Holy Spirit." To be baptized at that time, in the original Greek meaning, didn't mean to receive a few drops of water on your head. It meant full immersion in water. Jesus meant for us to be fully immersed in the life of the Trinity. This is Pentecost, my dear brothers and sisters. Are you starting to desire this? Because if you desire with an expectant faith, this is a gift you will receive. It is a formal promise of Jesus. "If you who are evil can give good things to your children, how much more will the heavenly Father give the Holy Spirit to those who ask him?" (Matthew 7:11).

I had a new understanding of Pentecost after receiving the Baptism in the Holy Spirit. The apostles went out and started proclaiming Jesus in such a way that 3,000 people were converted. The message went straight to their hearts. I imagine it was precisely at the moment when Peter—in the power and the anointing of the Spirit—announced the name of Jesus.

After explaining that the people filled with the Spirit were not drunk, Peter said, "Now, people, listen to me." Then he pronounced the name "Jesus of Nazareth." He wanted to be absolutely sure they understood of whom he was speaking. Many of these people had forgotten Jesus, or they didn't know Him at all. They were only present in Jerusalem to celebrate the feast of Pentecost.

Peter reminded them of the Messiah, Jesus, and the life He had led with goodness, love, and kindness to others. Then Peter said, "You have killed Him. You gave Him to the pagans and you had Him crucified, but be not in despair, God has raised Him. So the whole house of Israel, the whole world must know that God has made this Jesus, whom you have crucified, both Lord and Christ" (Acts 2).

The first fruits, the blessings of the anointing of the Holy Spirit, are a strong proclamation of Jesus. That day the apostles understood who Jesus truly was. The same experience happened to me. After receiving the

Baptism in the Holy Spirit, I discovered this new Jesus. I am not finished discovering Him. No one can ever finish discovering Jesus. It is impossible. It is so sweet. It is so enriching, so fulfilling to know Jesus. I recommend you ignite this fire in your own life.

Do you love Jesus? If your answer is "yes," Jesus is happy to hear people proclaim this truth. In reading these words you may experience this infilling of love. You are welcome to shout the words alone, or with believing people around you. Just say, "Jesus, I love You!" You will not remain the same after invoking these words with an open heart.

As I was preparing myself for this new ministry back in 1980, I received a phone call from Rome. My Superior General was on the other end of the line. "The Holy Father, John Paul II, has appointed you as the Preacher to the Papal Household," he told me. "Do you have any serious reason to say no?"

I was shocked by the request. I tried to find a reason, but I honestly couldn't think of any reason to avoid this appointment. I had to prepare myself within a few weeks to preach my first weekly meditation to the Papal Household.

You may consider this a strange ministry. I've been asked about it by people who are surprised to learn the pope listens to sermons given by a priest. The pope, by his example, gives us a tremendous sense of humility and respect to the Word of God.

There is a fixed ministry in the Vatican called the "Preacher to the Papal Household," which in the last three centuries has been given to the Capuchin order. Each Friday morning at 9:00 a.m., meditations are given to the pope, to his secretaries, to the cardinals of the Roman Curia, to the bishops and prelates, and to the superior generals of the various religious orders. In total about sixty or seventy people are in attendance.

Can you imagine preaching to the pope and the cardinals in attendance? However, as threatening an audience you may consider them to be, it is much more of a challenge for me to speak in America. I can speak Italian at the Vatican. In America, I must speak English.

After all these years the Lord still has me in this position. No preacher has lasted so long in the history of the Church, which accounts for the heroic patience of the popes. Pope John Paul II rarely missed a sermon, even when he was in bad health. One year he missed two Fridays because he was traveling around Central America. When he returned, he came straight to me and apologized for having missed the two sermons. I sometimes ask people, "Do *you* ever go to your parish priest apologizing for missing last Sunday's sermon?"

The Lord appointed this simple Capuchin priest to preach at the Vatican after he received the grace of the new Pentecost. This ministry allows me to make known at the heart of the Church what is going on among the people of God. On the other hand, it allows me to share with my fellow brothers wherever I am preaching about the concerns of the hierarchy, the concerns of the pope, and of the institutional Church. It has been a great blessing in my life.

Once a year, on Good Friday, the sermon is delivered in St. Peter's Basilica. This is the only occasion when the pope presides over the liturgy, but he doesn't preach. The Papal Preacher climbs the Papal altar to deliver the homily with the pope, the cardinals, the diplomatic body, and all the people present.

The first time I gave the homily, I had to speak very slowly because there was an echo in the Basilica. As a result, the sermon lasted ten minutes longer than the time allotted. The bishop in charge of the pope's schedule was nervous. He often looked at his watch, because after the service the pope must preside over The Way of the Cross in the coliseum.

I learned what happened later. The bishop shared the story with some religious sisters. After the liturgy, Pope John Paul II called him. Smiling, he said, "When a man of God is speaking to us, we should not be looking at our watches."

This is a lesson for us all. Don't look at your watches in church. You shouldn't be looking at your watches ... but the preacher should!

When the communist regime collapsed in 1989, I was giving meditations on the book of Exodus. Everyone considered John Paul II the new Moses, leading the people in his native Poland—and others—out of the communist regime. In one sermon I quoted this beautiful song in English, "Go down, Moses, in Egypt land. Tell old Pharaoh, 'Let my people go.'" Without saying it, I intended to apply this song to John Paul II.

After the sermon I met him, as usual. He was impressed and said to me, "Oh, how beautiful! You are right. 'Let go my people, let go my people.'" I corrected the pope in his English translation. "Let my people go, Your Holiness." "Oh, yes. Let my people go."

Since starting this ministry first at the Vatican, it has slowly expanded. After I left the university, I was invited to preach at bishops' conferences and to clergy in many dioceses. Once or twice a year I travel to the United States. There seems to be a special relationship between the United States and me. I feel indebted because I received my new birth in that country. I was baptized in the Holy Spirit in America.

I am also invited by many Protestant brothers to give retreats and to preach. It is a blessing. One year, I preached at a seminary in Kentucky and experienced an incredible unity. Another time, I was invited to give a retreat to 3,000 Lutherans in Sweden and felt an amazing spirit of unity. I have also been invited many times to preach in England. One day I gave a retreat to an Anglican community and felt obliged to present a sermon on Mary, the Blessed Mother. I admit it was a challenge teaching on Mary to our Protestant brothers.

I explained that we Catholics were partially responsible for their difficulty in accepting Mary's role because we have exalted her many times in a wrong way. I wanted to show how they too could develop a relationship with Mary and learn unwavering faith by her example by just reading the Scriptures. Starting from the Gospels, I spoke of Mary as she journeyed to Golgotha, watching her Son. She was the first believer. As a woman she was close to the other women at the time, walking beside them and encouraging them.

I believe this teaching brought about a healing in the community. It was such an experience to watch the people as I spoke. They were crying. Later that day, one lady told another, "Don't mention what we have heard this morning. Otherwise I will start crying again." It was a beautiful experience to consider Mary in a different light and bring healing in the relationship.

I believe it is important because I am directing this teaching to the Magnificat women's ministry. I wish to pay homage to the importance of women. I once gave this sermon on Good Friday, before the Holy Father, in regard to the importance of women in the gospel. Jesus chose women to be the apostles of the apostles. I am always impressed by this fact.

In the Bible we find many voices of God saying, "Go and speak to My people."

God directs Moses, "Go down, Moses, to My people in Egypt."

He says to Isaiah, "Go and speak to My people."

He directs the call to many people and finally to the apostles. All of these summons "to go" are directed toward men. There is only one passage in Scripture when "go" is addressed to women. Some may argue it is the most beautiful of all. It is the "go" Jesus pronounced Easter morning when He told the women, "Go to My disciples and tell them that I am alive."

Now, I dare to repeat this same charge: Go and tell the disciples of Jesus and the priests that God is alive.

You have an important role to play. Many of you love your priests. Your love is important to them. Because priests are celibate, they need sound relationships, ones not based on flesh and blood, the kind of relationship God reserves for married couples. This love is what God had in mind when He created man and women together.

What a marvelous plan of God! He wanted people on Earth to reflect what happens in the Trinity. In the Trinity there are two persons who love each other, the Father and the Son, and the love that overflows from them results in the Holy Spirit.

God wanted this to be repeated in many different ways. First, a man and a woman who love each other in marriage. Another way to express the love of God is a father and a son or daughter, or a mother and a daughter or son relationship. There is sister and sister, or brother and brother within a family, who express their love for each other.

Then there is the love outside of the family bond, between friends. This always involves two people. When two people love each other with God as the center, something miraculous takes place that reflects the sharing of the Trinity. What a marvelous project God began when He created man and woman. Unfortunately, we spoiled this project.

St. Francis and St. Clare are examples of a relationship close to what God had in mind, being man and woman, and a help for each other. Not an enemy, not a trap.

I leave you with this thought, this charge to "Go!" You have a special calling as women to be apostles to the apostles. The world needs you. Jesus needs you, and Jesus loves you. Receive the Holy Spirit to really do His work, and each day fulfill your calling as apostles to the apostles.

Bio–

Fr. Raniero Cantalamessa lived in Ascoli Piceno, Italy, and was ordained a Franciscan Capuchin priest in 1958. In 1980 he was appointed by Pope John Paul II as Preacher to the Papal Household, in which capacity he also served under Pope Benedict XVI and currently serves under Pope Francis. His official duties include preaching retreats to the pope, members of the Papal Household and Vatican officials. He is a Doctor of Divinity, a Doctor of Classical Literature, and former professor of History of Ancient Christianity, and Director of the Department of Religious Science at the Catholic University in Milan. He was a member of the International Theological Commission and has been a member of the Catholic delegation of the dialogue with Pentecostal churches for the last seventeen years. He runs a weekly program on the first channel of Italian state television on the gospel. Fr. Cantalamessa is frequently invited to speak at international and ecumenical conferences and rallies. He is a prolific writer and one of the greatest spiritual educators of our time. Father Raniero shared the above elements of his testimony with our Magnificat Chapter in Grapevine, Texas, on October 4, 2008, the feast day of St. Francis of Assisi!

Rev. Fr. Lou Cerulli

O ne of my concerns when sharing my journey and call to the priesthood is the tendency to bring the focus on myself. That is not my intent. My story is more about God than it is about me. Jesus said, "It was not you who chose me, but I who chose you" (John 15:16). I am blessed because I "believed that what was spoken to [me] by the Lord would be fulfilled" (Luke 1:45).

I pray you hear the Lord as you read these words, and that they touch your heart in the way the Lord means for them to touch your heart. I pray that all praise, honor, and glory is given to God, our Lord and Master.

My calling involved great faith, belief, discernment, and trust. I am reminded of a story that illustrates this point very well, because my call began with falling over a "cliff."

A man was driving his car along a mountain road. However, he was driving his car too fast. Traveling along a mountain road at high speed means something is bound to happen. Sure enough, something did happen. The driver came to a curve in the road. There was no way he could manipulate it. His car was going over the cliff, and it was going *down*. There was about a 3,000-foot drop.

Luckily, as his car plummeted down, a branch was sticking out. The man grabbed the branch, and the car went crashing all the way down to the bottom.

This guy was left hanging. He looked around. He couldn't go down. He couldn't go up. He couldn't go left, and he couldn't go right. The only thing left for him was prayer. "Oh, my God! God! Dear God! Please, please help me!"

The man suddenly heard a booming voice, and the Lord said, "Do you believe?"

"Oh, yeah! Yeah, yeah! I believe."

"Do you *really* believe?"

"Yeah, yeah, yeah. I really believe!"

"Do you *truly, really* believe?"

"Yeah, yeah! I really, truly believe. Please help me!"

"Let go!"

"No way!"

So, there is the call and the response. Isn't that typical? We want to hold on to that branch all the time. We may let go occasionally, but we don't like to move too far away … just in case we need to grab the branch again. It's okay if that branch is God. We can hang on to Him, but all other branches need to go.

I will share my story in the way I believe the Lord is asking me. Of course, it all started when the Lord decided I would be born, but I won't go back that far.

I was married in 1966. Renata, my daughter, was born in 1968, and I was divorced in 1971. My divorce is the "cliff" in my story. I made a Cursillo in 1972, and in 1973, I initiated the process to obtain a Decree of Nullity. My first try for the process of annulment was answered with "no." Three years later, I tried again, and the answer was still "no." I tried again in 1977. The answer? "No."

During this same year, the Lord led me to the Charismatic Renewal. My life was never the same after I encountered the Holy Spirit and His gifts and power in my life. The Holy Spirit began a process of healing me from all the grief and wounds of my past, and He continues to heal me through tears and laughter.

After my initial encounter with the Holy Spirit, which was very intense and dramatic, I became involved in a prayer group that became my home and family. I would not be here today, and I would not be a priest today, if it were not for those wonderful people, the Holy Spirit, and my daughter, who was my greatest supporter. From my first encounter, I was filled with a hunger and thirst for the Scriptures, for more knowledge and wisdom, and for more of the Lord and the Holy Spirit. I soon became a leader in the prayer group and healing ministry. I also spoke to the auxiliary bishop about the diaconate, but I was told it was impossible.

However, I no longer believe that anything is impossible.

In 1978, I became one of the group of pioneers of the Christian Training Program (CTP). Then, in 1979 I had the blessing of being called to make a thirty-day retreat in Mississauga, Ontario, at a place called Mary Queen of Apostles. It was six years after my first petition for annulment, when the auxiliary bishop encouraged me to try again. So in 1981, eight years after my first petition and three failed attempts, I tried again. The case was finally heard in 1982, nine years after the first try. The next year—ten years from the start—the annulment was finally granted.

My annulment opened many possibilities for me. In 1985, my now seventeen-year-old daughter went to live with her mom in South Africa. She was about two years old when her mom left, and I was blessed to have been able to raise her.

I entered St. Paul's Seminary in Ottawa, Ontario, this same year. On December 4, 1990, I was ordained to the transitional diaconate and was ordained to the priesthood one year later. Thank God!

Please bear in mind as you continue your own journey that God, the Lord, is with you, loves you, is guiding you, and is blessing you. He will continue to remain with you always. That is guaranteed. That is a given. That is a promise. God walks in the corridor of your heart, and God rests on the altar of your soul. God is with you. He is ever faithful, ever loving, and is always a steadfast God.

My divorce was a struggle. First of all, I had to deal with the whole area of being Italian—you can't get divorced, and being Catholic—you can't get divorced, and what to do in terms of activities in the church, including receiving Holy Communion.

The entire process was very painful. I could not come to grips with the pain, and it took me many years to allow the Lord to come in and heal that part of my life. But one thing was very, very clear in my mind: my daughter must stay with me! That was my prayer. The rest of the stuff I could deal with or handle, but about my daughter I prayed, "Lord, if nothing else, please let her stay with me."

The Lord honored that prayer, and she stayed with me. She was only two years old, but I realized there could come a time in her life when she might decide to live with her mother. That was something I would never interfere with. It is important for mother and daughter—for both of their souls—to work out their relationship.

Once the divorce took place, my relationships with women became difficult. It never worked out well. I have come to grips with this fact. The Lord revealed, blessed, and healed me. But there were a few of whom I thought, *God, You know if I ever did remarry, this is the type of woman I would want to marry.*

There was one woman, an Italian. She even spoke Italian. Her parents were from Italy, did all the cooking, and she loved me like crazy. I had feelings for her, but I was struggling, not too sure why or what I was feeling. It got to the point where she started talking about the wedding cake and the wedding dress. We had never talked about getting married, so I figured I'd better say something.

I'm a romantic, so I invited her for a walk up on Mount Royal. "I need to tell you something," I said. "You're talking about wedding cakes and wedding dresses, but you and I have never talked about getting married. So, I'm having a bit of difficulty."

Then I added, "My problem is this. I'm not sure what God wants of me. Does He want me to remain single and celibate? Should I marry, or is God calling me to priesthood? Until I know, I don't feel I can be in a relationship with you. Maybe this is the relationship for me. Maybe you are the best thing that ever happened to me, but I simply don't know.

"What I do know is that I can't make a commitment until I discern the Lord's calling. Now, if that is okay with you—assuming the relationship may change—then that's fine. I don't mind being in a relationship with you. If not, then that's okay too. I understand."

"No," she said. "I can't deal with that."

We parted company. As I walked away, I thought, *What if this is the woman? What if the Lord is calling me to marriage and now I am messing up again?* I also thought, *Well, I can only do the best I can, and I have to follow where I believe the Lord is calling.*

There had been different signs along the way, but I didn't recognize them while this relationship was going on. I didn't have a good spiritual director, which is so valuable. I would encourage you to find a spiritual director and make sure you avail yourself of the grace of spiritual direction.

At times, I'm slow to catch on to what is happening around me. People would approach me and ask, "Are you a priest?"

"No."

"Have you ever thought of becoming a priest?"

"No."

"You should be a priest."

This went on for years. Finally, I thought, *Why do people keep asking if I'm a priest?* Sometimes I am very, *very* slow. *Testa Dura* (in Italian) means "hard head."

I decided if anyone asked me again, I would find out why. Sure enough, it happened again. "Why do you say that?" I asked.

"Oh, I don't know. Because you act like a priest. You look like a priest. You look like you would make a good priest. I find it easy to talk to you. I am comfortable with you."

I remember taking a course at Loyola as part of the Christian Training Program (CTP) program. A certain lady in the class and I had never said anything more than "hi," "hello," or "how are you" as we passed each other. One night in the cafeteria—and somehow by the grace of God—she and I ended up sitting at the same table. She began pouring out her life story and then said, "I don't know why I am telling you any of this."

That was another familiar phrase I kept hearing: "I've never said this to anybody before." "I didn't plan to tell you any of this." "I don't even know you. I don't know why I'm telling you all of this stuff."

I would think, *Neither do I.*

Somehow, though, I instinctively knew to be present and to listen. I believe these were all indications. Of course, that alone doesn't mean I was called to be a priest. I could still do the same thing, and people would still have the same feelings in their relationship with me if I were not a priest.

This is part of the discernment process. To ask: What does this mean? Where do these experiences come from, and where is it leading me?

The auxiliary bishop—God bless him—was very instrumental in my life. I had an office in the Sun Life building in downtown Montreal, and I attended Mass in the Cathedral every morning. I didn't know the celebrant was actually the bishop. I thought he was just a priest. I wondered about him as he celebrated Mass. I had been thinking for some time about the possibility of the diaconate. I had read about different diaconate programs in different places and I thought, *I'm going to ask somebody.*

After Mass, I introduced myself to this priest.

I was surprised. I didn't realize he was the bishop! After our introductions, I explained my desire to find out more about a diaconate program.

"Tell me a little bit about yourself," he said.

"I'm divorced, I have a daughter, and I'm in debt up to here." I told him one problem after another.

He listened to me then said, "Oh, it will never be possible. Besides, we don't have a diaconate program here in Montreal."

Now, in addition to being a little slow, I can also be a bit naïve and ignorant. Sometimes that can be bliss. While the bishop was telling me it would never be possible, I was thinking, *If it is what the Lord wants, it is going to happen.*

That was a grace from God because in the back of my mind I somehow also had the idea of the priesthood. Certainly, it was not possible so long as I didn't have a Decree of Nullity for my divorce. I slowly begin to prepare myself just in case this was where the Lord was calling me. If not, the teaching and the training would still be helpful. The idea of priesthood would not leave, however. Somewhere along the line, the Lord had planted that desire and that grace in my heart.

About a year or two later, the diocese did begin the Christian Training Program. I had been told "no," but I decided to go anyway and see what happened. Surprisingly, I was accepted into the program, and I figured it was a good start!

However, I believed I should never express the real reason I was there—the desire for priesthood. I didn't trust myself enough, especially if this desire to become a priest came from me and not from God. It would not be a good thing, and I would be off track. I thought the journey to the priesthood must come from the outside.

At one point during the Christian Training Program, I was asked to apply to be accepted as a candidate. Before that happened, someone in the program came to me one day and said, "Lou, have you ever thought of the priesthood?"

Ah, I thought, *this is from the outside.* "That is why I am here." That's all I said.

That person happened to be the auxiliary bishop's administrative assistant.

Several months after that, we were asked to apply for candidacy, so I did. I figured, *I don't know where this is going, but I'm going to take the next step.* Subsequently, there was a Bible study day at the Sacred Heart Convent at Atwater. The bishop was there. He came over to me at one point and said, "I'd like to talk to you."

"Sure. When would you like me to come?"

"No," he said. "I would like to talk to you today."

"Okay, fine."

This was in the morning. When the lunch break arrived, the bishop said, "Why don't you and I sit together?"

Now, you know that when the bishop is around everybody wants to talk to him and have a chance to say "hello." The bishop and I sat down for lunch. There were over 150 people at the luncheon that day, but not one person came anywhere near us the whole time we were having our meal. The moment our conversation ended, it was as if someone rang a bell. Suddenly, people came over to greet the bishop.

This might not mean much to you, but I experienced it and could not believe it. I couldn't get over that seemingly inconsequential incident. It spoke very powerfully to me. Somehow, I had experienced the hand of the Lord.

The bishop said, "We have received your letter to be accepted as a candidate, but we decided we are not going to process it."

My heart stopped for a second.

"The reason," he explained, "is because I've researched your file, and I believe you do have grounds for an annulment. I sent your file to a friend of mine in Ottawa, and he concurs that you do. I would encourage you to continue to pursue your annulment so that we can get you your freedom in order to study for the priesthood."

I sat there, stunned. *If you only knew, you are the very same person who told me four or five years ago that I couldn't even be a deacon.* My heart and soul were smiling. *You told me this could never be possible.*

Now, here was the very person who was most instrumental in eventually getting me into the seminary. I was continuously turned down for the annulment, and here I could not help but see the hand of God.

Prior to this, my life had been hit or miss, wandering and wondering like a lost soul. I thought, *Maybe I'll try this way. Oops! No, not that way. Well then, maybe this way. Oops! No, not here!*

I received so many "bumps" on my head that the wise decision was to stop and pray first. At that time, I made a thirty-day Ignatian retreat. I was in a business at that point, and I wasn't happy. Things were not going well. So I said to myself, *This is it!*

I began a process of prayer and discernment and came to the conclusion that I had to leave the job. But I didn't know where I was going from there. It was something like Abraham when the Lord said, "Go." He didn't ask, "Where do you want me to go?" The Lord said, "Go." So he said, "Okay, I'll go." Abraham didn't know where he was going or what was going to happen, but the desire was there.

The Lord blessed me with that desire too. But my thinking was, *Lord, I have been trying it my way up to this point and messed up so badly. Maybe it might be a good idea if I put things in Your hands and see what You want.*

I went on the thirty-day retreat as a part of that process, to put the prayer into effect. That is grace to be able to make a retreat, and the Lord continues to bless you for the rest of your life through your willingness to let go and discern.

I came back from the retreat uncertain except for the notion of not doing anything. That was until it became clear what direction the Lord was calling me. I had no money. I was still in debt. I did not know what I was going to do. I didn't know how I was going to live. I didn't know how I was going to raise my daughter. I didn't know how I was going to pay the rent. You know, all of the struggles most of us live with daily. But my heart felt no reservations. *Lou, you have to do this.*

It is important to emphasize that from this point onward not everything I did, said, thought, or decided was right. I still made many mistakes. The difference was that my motivation and my heart were in the right place.

Finally, after much waiting, an opportunity for a job was presented. *This job is for me,* I thought.

The job requirements included language fluency—being bilingual—a university degree, and that you send your Curriculum Vitae (CV/resume) to a post office box address. Instead, I learned where the company office was located and appeared in person to present my CV face to face. Never mind that I wasn't qualified. I was not bilingual, and I didn't have a university degree. Yet, I believed this was the job for me. I could do this, and it was right.

The company received 150 applicants for the job, and I got the job!

During the interview, the talk turned to money. I had about as much money in my pocket then as I do today— $1.25. As I sat across from the man interviewing me, he said, "We can see by your resume and work history that you have accomplished what we are looking for, and we would very much like to have you as a member of our organization. We would like to offer you work as a freelance trainer, but"—he paused—"we can only afford to pay you about $250 a day. Would that be okay?"

I was gripping the bottom of my chair. *Wow! Would that be okay?* I calmly said, "I suppose we could start at that rate. Sure, it's okay." *I've never earned that much in my life,* I thought. *Even if they only gave me one day a week or two days a month, it would be fine.*

I got the job, and they kept me busy by giving me quite a bit of business. I was good at this type of work. By the grace of God, I am good at what I do.

Before entering the seminary, the Lord had other plans. The company I worked for received a big contract with Air Canada, and they needed a project manager. I received a call to come into the office. "We would like to ask you to consider working with us full time," they said.

I had learned the skill of a terrific negotiator by now. "Well, I'll consider it. What can you offer?"

"The bottom line? The best we could do at this point is offer you $30,000 a year."

This was in the 1980s. Once again, I was gripping the bottom of my chair. *Wow, $30,000 a year!* "That's a good place to start," I answered calmly.

I started at $30,000 a year. About seven months later, I received a $6,000 raise. I eventually ended up making $40,000 a year. This job afforded me an opportunity to earn much, much more than I had ever earned. I could have gone on to a larger organization.

One of my friends said, "Lou, apply to this other company. They will hire you at $60,000 a year."

The company I was working for asked me to go to Toronto to open an office there, and they wanted me to become a partner. This opened all kinds of possibilities in terms of income and the accompanying perks. Yet, all the time I spent in that job, I had a sense that it was a temporary position. What was most important to me was the welfare of my daughter and time to continue attending church activities.

I couldn't get too involved with work. The minute I accepted a salary beyond $40,000 a year, they would expect me to work twenty hours a day, ten days a week, and they would own me. I was not prepared to pay that price.

Truthfully, it was very enticing, and it was part of the struggle before entering the seminary, especially the opportunity in Toronto. *The possibilities!* I thought. Especially when I considered how much money I could earn, the kind of life style I could live, and the benefits they were offering.

While it was painful, and I really struggled, there was something that did not sit well with me. I thought maybe I was making another mistake, but as I struggled, I didn't think it was a mistake. I *hoped* it was not a mistake, but I decided to say "no."

During the possibility for promotions, my daughter was seventeen. By this time, it was becoming clearer to me that the Lord was indeed calling me to the priesthood. I felt my daughter was still young and needed me at that time. On occasion, we briefly discussed my calling to become a priest, yet I was adamant that she should never feel like she was being forced out of the house.

Before I made a final decision or even thought of doing anything permanent, I wanted her to make her own decision about her life. Whether that was a decision to get married, to move out on her own, to live with her mother, to work, or to attend a university—whatever she wanted to do—I wanted her to do that first. Once she made her decision, I would then be free to go wherever the Lord was calling me.

I figured it would take anywhere from five to seven years for her to be settled. She would be in her twenties. I was happy with the decision because that was my place as a father. That was my vocation, the desire of my heart, and where I belonged.

Then suddenly I began to sense there were other things happening in my daughter's life. One night we went out for supper. "You know," I said. "Lately I've been feeling you may be thinking about going to live with Mummy, but you are not telling me because you're afraid of how I am going to react."

"Well, Dad," she replied. "If I did that, then what are you going to do?"

"For me it is simple. If you go and live with Mummy, then I'll go to the seminary."

"Oh," she said. "If you do that, then I won't worry about you. I know someone will look after you, make your meals, and you'll have a place to sleep."

God bless her! She was only seventeen, but she was concerned about me. I had a picture in mind of how things might evolve, but there was a need to be open to the work that the Lord was doing. I'd been figuring it would be years before I could leave my daughter, but the Lord said, "No, kid. Now is the time."

Those of you with children know the normal pain and struggle when you must let your children go. But under the circumstances in which my daughter and I were parting, I began to think, *What kind of a father am I? How can I be a good father? What if it doesn't work out for her?* I worried until the Lord healed me and as I remembered to trust in Him.

My daughter went to live with her mother in South Africa. I went to the seminary in Ottawa—not as exotic. I assured her that if she needed to come home, I had money for her in the bank.

And that's what happened. She phoned one day. "Dad, I want to come home."

"No problem. Just tell me when."

It was the summer, yet she said, "I'll come home in December."

I was confused. "I don't understand. If it's not working out and you're not happy, why are you waiting until December?"

"As long as I know I'm coming home, I can stay here a few more months. But when I started thinking I must stay for five years, and under these circumstances, then I wasn't happy."

"Okay, no problem." I sent her a plane ticket for her return flight.

I thought, *Lord, what is this all about? What do I do now?*

When I came to the seminary, it was under the circumstances that she was with a parent, that she was provided for, looked after, and with family. Now she was coming home. What would I do? What did that mean in terms of my staying in the seminary?

When I finally stopped to think about it, I realized that I had four or five more months to finish the first year. *Well, that makes good sense. It's only a few months.* A couple of friends in Montreal offered to have her live with them, and she did.

I came home that summer, and my daughter and I discussed the situation. We talked about her feelings with having her father in the seminary, and what we should do about her situation and mine. I invited her to come to Ottawa, live there, and perhaps attend the university. I also offered to leave the seminary. My love for her, my sense of responsibility, the desire to protect her and to be there for her were lodged in the depth of my heart.

It is easier to talk about it now, but it was very hard when I was going through it.

A priest friend was one of the blessings in my life, and he helped me tremendously. It began to evolve from there, but it was very difficult to let go. The first three years were really, really painful. I had difficulty letting go and trusting that my daughter would be all right.

After seminary, the years have been absolute joy, absolute bliss. The Lord has blessed me, taken away the guilt and worry, and He has healed me. He gave me the grace I needed, and it has been a joy. That doesn't mean I have no problems, or at times that I don't second-guess my decisions, but they are inconsequential. I mean ... God is God. God is Lord. God loves us and is in charge, so how can things go wrong? When I do have a bad moment, it's just a "moment," because that's about how long it lasts. I remind myself, *Wait a minute, I am not God.*

It was a gradual drawing me along over the years.

When I entered the seminary in 1985, I was forty-five years old. The seminary was not suited for older vocations, nor did it recognize that more and more men would enter later in life. You cannot bring a forty-five-year-old man into a system that is setup for twenty-year-olds and expect them to live as a twenty-year-old, yet that is basically what happened.

This set the scene for many serious problems. At forty-five, I came in with a whole set of life experiences the Lord had brought me through. They needed to be recognized, acknowledged, accepted, and utilized. The reason this is important is because I finished my first year and received a good evaluation.

When I completed my second year, it was as if I was a different person—the first-year seminarian didn't exist to the evaluators. I was excited about receiving my evaluation to see how things were progressing. I saw tremendous growth in myself. Healing and changes were taking place in my life.

When I sat down in front of the rector, he began stalling. He hemmed and hawed.

"Father," I said. "What are you trying to tell me? You must be clearer, because I am not getting the message."

He hemmed and hawed a little more then said, "Basically, the staff evaluation is that you are not welcome to come back to the seminary."

I'm through! I thought. *Well, that was pretty clear. I do not necessarily agree, but it's clear.*

The rector then proceeded to list an entire litany of grievances—the reasons why I should not return. The recommendation was that Lou should discontinue his vocation project. Lou has such deep psychological problems that even if he attended counseling for an extended period it would not make any difference.

I objected. "Father, there is no one on the faculty at this seminary who is qualified to make that kind of psychological judgment against me." I then asked, "Father, where is the hope in all you just told me?"

He replied, "There is none."

My heart sank. "When I came here, I saw this as a place and a time for learning and healing. I felt it was my responsibility to do the best I could, while also addressing the areas of my life that need healing and deal with them so that once I am ordained I will not inflict any of my brokenness on the parishioners. I saw this as a house of healing."

"Oh, no, it's not that," he replied. "We make priests here."

That is just a small portion of what I was told. The details are not important other than to give a sense of what happened. I would add that most of the people I encountered in the seminary at the time were honest and sincere in their efforts.

Needless to say, I had a difficult night. My soul encountered the darkest depths ever in my entire life. I could not fathom what was happening. *Lord, I don't understand it. It does not make sense. I know they are wrong! I know You are healing me. Obviously, they cannot see it, but they are not even asking. What am I to do?*

I sat quietly in my room in desperation and pain. I decided to look at this logically. Was there anything I needed to acknowledge? Was there a thread of truth in what I'd been told? I sifted through the conversation, recalling it as best I could.

Then it hit me, *Wait a minute! How did I get here in the first place?*

When I considered all that had preceded and made my entry into the seminary possible; when I recalled all the insurmountable obstacles and road blocks, all the prayers, discernment, and conversations that had gotten me here … *How could all that be wrong? Either the discernment was wrong, or it is wrong now.*

That wasn't necessarily the case, but given those circumstances, I began to question my vocation. The next thing that happened was a question I believe the Holy Spirit placed in my heart. "*Lou, do you believe this is what the Lord wants of you?*" My immediate reply? "Yes!"

Then came the prayer, the answer. "By the grace of God it can be done!"

This situation took place as we were preparing for exams, and everyone was under stress. I'd had the best exam session up to that point. I knew many people were praying for me, and I had the prayer the Lord had given me—the prayer that kept me going. "By the grace of God it can be done!" The answer to the question: "Yes!"

I prayed all day long in the middle of classes, in the middle of meals. I was so broken. I was so devastated, and there was no one to talk to, nowhere to turn other than to God.

I returned to Montreal and traveled to the chancery office to see someone to discuss my dismay. The scenario went something like this:

"Well, you gave it a good shot."

"Yes, I did."

"You really tried."

"Yes, I did." Again, I said, "If there is something you are trying to tell me, you need to be much clearer, because I am not getting the message."

"If the seminary says you are not welcome back, then you can no longer continue to study for the priesthood for this diocese."

"Why not? What's the problem?" In Ottawa, I had witnessed men from other dioceses living outside of the seminary and studying for the priesthood. *Why can't I do that?* "I've completed two years," I said. "I believe canon law requires two years in the seminary."

"No," came the answer. "The archbishop here requires that you complete all of your years of formation in the seminary. If the seminary won't accept you back, then you can't continue to study."

Hold on a second, I thought. "Okay, that is how the archbishop feels. Fine. Then what I suggest is to sit down and look at the file I have prepared for the bishop. I figure if I were the bishop, what would I be looking for? I would look for a balanced view in this situation. You have the seminary's point of view. The balance would be to get Lou Cerulli's point of view."

I had compiled a file, as well as letters and evaluations from people I had worked with at the seminary. "In this envelope you will find documents supporting my cause for the priesthood. Take it, read it, study it. Then let me know when you are ready to meet so I can answer any questions for clarification. At that time we can figure out the necessary steps and make a presentation before the bishop."

"It won't do any good. Don't bother."

"What do you mean *it won't do any good?*"

"I know him. I know what he is like, and I know it won't do any good."

"I think there is something you should understand," I said. "My one desire, the desire of my heart, is to do the Lord's will. I am not locked into the priesthood as the only way. If the Lord's will for me is to be ordained a priest, terrific. If the Lord's will is 'no,' then great. I can't lose. I want to be where the Lord is calling me. I am standing up for justice, but I don't feel I'm receiving justice in this situation."

For me to stand strong, to say what I did under those circumstances, had to be the work of the Lord. This was so out of character for me. I would not have had the courage nor the strength.

The doors were closing—*boom, boom, boom!* As they were closing, I felt like I had received a kick in the head. I kept bringing it back to the Lord in prayer, "Lord, what do I do about this?" What kept coming to me was the thought, *As long as there is no one who will stand up for you, then you keep knocking on the door.*

That is what I did. I kept knocking and knocking. Finally, there came someone who took enough of an interest to go through the file, check the facts, research personally, and take the time to ask me for additional information. The mess was straightened out, thank God! Another seminary, St. Peter's in London, Ontario, is where I went to complete my seminary formation. The last year I interned at the Ignatius Center.

The word started to circulate about my situation and difficulty. People, especially priests, asked, "Lou, you went through an ordeal, and you still want to be a priest?"

"Yes. It is almost as if I have no choice. This is what the Lord wants."

Lord, my desire is to do Your will. You know all my problems, and there is only so much that I can do. Yours is a bigger job that only You can accomplish.

From the first time I had spoken with the bishop and he said "no" to the diaconate program—one by one, the problems were wiped away. Incredible obstacles began to dissolve. It would take pages and pages to share all the things that happened. If you are in God's will, somehow the Lord will touch your heart with whatever it is you need for the day.

Forget about me. Forget about my journey, the difficulties, and even the amazing outcome I have shared. Concentrate on the blessings from the Lord for you as He touches your heart. Listen and go with that.

It is only by the grace of God that this happened, and help from others as well. Many graces sent by the Lord were sent in the form of people. Good people, good friends when I needed them to be there, at the perfect time. Ultimately, though, my life and my vocation is a journey and a responsibility I made on my own.

Holding on to the branch that is Jesus Christ is all the help I need. It is a personal relationship between Jesus Christ and me in the quiet of my heart. He sees the pain, the desolation, and the darkness, and then He provides the light and the consolation.

This can happen for you, and it is personal between you and Jesus Christ. While other people will be there when you need help, the bottom line is there is a time, or a moment of truth, when it is you and Jesus Christ—and it is your decision to do His will. Are you going to sink or swim? If you latch on to Christ, then you know you are going to swim.

Of course, prayer helps. Without my own prayer life and the prayers of many people, I would not be here today. Sacred Scripture, spiritual direction, and your faith—all of this helps. Keeping a journal is also very helpful, and I do this as well.

Another key point that helped me on my journey was to examine my past. There was a turning point, which I examined. It was my call to the priesthood. I looked back at the turmoil and the obstacles, examining situations and trying to discern the meaning—was I supposed to leave? Was I supposed to live with my daughter? Would she move nearby if I wasn't accepted back into the seminary? What if the bishop said I could not go back? What would I do?

I could see that turning point in my past, realize how powerful the desire was to become a priest, and believe the Lord—believe that He was calling me to be a priest despite the hardships and the obstacles. If He willed it, it would come to pass. "With God all things are possible" (Matthew 19:26).

When I was finally ordained to the priesthood in 1991, God took the natural gifts, talents, and abilities He had given me and ordained them for His own good purposes. I still use the gifts I applied in my work life in the training and development industry, but now it is all for the Lord.

I urge you to go back and examine the turning point in your life. It consists of two things. One, your heart. What is your heart's desire? Second, learn to recognize the sound of your heart's desire and the voice of the Spirit at work in you. And listen. In my life, it was too powerful for me to ignore. I could not say, "That's it, I give up. I need to forget it."

By the grace of God, the Lord helped me to hang in there. I am so thankful to the Lord every day. I am very, *very* grateful. I am grateful to you for your prayers, for your support, and for those who reached out to help look after my daughter when that was needed. I am also grateful that I have been blessed financially.

I hope that at least one word—something I have shared in these pages—will plant a seed in your heart. Remember, God walks in the corridors of your heart. God rests on the altar of your soul. You are in the hands of the Lord—a Lord who loves you and cares about you.

I pray God's blessings upon you all.

Bio–

After years of working as a consultant designing and conducting seminars on management and communication skills for major companies and industries, Father Lou Cerulli entered St. Peter's Seminary, London, Ontario, Canada, as a late vocation in 1985. He received a Master of Divinity in 1990 from the University of Western Ontario and was ordained August 30, 1991, in the Archdiocese of Montreal.

Since Fr. Lou's ordination, he has been active in parish ministry teaching internationally, as well as ministering through retreats, workshops, days of reflection, speaking engagements, and healing services. He has also participated in Cursillo and the Charismatic Renewal since the early 70s.

One of Fr. Lou's desires is to share his experiences and love of the Eucharist and the healing power of the sacrament. In 1992, he developed a series called "Healing in The Eucharist," which confirms the Church's teaching that the Eucharist is the source and summit of our faith.

Rev. Fr. Harold Cohen, S.J., S.T.L.

$$\sim\!\!\diamond\!\!\sim$$

My favorite Scripture passage is Ephesians 3:20–21, which clearly expresses what is in my heart: "Glory be to Him whose power working in us can do infinitely more than we can ask or imagine. Glory be to Him from generation to generation in the Church and in Christ Jesus forever and ever." Amen. Alleluia.

Second Corinthians 12:9 is also a special passage of mine. "My grace is sufficient for you. For My power is at its best in weakness." I will sing the mercies of the Lord forever, and you and I in heaven will sing His mercies forever.

As I share these verses with you, I want to sing His mercies, His love, His goodness, His faithfulness, and His power working in and through my weaknesses, of which I am very conscious. Two images occurred to me when I was preparing my testimony, one which I have shared a number of times.

I picture myself as a little boy going off to kindergarten or first grade with his father gently tugging him along the sidewalk. The little boy is looking around at butterflies and garbage cans, cars passing by, and whatever else catches his attention, not very anxious to go to school. The father continues to gently move him along, however, and finally gets the little boy to where he wants him to go.

During my life, God my Father has been that way with me. I have been distracted, looking at all kinds of things, but He gently keeps moving me along the way He wants me to go.

The other image is the story in John's Gospel about the multiplication of the loaves. Andrew found a little boy who had five loaves and two fish and was willing to give them to Jesus for the crowd. Five loaves and two fish can't feed many people, but five loaves and two fish in the hands of Jesus can feed a multitude. I feel what I have tried to do in my life is give what I have to Jesus and let Him feed others—to feed *many* others—because He can do that with the little we give Him.

I was born November 30, 1929, in New Orleans at Hotel Dieu, the only child of Harold "Babe" Cohen and Sarah Brown of Baton Rouge. I was baptized at Our Lady of Lourdes Church in New Orleans not long afterwards. At the time I was born and for many years afterward, my father was a non-practicing Catholic. He was a traveling salesman and went to Mass when he was in town because my grandmother corralled him, his brother Clarence, and—as I grew up—me as well. She made sure we got to Sunday Mass at St. Stephen's.

Dad was a traveling salesman for RKO Pictures (movies). He loved to gamble, especially on the horses and poker games. He loved to party, and he loved to drink. He was a friendly, outgoing man.

I had a wonderful relationship with my father, even though he was out of town a lot. I always felt warm and affectionate with him. Beginning as a child, perhaps at the age of two or three, we played games. I'd be in the bedroom with him and he would say, "Harold, run into the other room and see if I am there."

I'd run and then come back and say, "No, Daddy, you are not there." I knew it was a game, but I was never sure if he knew that I knew it was a game.

Growing up, Dad and I played games like the football games where you roll dice and your team moves so many yards—things like that. He didn't teach me to hunt and fish, but he taught me to play poker. He also taught me to mix drinks for the parties at home.

From this wonderful relationship with my father, I felt very much affirmed. It isn't that he didn't have a temper, and not that I didn't do things to provoke his temper from time to time, but from this bond with my father, I easily passed to a wonderful love with God my Father, which has been one of the special graces of my life.

My mom was a non-practicing Episcopalian. She had come from a broken home of divorced parents. Mother loved Bridge parties with her friends. She was less warm in her relationship with me and was more intellectual. Not intellectual in the sense of a great scholar, but she was more aloof, less affectionate due to her own family upbringing. Our association wasn't the warm relationship I had with my father.

I believe my mother and father were my strength and my struggle. My connection with my father was a great strength in my life. Yet, the lack of affection I felt from my mother led to insecurity and a lack of self-confidence as I grew up, and later in life.

I was a pugnacious kid. I was always fighting with other kids on the block. We had a game called McDonogh 14, in which we had to bring kids to our "dens." The dens were rows of benches around trees. I remember playing this as a little kid against the big kids. My friends and I loved to jump on the bigger kids and bring them down to the ground, and then they would have to come to our den. I liked that kind of game.

As a kid I also loved playing sandlot football and wrestling and anything aggressive. I was often punished at school. I remember my sixth-grade teacher saying, "Harold, wouldn't you like to raise the flag and wear one of those rifle things across your chest?"

"Yeah, I would love to do that," I said.

"If you quit talking in class, you can do that."

Well, I never made it.

It must have been sixth or seventh grade when one of my teachers told me about a Jesuit who had been martyred in Mexico—Father Miguel Pro. She said, "Father Pro always used to cut up a lot." I think she added something like, "Harold, there is hope for you."

This stuck with me.

About this time, I got a pass to the United Theater since my father worked for RKO Pictures. God have mercy on them. It was a pass for the entire family—for Mr. and Mrs. Harold Cohen and son. I invited two of my buddies. We went to the Prytania Theater, and they let the three of us in on the pass. After the movie began, we started horsing around so they would have to kick us out. We then demanded our money back, which we hadn't paid in the first place.

I made my First Communion when I was in seventh grade. I had gone to church periodically on Sundays, but one of the good things about waiting that long was that I had a hunger for God because my other friends had made their First Communion and Confirmation.

My good friend Jack Deeves—who later became a Jesuit priest—and I entered together. His aunt had given him a medal with a dove on it for his Confirmation.

That dove made an indelible impression on me. I was so envious of Jack. I wished I had a dove. I wished I could make my Confirmation. Finally, when I was brought to St. Stephen's to make my First Communion, I was very happy. I was a little embarrassed too, to be in class with first graders when I was in seventh grade.

God bless her, Sister Celestine—now Sister Mary Joseph—back in New Orleans, took me aside and instructed me. I made my First Communion on December 8, 1940. I made my Confirmation at St. Stephen's on April 7, 1941.

I thought it was cool to make it at St. Stephen's Church. My dad's confirmation name had been Stephen, and his dad's name had been Stephen, so I chose Stephen for my dad, and I chose Stephen for the church. I had heard that Stephen was the first martyr. I thought it was neat to be named after him. I was Harold Francis Stephen Cohen.

I became caught up in my religious instruction. I wanted to become a Vincentian priest and go to their seminary at the end of seventh grade. As you might know, all Louisiana students were precocious in those days. We didn't have to go to eighth grade. We went right from seventh grade to high school. Yet, I wanted to go right to the seminary.

Mother and Dad were upset by this idea. They talked to Dr. Willoughby, who lived in the same apartment house as we did. He knew a Jesuit because he had operated on the Jesuits and introduced us to Father Aferton. He and I started talking about football, and Father Aferton showed me his big legs. I guess it was to prove to me that he could have been a good football player.

Father Aferton thought it would be a good idea if I went to Jesuit High. If I wanted to become a priest afterward I could. He explained that I would receive good religious instruction. So, I attended Jesuit High School.

It was amazing that at Jesuit, even though I'd had no Catholic school training, I did much better than most kids in religion because it was all brand new to me. The other kids were tired of Catechism, whereas for me it was a whole new ballgame, and I liked it. I did well.

During high school I became more proficient at poker, at dice, and at organizing parties. I *loved* to organize parties. We'd rent the Audubon Tea Room, and I was often the instigator to buy wax that you put on the floor. We'd rent a jukebox and get Cokes and beer and plan a party.

I became very interested in girls from grammar school on, but in high school I became especially enthralled with them. I used my movie pass again, but this time we went to drive-ins. I'd introduce myself and my date by saying, "I'm Mr. Cohen, and this is Mrs. Cohen. That is my son in the backseat with his date." Therefore, we only paid one fare.

They usually laughed and let us in.

One of my first mishaps while driving occurred one night when I was returning home with my date. I thought it would be a good idea to kiss her while driving, but I didn't notice the traffic circle in front of us. I guess it was a longer kiss than it should have been. The next thing I knew the front tire had blown out on the curb.

My friends and I used to play a game at Loyola called Slaughter House. We were pretty good, generally speaking. We would gather twenty or thirty kids on a rather small triangle of grass so that there wasn't much room to move. Then we threw the football up. Somebody would catch it, and then everybody would tackle him and pile on. We loved to play that whenever we could. We also loved to play football at Audubon Park on rainy days and use any excuse to fall in the mud.

I remember one time bringing a white rat to Mr. Cutcliff's class. He was a Jesuit scholastic. I sat in the back row with the rat in my pocket. Somehow, the rat slipped out of my pocket and ran down the back of the classroom. Stealthily (or so I thought), I got out of my chair, ran down the back of the classroom, caught the rat, and put him back in my pocket.

Mr. Cutcliff didn't say anything at the time, but about two weeks later he said, "You know, a lot of things go on in the classroom that students don't believe anyone notices. Somebody might do this or that, and somebody might bring a white rat to class."

Fortunately, he didn't punish me.

I had a good friend, Randy Newman. I used to get Randy into various escapades that I think he would rather have avoided. One was making what was called Kick-a-Poo Georges. Randy's father had an ample liquor cabinet. Before our dates, Randy and I would take empty bottles and go to his dad's liquor cabinet to fill ours with a little of whatever we could find. A little gin, a little Scotch, and that would make our Kick-a-Poo Georges. Then we raised the level of the bottles of liquor we had used with water and replaced them in the cabinet so his father wouldn't notice any missing.

Those Kick-a-Poo Georges sure packed a punch!

My last year of high school, our gang, the "Little Crew," not to be confused with the "Big Crew," decided to go across the lake for a weekend. It was the summer of 1945, and someone said they had a house where we could stay. What little money I had, I lost in a dice game at Benny French's. The house plan fell through, so some of us slept in empty cars at a hotel parking lot and then on a bench.

The next night we went to the back porch of a sorority house and Lorraine, being my confidante in high school, took pity on me and provided food for me. At least I didn't starve because of the money I had lost at Benny French's.

I dated many, many girls during high school. One time I thought about doing something different. I double dated with Don Ford, a football player at Jesuit. "Don," I said, "why don't we go to the morgue tonight."

"The morgue?"

"Yeah, just to do something different. We always do the same old thing."

"Okay," he agreed.

We picked up our dates and went to Charity Hospital. I introduced ourselves as Tulane students and said we wanted to show our dates around the morgue.

The night watchman said, "Fine, go on in. Help yourself."

We had a lively time at the morgue that night.

Of the many girls I dated there were two in particular who stand out in my memory. One was Doris Charbonnet, my best friend Bobby Charbonnet's sister, and the other was Toby Francis, who is now Bobby's wife. Before I left for the seminary, I told him to look after her, and he did that very well.

Amazingly, both girls married, and between them they had nineteen children. Doris had ten, and Toby had nine. Looking back, I think the Lord wanted me to be fruitful in another way. In the midst of all the drinking, partying, girlfriends, and shenanigans, the priestly vocation stayed in the back of my mind, due to the mercy of God.

Another side of me during high school was learning Latin, and to be an altar boy. In the past there were so many priests living at Loyola that Holy Name Church had five altars to accommodate them—which they still have today. At times there would be five Masses said starting at 5:30, 6:00, 6:30, 7:00, and 7:30 because concelebrating was not performed in those days. Sometimes I served as many as five Masses in a morning. I arrived at 5:30 and served right up to 7:30. Now and then Brother Matlan treated me with a quarter for breakfast after serving five Masses.

I must say that did make an impression on me!

The idea of becoming a priest had never left, and it now became my focus. When I went to the Manresa House of Retreats for my senior retreat, I said, "Lord, I really want You to show me what You want me to do."

The Lord worked on me in a few ways. One was a picture that came to mind a number of times. I pictured myself married with my children and my wife in Holy Name Church, attending Mass on Sunday. The thought of being married and having a family appealed to me as an only child, since I was often lonely as a kid.

Then I pictured myself at Holy Name saying Mass and looking out at the congregation. I knew in my heart that if I got married—although that was very appealing—when I attended Mass on Sundays I would always wish I was saying Mass and not sitting in the pews. When I thought of myself as being a priest, I always thought that was where I belonged.

On that retreat I thought a lot about it, and I experienced great consolation from the Lord. I experienced Him touching my heart. I went into the woods and read a little pamphlet about the Sacred Heart. It had nothing to do with vocations as far as I can remember, but the Lord filled me with His love during that time. I made my decision then and decided that I would enter Grand Coteau.

Sometime after that, but definitely during my senior year, the Blue Jay Marines visited Jesuit High School. There was a crack platoon drilling one day, and my platoon was not a crack platoon. I stood at the back of my platoon while the crack platoon was drilling. Most of the kids were around the yard in their platoons, and I was picking up pebbles and throwing them at the kids in front of me.

Mr. Dan O'Callaghan, a Jesuit scholastic, was up in the window looking down on the grounds. He saw me and called me over. "Son, what do you expect to do with your life after you get out of high school?"

"Well, I was thinking about becoming a Jesuit."

That kind of threw him, but he gave me some good advice. "When you get through with all the fun and games, you have to be serious when you go there."

I remember one Sunday morning when Dad was lying in bed. He called me over. I lay down beside him.

"Son," he said, "where do you want to go to college?"

I told him I wanted to become a Jesuit.

He was shocked. When he later told Mother, she was shocked as well. I really thank God for the gift of my parents saying "yes," especially given their history of not practicing their faith. They gave up their only son to become a priest when it was impossible for them to understand my calling.

The plan was to enter the seminary on the feast of St. Ignatius, July 31, but after my physical examination, I learned my kidneys were in bad shape. I honestly think it was from my excessive drinking. After my diagnosis I attended a party at Toby Francis's house. The doctor had ordered me to cease drinking, but here I was with the gang, who drank like fish.

Toby's mother noticed me drinking a Coke. "You are such a wonderful young man, so different from the rest of these kids."

"Yeah, you know how it is," I replied.

Entry to the seminary was postponed until September 8th, which is Our Lady's Nativity, so God drew good out of evil, and I entered on a feast of Our Lady. The day I entered the Jesuit order was surreal. I had been praying for years that I would become a priest. In the midst of all the prayers and longing, I'd also prayed that Mom and Dad would be converted, and that Dad would come back to the Catholic faith.

The day I entered the order, Dad went to communion. He'd gone to confession the day before, and for the first time in many years he received the sacraments. This was a tremendous consolation to me.

The two years of the novitiate were the hardest years of my life. I was homesick, and I threw myself into scrupulously obeying the rules. I had tremendous temptations against my faith. Thoughts such as, *This is not worth believing,* etc. came to mind. I thank God for my novice master, Father Mangiacina, who became both father and mother to me. Without him I would never have made it.

At the end of the two years of real purification and a long thirty-day retreat, I made a commitment of my life to God, my Father, and to Jesus, my Lord, when I took my first vows of poverty, chastity, and obedience. I thank God for that grace. I believe if I had entered the Vincentians minor seminary at the end of grammar school, or had gone on to college after high school, I would have been messed up. The road I had been on was not one leading to the seminary. I thank God, and I am deeply grateful for His perfect timing.

In the novitiate, we preached sermons in the dining room while several Jesuits were eating. We would stand up in the pulpit and give a homily. Out of the four required, I gave one on Mark 16: "These signs shall follow those who believe. They shall lay their hands on the sick and they shall be healed." I was interested way back then in the Charismatic dimension of the Church, and I spoke about the miracles at Lourdes.

I went to Spring Hill for three years to study philosophy. There at a Jesuit high school in Tampa I taught Spanish. About half of the students spoke Spanish, and I learned to speak their native language after class. I tried to teach them grammar, which they didn't know, and they taught me to speak correctly.

I thank God for my Jesuit life, a sound religious and spiritual training. It was a life of regular prayer, with an hour of meditation every morning, Mass and communion every day, an eight-day retreat every year, spiritual direction, and later a study of philosophy and theology. At the end of my three years in Tampa, I asked my provincial if I could study theology in Latin American so I could learn Spanish really well.

"Why don't you go to Spain and see some of Europe?" he suggested.

I studied two years of theology in Spain, where the people were very warm. Learning Spanish was a wonderful experience but it was also difficult. I weighed the most I'd ever weighed when I left Tampa (190 pounds), but I weighed only 150 pounds two years later when I came back from Spain.

I had one of the most extraordinary experiences of my life in 1955. It occurred on Christmas Eve in Spain, right at the beginning of midnight Mass. I felt Jesus—not in an audible voice but in my spirit—bathing me with His love and saying, *"You have not chosen Me, I have chosen you. You have not chosen Me, I have chosen you. You have not chosen Me, I have chosen you."* Over and over again.

In January 1957 we were reading in the dining room *The Life of Edith Stein*, the German Jewish martyr, and I felt the Lord speaking to my heart. *"Are you willing to say 'yes' to Me?"*

I didn't know what I was saying yes to, but I agreed. "Yes, Lord, I am willing."

The next day I left to teach catechism as planned, on a Thursday. As we rode our bicycles, I began to pray, "Lord, into Your hands I commend my spirit." When I arrived home, I learned that my father had died. That was an extremely difficult time in my life. I was so far away when he died and away from Mother. In those days the superiors didn't allow you hop on the next plane and go home.

However, I was thankful to God that my father had become a fervent Catholic. For ten years he was a frequent communicant, a retreat captain at Manresa, and even when his heart was bad and I encouraged him to give up his position, he wouldn't. He said, "No, son, I will give up everything else, but God has been so good to me. I'm going to do all I can to bring other people to Him as long as I have life." Which he did.

I returned to the U.S. and was ordained at Spring Hill College in 1958, and I thank God for the gift of the priesthood. To celebrate the Eucharist every day is an extraordinary grace. I am not worthy of it. Nobody is worthy of it, but to hold the Body and Blood of Christ in your hands! When I have intentions to intercede for you and I hold up the cup, just the ability to plead the blood of Jesus on those things is an extraordinary grace. Eucharist really sums up the thrust I want to have in my life: "In the Spirit, through Jesus, to the Father."

When I celebrate Mass, at the end of the Eucharistic prayer I say, "Through Him, with Him, and in Him, in the unity of the Holy Spirit all glory and honor is Yours, Almighty Father." This reflects the way the early Church celebrated. "Glory be to the Father, through the Son, in the Spirit," and I would add *with Mary.* That is the focus of my life, and what I wish to say is, "Yes to the Father with Mary, in the Spirit, through Jesus."

It has been a joy for me to preach, to hear confessions, to celebrate the Eucharist, and to give Holy Communion to little children.

After I finished theology, I went to Jesuit High as a guidance counselor and a teacher of religion and speech. I got the nickname "Happy Harry" from my students. I went to Loyola in 1969 as the university chaplain and instructor of psychology. Once I graduated from the seminary, and we didn't have a structured time of prayer, I became too busy or too tired to pray as I should. I prayed a minimum. I never was completely away from prayer, but my prayer life really slowed down, and it became evident.

There was a book my father used to quote saying, "Life begins at forty." I was stationed at Loyola on my fortieth birthday along with a group of students at a retreat house on the Mississippi Gulf Coast. I slipped away from the students and prayed, "Lord, I am really, really dissatisfied with my life as a priest. I am self-centered. I don't pray as I should. I make retreats every year but nothing happens. Only You can change me." I think I quoted Ephesians 3:20: "Glory be to Him whose power working in us can do infinitely more than we can ask or imagine." I said, "Lord, I can't do it. You can."

In April of 1969, a young man named Jim Warnke arrived from Fordham to be interviewed for the Society of Jesus. I was one of the interviewers for those entering the Jesuit order. He was blind in one eye and legally blind in the other. The New York province had rejected him, but the Jesuits at Fordham told him, "Go down to South. They will take anybody." In the biography he'd sent ahead, Jim said he was in a Catholic Pentecostal group at Fordham.

I had read about a Pentecostal group at Notre Dame in South Bend, and I was both intrigued and intimidated by what I read. "If I ever go that way, I will stand on the fringe of this group and see what is happening." We met on Good Friday of 1969, and I used this as an ice breaker, but we had to complete the interview first.

Jim and I made an appointment to talk on Easter Monday, April 7, 1969. I had many problems over the weekend. I couldn't understand why at the time. Looking back, I know that when the Lord is about to call us, the evil one learns about it and gives us a hard time.

On Easter Monday, still seeking information about this Baptism in the Spirit, I talked to Jim. We went to Mass first in Thomas Hall and then to my office. While I was talking to him and asking questions, a thought came that had not entered my mind before. *Does God want me to ask this kid to pray with me for the Baptism in the Spirit?*

I tried to pray and discern while I was talking to Jim. *Lord, if you want me to ask him, please show me.*

After that, it appeared He wanted me to ask for prayer. *Lord, give me the guts to ask him,* I prayed. Jim had shared he had 2,000 people praying for this interview. I think he had called a lot of prayer groups.

As it turned out, he did not get accepted into the Southern Jesuits, contrary to the advice he had received from the Fordham Jesuits. But his purpose for coming was for me. I received the gift of the infilling of the Holy Spirit, which is—next to my sacraments and my vocation—the greatest grace of my life.

I knelt on the floor and asked Jim if he would pray with me for the Baptism in the Holy Spirit. He told me to recommit my life to Christ as I had done when I took my vows and as I had done when I was ordained.

I did. I was hoping and expecting some great manifestation of God. I expected to be zapped, certainly *hoping* to be zapped—to start speaking in tongues and have a tremendous experience of God.

There I knelt with this kid praying over me in English, and then in tongues ... and all I felt was dumb. I felt dumb kneeling on my office floor with this kid praying. For those of you who have sought the Baptism in the Holy Spirit and felt nothing at the time, or for those of you in the future who don't feel anything at the time, don't let the lack of "feeling" disturb you. Again, next to the sacraments and my vocation to the priesthood, this was the greatest grace of my life. It completely changed my life.

Later, Jim and I went to the park and said the Rosary. That night I went to the chapel, where I entered into a depth of prayer that hadn't taken place in years. "I think something happened," I said. I began to be faithful to prayer, and when I preached, people were being touched because there was more of Jesus and less of Harold.

I went to the third international conference in Notre Dame a week afterward and met Al Mansfield. There were 500 people in attendance. Sometime later, I received the gift of tongues, which I started praying regularly. I gathered a group of students together to form a Charismatic prayer meeting. When they went home for vacation, I gathered a group of adults.

I hoped this group would grow, take over, and sweep throughout Loyola. However, the group at Loyola always stayed small, but the group in New Orleans grew and spread to other places in the South. The Lord began to use me. I spoke Spanish, so He sent me to Mexico, Guatemala, Honduras, the Dominican Republic, and Brazil (where they speak Portuguese) for the Charismatic Renewal.

Being baptized in the Holy Spirit doesn't mean you no longer have the "cross" in your life. Many times I have wanted to say to Jesus, "Move over, Jesus. I am going to lie beside You." Or I'd say, "Father, if it is possible, take this from me, but not my will but Your will be done." I also remember saying, "Lord, You can take back this Charismatic Renewal. I am tired of all the problems." But God was faithful when I said, "Yes." And He was faithful to me in His mercy.

A passage I received early in my work with the Charismatic Renewal was Revelation 3:8. That passage was prophetic for my life. The Lord says, "Behold, I have set before you an open door which no one is able to shut. I know that you have little power, and yet you have kept My Word and have not denied My Name."

I do have little power. He knows I am weak, but He opened the door for me just the same.

At a pastoral team meeting one night, Al said, "Harold, why don't you get on the radio?" Within two weeks I started *My Closer Walk*, broadcast on WWL TV in 1981. In 1982 and 1983 I created thirteen TV shows with Mother Angelica on EWTN. In 1984, when things were going very well, I came close to burning out. I took a sabbatical in West Palm Beach. While it is a very nice place to visit, I felt in exile nonetheless.

Everything died. The entire ministry died, but the provincial encouraged me to find a place where I could continue to spread God's Word, and he would grant permission. Archbishop Hannan visited West Palm Beach to see his niece, and he said Mass at our church. I spoke to him afterwards.

When he returned to New Orleans, I wrote and asked if he could use me to teach on WLAE, a Catholic television station in New Orleans. He wrote to Jerry Romig, a popular media person in New Orleans known as the "voice of the [New Orleans] Saints." That opened the door for my show on TV. Providence helped me get back to New Orleans.

Just a few years later, I was amazed at the way God brought me to nothing and then lifted me up, and in such a way that I knew it was God's work. In New Orleans, I was on TV twenty-five times a week. I found it hard to believe—twenty-five times a week!

I was on the radio ten times a week in New Orleans. I appeared on EWTN, Mother Angelica's broadcast network, which went across Canada, the Caribbean, the U.S., and beyond. I had meetings in Bogota, and doors around the world opened up for radio and TV in Africa, Asia, the Virgin Islands, and more.

It is extraordinary. God can do so much more than we can imagine!

One of the many graces from God was my secretary Virgie, her husband, Lenny, and another secretary, Diane, in addition to the many volunteers that I called my "angels." Virgie was my archangel, and the rest were angels who worked in my office. One of the things Virgie would never tell anyone is that I'm not the most organized person in the world. But God provides many gifts in the Body. Virgie made up for my lack of gifts in many areas.

Some of the other graces in my life I would call, "Baptism into Mary." The Holy Father, Saint John Paul II's motto was *Totus Tuus, Maria,* "All yours, Mary." I am very grateful that God has brought me to a new depth of union with Mary that leads to a deeper life with Christ.

Another great grace in my life has been discovering the Mercy of God devotion. There are little pictures depicting God's mercy. The rays stand for the blood and water that came from the heart of Christ. This Divine Mercy image had a great impact on me. It is the image I saw when I was a kid, represented in another person.

I had gone across the lake with my uncle to a Dr. Batalora's house. Mrs. Batalora had a child, around ten years old, who was totally incapable of doing anything for himself. He couldn't speak. He couldn't walk. He couldn't feed himself. But he was tremendously affectionate and attached to his mother. If she put him down, he cried for her. That woman was a real martyr.

When thinking about the mercy of God, I look at myself as that helpless child. God is merciful. He is merciful as a father and merciful as a mother. He sustains me in my total weakness. As a loving Father, He does so much in and through me.

The Lord told Blessed Claude de la Colombiere, "He is all powerful and he completely distrusts himself to place his trust in Me alone." That is where God is bringing me. Total lack of trust in me and more and more trust in Him.

Another grace in my life has been the Right to Life movement. I always wear a pin of the little feet, representing a child. I am so happy to be involved with them, and the members of our prayer group. We regularly picket abortion clinics in New Orleans and Metairie.

I feel the abortion situation is comparable to the holocaust of Nazi Germany. Over fifty-eight million unborn infants (2016) sacrificed since 1973. If there are any women or men who have cooperated in an abortion, or any women who have had an abortion, know that God's mercy is infinite. This is a terrible situation, and I am glad to take a stand against it in the power of the Spirit.

I would like to share a special prayer from Ephesians 3:14–21. "For this reason I kneel before the Father from whom every family in heaven and on earth is named, that he may grant you in accord with the riches of His glory to be strengthened in the inner self and that Christ may dwell in your hearts through faith; that you, rooted and grounded in love, may have the strength to comprehend with all the holy ones what is the breadth and length and height and depth, and to know the love of Christ that surpasses knowledge, so that you may be filled with all the fullness of God. Now to him who is able to accomplish far more that we can ask or imagine, by the power at work within us, to him be glory in the Church and in Christ Jesus for all generations, for ever and ever. Amen."

The following comments come from people who knew Father well and have shared what he meant to them.

"Working with Father Cohen was a learning and growth experience, not only being exposed to his preaching and teaching, but also in observing

how he related and handled different situations. I know how I would react in those situations, and then I observed the very Christ-like way he dealt with it."
—Virgie Maretta, Father Cohen's personal secretary

"From Isaiah 51:2. 'Look to Abraham, your Father, when he was but one I called him. I blessed him and made him many.' Father Cohen had a nickname among many Jesuits—Abie—taken from the name Abraham. It is a name very appropriate to him for truly like Abraham, God blessed him and made him many. He was a father in the Spirit to many in this area and throughout the world. Many were inspired by his words and by his example to commit their lives to Jesus. It was our special privilege to have known him, loved him, and been a support to him in Christ."
—Pete and Marilyn Quirk

"It is truly marvelous when we observe how God's grace worked in and through Fr. Cohen. How much God must love him to have used him so widely and in such a mighty way in the life of the Church and in so many people's lives! These few words are meant merely as a sign, a symbol, and a token of the many unspoken thoughts and affections in our hearts."
—Al and Patti Mansfield

"Our friendship started about fifty years ago and was a blessing to our family: from helping us put Santa's toys under the tree on Christmas Eve to being a counselor. He converted Jack's father to the Catholic Church, married our children, baptized their children, and buried our loved ones. He performed priestly duties for all of us all over the years, but more important to Jack and me, he was always a true and loyal friend. We watched him grow in holiness and fame. The only quality that showed no sign of improvement during those wonderful years was his singing voice, but we never gave up hope even for that."
—Jack and Lorraine Levine

"Jesus gave us the new commandment, 'Love one another as I love you.' As many of you know, Father lived that commandment. He was never too busy to give us a smile, to take time out to speak a kind word to us, or to really listen to what we were saying. Regardless of our weaknesses or inabilities, he always confirmed and reaffirmed us and continually spurred us on to holiness. God, Who ordained His Son, Jesus, High Priest, also chose Father to be His high priest and steward of His mysteries. Father was

faithful to his call, an obedient servant, and brought Jesus into the lives of many of us. We can all attest to the fact that 'to know him is to love him.'"
　　—Beverly Carriles

Bio–

Father Harold Cohen was a native of New Orleans. He was ordained a Jesuit priest 1958. He had an S.T.L. in theology and a Master's Degree in Educational Psychology. He was the first representative of the Archbishop of New Orleans to the Catholic Charismatic Renewal. At the time of his beginning involvement in the Catholic Charismatic Renewal, he served as the student body chaplain at Loyola University in New Orleans. To evangelize, Fr. Cohen began *A Closer Walk* on radio in 1981 and later on TV with EWTN. He also did a series of half-hour shows, *Catholics, the Bible, and the Early Church.* He was the first Spiritual Advisor to the mother chapter of Magnificat and later the first Spiritual Advisor to the Central Service Team of Magnificat until his death January 16, 2001.

Archbishop Salvatore Cordileone

My story is the account of my *fiat*, which is comprised of my journey to the priesthood and how this openness to God's will has continued since my ordination. St. Luke recounts the call of St. Peter:

> While the crowd was pressing in on Jesus and listening to the Word of God, he was standing by the Lake of Gennesaret. He saw two boats alongside the lake. The fishermen had disembarked and were washing their nets. Getting into one of the boats, the one belonging to Simon, he asked him to put out a short distance from the shore. Then he sat down and taught the crowds from the boat. After he had finished speaking he said to Simon, 'Put out into deep water and lower your nets for a catch.' Simon said in reply, 'Master, we have worked hard all night and have caught nothing but at your command I will lower the nets.' When they had done this, they caught a great number of fish and their nets were tearing. They signaled to their partners in the other boat to come to help them. They came and filled both boats so that they were in danger of sinking. When Simon Peter saw this he fell at the knees of Jesus and said, 'Depart from me, Lord, as I am a sinful man.' For astonishment at the catch of fish they had made seized him and all those with him and likewise James and John, the sons of Zebedee, who were partners of Simon. Jesus said to Simon, 'Do not be afraid. From now on you will be a fisher of men.' When they brought their boats to the shore, they left everything and followed him. (Luke 5:1–11)

The fisherman theme is one I relate to in both a spiritual and very personal way, because my father was a commercial fisherman. He inherited the trade from my paternal grandfather, who was a fisherman who first immigrated from a fishing village in Sicily to San Francisco, where my father was born. Shortly thereafter he moved his family to San Diego, where he could continue his work as a fisherman in a warmer, drier climate. All four sons of the family, my father included, grew up helping their father with his work in the fishing profession and eventually entered that profession themselves. That is why I am fond of saying, "I am the only grandson who is carrying on the family trade."

My mother's parents also came from Sicily, and so my roots are Sicilian through and through. In our culture, like in so many others, the sense of family and family unity is deeply ingrained. If you have ever seen the film, *My Big Fat Greek Wedding*, and remember how it ends—well, that was my family. I literally grew up in the house next door to my grandparents. Those were my father's parents. My mother's parents lived only a few miles away.

The proximity of both sets of grandparents allowed my siblings and me to enjoy many sleepovers at their homes. In addition, all of the cousins on both sides of the family lived within a few miles of each other, and so the extended family got together all the time. In fact, on Sundays, after our family dinner at 1:00—as they do in Italy—we visited older relatives, usually my mother's aunts and uncles. Later in the evening, we spent time at my maternal grandparents' home, where that whole side of the family gathered.

Family and the security and unity that flowed from it were and are the foundational formation of my life. Along with my extended family's support, my parents and the example they set reinforced the value of family life at home. Every member of our family had an established role, and we knew the expectations of these roles and the commitment it required from each of us.

Considering the era and the strong family dynamics I was raised in, divorce was a foreign concept to me growing up. I still remember the first time I heard the word "divorce." I was in the third grade, and as we were returning from recess, a classmate told me that his parents were divorced. "What's that?" I asked. I still remember what he told me: "It's when your parents have a big argument and they break up." Sadly today, the wreckage of divorce permeates into our culture and society and now affects all families, even my own. Nevertheless, the security that comes from family cohesiveness is something that has defined me, as well as certain virtues like hard work.

Since the time I was born, my father owned his own albacore boat, a smaller vessel used for seasonal fishing, which he operated during the months of May to September. During the winter, he worked on a dredge or found other work on the bay. Sometimes he worked long hours, especially in the springtime when he was preparing his boat for the fishing season. We almost always waited until he arrived home to have dinner, but occasionally, when it got to be extremely late, my mother would reluctantly serve us dinner while we waited for him to return home.

My father's leadership in our family helped me to understand the importance of fathers in every family, especially their effect on children and their relationship with Christ. One of my earliest childhood memories is of those few times we started dinner before my father arrived home. While sitting at the dinner table, my little sister and I would hear his footsteps coming up the stairs to the back door; we would then push our chairs back from the table, jump up, and run to the back door waving our arms and yelling, "Daddy!" No matter how tired he was, our father had enough strength to pick us both up at the same time, one in each arm. That memory of my own father has stayed with me very vividly, and mirrors such a powerful image of the love and tenderness of God as our Father.

I attended public school from elementary through high school. Although I didn't attend a Catholic school, I understood that our faith was central in our lives. By today's standards, I suppose we would have been considered a religiously observant family, but by the standards of that time, which was a more religiously oriented society, we were pretty typical. My mother saw to it that we attended catechism classes and Mass, and she took us to Confession every couple of months. Along with her insistence on our Catholic religious education and upbringing, our Sicilian heritage itself, heavily rooted in the Church, carried its own Catholic traditions.

One of these traditions is the celebration of the feast day of St. Joseph, to whom Sicilians have a very strong devotion. When I was young, my grandmother's cousin would prepare the St. Joseph's Day celebration and host it at her home in Glendale, which was roughly a two-hour drive from our home. After she passed away, we continued to celebrate the tradition back in San Diego. For the traditional celebration, special foods are prepared, and a table is set up as an altar. Three loaves of bread are baked to represent the Holy Family: one in the form of a braid to represent Mary's hair, one as a staff to represent St. Joseph, and one as a crown to represent Jesus. No one sat at this table except the three people representing the Holy Family, and no one could start any of the courses until after the representatives of the Holy Family had eaten from them first.

At the start of the celebration, the Holy Family would appear at the door, much like in the Mexican posada. An older man representing St. Joseph would knock and ask to be admitted. The lady of the house would open the door and say, "No, you can't come in." Then she would slam the door shut. They did this a few times until the Holy Family was finally welcomed into the house, with everyone shouting, *"Viva San Giuseppe!"* The Holy Family would then sit down at the head table, and Jesus, the little boy, would bless the food, and then the meal would begin. (Coincidentally,

I played the role of Jesus a few times.) This ritual and others like it were ingrained in us and very much part of my culture.

During the spring when my father prepared his boat for the fishing season, I occasionally accompanied him to the dock at Point Loma. On the way, we would drive past the Naval Training Center, which was still in use at the time. It bustled with military activity, and I would observe it as we drove by. It very much captivated me. In addition to this, my father had served in the Navy during World War II, and so I grew up with a fascination of the sea, the Navy, and a life of service. It instilled in me a desire to pursue that kind of life. By the time I was in elementary school, I knew what I was supposed to do with my life—have a career in the Navy. I was enthralled with this idea and even created a scrapbook. As I grew older I looked into the possibility of applying to the Naval Academy.

Knowing the rigorous requirements of admittance into the Naval Academy, I prioritized my academic studies and took advanced courses, with lots of science and math. Despite my best efforts, however, I realized that my plans for a career in the Navy were not going to materialize. The setback was my colorblindness; although only slight, it was enough to disqualify me from admittance. Service academies can make certain exceptions to this rule for students who are real geniuses or exceptional athletes, but I didn't fall into either of these categories.

Later into high school, my real interest was in the area of music, but my strength was math. Toward the end of my high school years, I began to discern my calling, "What am I called to do?" I thought it was the military but perhaps, I thought, there was another way to pursue that path, perhaps as a staff officer. Being good in math was necessary, but I felt a tug toward music. My instrument was the saxophone, and so I played in the marching band, the concert band, and the stage band. Also, since one must exhibit leadership to be accepted into any of the service academies, I became the drum major in my senior year of high school. Later at my episcopal ordination, a number of my Crawford High School classmates were there. One of them was a good friend who had played the trombone in the band. "You know, Sam," he said to me afterward, "you always had a thing about being out in front leading the group with a stick and a tall hat."

I didn't recognize it at the time, but I can see in retrospect the signs of a priestly vocation. For one thing, my faith was always important to me. I never drifted away as some of my friends did. Even some of my friends in the seminary strayed and then came back. My mother didn't force me to go to Mass. As a teenager I attended even when I had to go alone. On occasion, I stopped at church on my way home from school to pray.

The virtue of hard work was instilled early on, and I had several jobs over the years. When I had a paper route and went collecting from my customers, I would sometimes linger and visit with them, especially the older ones. I would also help them out with chores around the house. One older couple in particular used to like to stay up late and visit with me and tell stories when I went to collect from them. One time they talked so long that it was midnight before I finally got out of their house and went home. My mother was worried, and there were no cell phones back then to let her know I was all right!

Another sign of my vocation is that as a child I found catechism class to be interesting. I wouldn't admit that to anyone, however, because little boys are not supposed to be interested in religion. I was inspired by the Church's tradition, the solemnity of the liturgy, and the figure of the priest—as a man in the community. I didn't consider the priesthood as my calling, though. I thought it was marriage. I remembered praying to the Lord, "Send me someone special in my life, preferably Catholic, but at least a very good Christian girl."

It was right around that time that I met my high school sweetheart. Her life goals and mine seemed to be in sync. She had good values and came from a religiously observant family, although they were Lutheran. We often attended Mass together at my church, and about a year after we started going together, she took instruction from the associate pastor of our parish and was received into the Catholic Church. So, I like to think that her conversion was my first pastoral success, even before I entered the seminary!

Toward the end of high school and the beginning of college, I began to seriously reflect on what I really should do with my life and what God was calling me to do. I was still considering a career in the military in some way and I was headed toward being a math major, but I was also interested in studying music. And now with my new budding relationship, marriage seemed like a real possibility. My high school sweetheart's real desire in life was to get married, make a home, and have lots of children. I appreciated that and liked the idea, and I especially liked that she wanted to do it in that order! But I wasn't ready for that anytime soon, and like most young adults at that age, I couldn't quite pinpoint what direction my life was supposed to take. I knew I wanted to do something different with my life. I wanted to live my life for others and serve something beyond myself.

I believe this explained my desire for a military career—to serve a cause greater than myself by serving my country in unity with others. I began to focus on what makes a difference in a person's life. At the time, the associate pastor at my parish was a young priest in our diocese. When I attended Mass, I remember having a desire to be up on the altar with him. His homilies were excellent and still are. (Some time ago, I was privileged to speak at the celebration of the 40th anniversary of his priesthood.) He always seemed to address what I was thinking about and trying to grapple with that week. More and more I began to think that maybe God was calling me to the priesthood.

It was difficult to reconcile myself to the thought of becoming a priest, but I had a defining moment during a job experience. I was working as a host at a diner, seating people and running the cash register. I worked the graveyard shift, so it was early in the morning. A customer returned and said I had made a mistake when giving him his change. He claimed to have given me a one-hundred-dollar bill, but I gave him change for a fifty.

I didn't remember it that way, but okay. I was young and naïve about these things, so I gave him the fifty dollars. I concluded my shift, went home, took a shower, and went to bed. Then I heard the phone ring. I thought, *I'll just let it ring and whoever it is will hang up.* But the phone kept ringing. There were no answering machines back in those days. It must have rung for at least five minutes. I finally got out of bed and answered the phone. Yes, it was my boss and, yes, he told me I had been swindled out of fifty dollars. I felt so bad and so stupid, but it made me think about the emptiness of material things, and why anyone would lose their honor for something as meaningless as fifty dollars. It enforced in me a strong distaste for worldly things.

The idea of the priesthood became stronger, and I finally worked up the nerve to talk to my associate pastor. He told me about a weekend retreat at the seminary for young men interested in the priesthood. I decided to go and quickly became friends with the seminarians. I also met young men who were considering a vocation to the priesthood. This was helpful, since up until then I felt I was the only one in the world with this crazy idea. When I spoke to the others and heard their stories, I felt a sense of solidarity.

I also learned that the seminary is the place to *discern* a vocation, not the place one goes when one has already made up his mind. And the discernment is on the part of both the candidate and the seminary faculty. This made the decision to enter a lot easier for me, since I would have the opportunity to seriously consider this life-changing decision without the need to make an immediate commitment.

As part of my preparation for entering the seminary, my associate pastor recommended that I become detached from my current life in all ways. Serious and active discernment requires an undivided heart, and I understood that freedom from my own attachments would allow me to discover His plan for my life with greater ease and clarity. One of those ways, obviously, meant that I had to break up with my high school sweetheart. It was awkward and painful, but while it was difficult at the time, there was a happy ending. She ended up marrying the first seminarian who befriended me, who left the seminary shortly after I entered to marry her! About fifteen years later, after they had moved to another part of the country, they drove back for a visit. I was a pastor in the area at the time, and they visited me. They were happily married, had six kids, and were hoping to have more.

Praise God! He leads us to the path He desires for our life, and we ultimately arrive if we pay attention to Him and do what He asks. Saying yes and taking the plunge to enter the seminary was my first *fiat*.

My initial feeling when I entered the seminary—which may seem strange—was, *this is a lot of fun.* The other seminarians were creative, bright individuals, and I felt like I fit in well. But there was still a pull between the priesthood and the vocation of marriage. Again, God's pull was stronger. He would not let me have peace with any other decision.

After earning my bachelor's degree in philosophy from the University of San Diego, I felt secure enough in my vocation to pursue studies in sacred theology. I requested to study in Rome for several reasons. Aside from its cultural richness and being the heart of the Church, studying in Rome afforded me the opportunity to explore my heritage and visit relatives my family was still in touch with who lived in different parts of Italy. Fortunately, the seminary faculty agreed, and so I made the move to study at the Pontifical North American College in September of 1978.

The timing of my arrival in Rome could not have been better, and looking back, I know God must have had a hand in it. I was able to be an eyewitness to some pivotal events in Church history. My class arrived in Rome the day before Pope John Paul I's installation as Holy Father, and as it turned out, it was the very first Mass I attended in Rome. Then we were there during Pope John Paul I's untimely death, his funeral, and the election of Pope John Paul II. The Lord blessed me with the opportunity to be present in St. Peter's square the night John Paul II was elected. It was an omen of things to come, and of the influence his papacy would have on me.

Many years later, right after his death, the editor of our diocesan paper asked me to write a reflection on Pope John Paul II. It wasn't until then that I realized I had a point of encounter with him at every step along my priesthood journey, in accordance to my state at the time: during my first year in the seminary, I served Midnight Mass for him; then during my last year in seminary, as a deacon, I served as one of the deacons of the oils at the Chrism Mass he celebrated; as a priest in graduate studies, I concelebrated Mass with him in his private chapel; later, when I became a bishop, I was part of the fifteen-minute private audience that the diocesan bishop, under whom I was serving as auxiliary, had with him for his *ad limina* visit. These encounters with Pope Saint John Paul II and his papacy would have a tremendous impact on my ministry.

The Lord provided special opportunities for me and gave me support through the priests of our diocese. This included the two priests who were my rectors at the seminary in San Diego, the vocations director for the diocese, and my associate pastor. Through their support I thrived. However, there was a struggle in my mind to make the ultimate *fiat*—becoming a priest.

I knew this decision was a supernatural calling. I couldn't do it on my own using human resources alone. I had to rely on prayer. I had to rely on healthy relationships, priest friends, family, and healthy relationships with lay friends. I had to rely on spiritual direction and a serious commitment to ministry in giving myself over to whatever the Lord wanted from me. When I arrived at that realization and finally handed myself completely over to God, trusting in His providence to help me persevere, I experienced a tremendous sense of freedom. That sense of freedom was the confirmation for me that this was my call.

At the end of my four years of theology studies, it was time to leave Rome and return home. I remember this event clearly. It was a nostalgic time for me since I had enjoyed studying and being in Italy. I enjoyed my classmates, the other guys I studied with, getting to know my relatives who lived in different parts of Italy, and all there is to experience in Rome and in the Church there. Yet I knew it was the right time to leave. It was a "kairos" moment. It was time to start a new chapter in my life. I left Rome with a sense of freedom and joy to return home to be ordained a priest.

God continued to provide. A priest's first assignment is critical for his path through the priesthood. Thank God for the bishop who assigned me to a good Irish pastor. He was patient with me, hard-working, and prayerful. He set a good example of what it means to love and shepherd God's people with generosity and sensitivity. Still, there was a period of adjustment I had to go through as I learned to put theory into practice. For one thing, the liturgies in the seminary were always well done, with everyone singing and participating with all their heart. Not all of the Masses at the parish were that way.

Marriage preparation presented another serious challenge for me. Even back then I was aware of the sad reality that many couples lived together before marriage; I wasn't that naïve. However, I was naïve enough to believe that people would be reasonable and logical when I explained marriage in the Catholic Church. It meant living as a Catholic, taking it seriously and being true to your word, understanding and believing in the gift of marriage and its sacredness, and making the appropriate changes.

I soon realized that not everyone is reasonable.

There are real challenges when a priest comes face to face with the culture. It took me a couple of years to find the pieces of my new life as a priest falling into place. By my third year in my first assignment I felt settled into my priesthood. I knew how to minister well and I was finding my stride and coming into my own.

Then Rome intervened once again.

I was ordained a priest in 1982. The revised Code of Canon Law was promulgated by Pope John Paul II in 1983. That meant that bishops from all over the country were sending priests to study canon law at that time, in order to be updated with the new Code. The priest from our diocese who was initially selected by our bishop, was instead chosen by the Vatican Diplomatic Corps to become a Vatican diplomat. I was still newly ordained and could readily transition back into studies, and the bishop wanted to send a priest to Rome for canon law studies, so I was selected as the replacement.

I liked the idea of graduate studies and hoped I would have that opportunity someday, but canon law was not at the top of my list of disciplines I wanted to study. Plus, I thought I needed a few more years of parish experience to really capitalize on what I had learned. However, this was another *fiat* moment. With mixed feelings, I took the opportunity and returned to Rome to complete graduate studies in canon law. I worked on my doctoral degree from 1985 to 1989. Those were years of continued growth and maturity, and a time to know my professors better, especially my thesis director, a Jesuit. I observed the holy life the Jesuits lived and found it inspiring.

The traditional Jesuit model consists of thorough religious and academic formation. They are cultured and brilliant. Yet, the professors I got to know in Rome lived rather Spartan lives, with few amenities. It is a life dedicated to learning, studying, and teaching. In addition to learning the course material, there is an emphasis on learning to think with a canonical mind, which is important. I came to appreciate my mentor's religious order and found the Jesuit way of life to have a profound effect on me in regard to my own priesthood.

As I was finishing my studies in Rome, a coadjutor bishop by the name of Robert Brom was assigned to our diocese. Our previous bishop, Bishop Maher, was near retirement, so they selected a bishop to be coadjutor, which means he was an assistant bishop who would take over as the diocesan bishop upon the retirement of his predecessor. The news was announced just as Bishop Brom was about to take a trip he had planned to Rome in May of 1989, before he knew of this news, to celebrate his 25th anniversary of priestly ordination. That meant I was the first priest of the diocese to meet him after the news came out.

Shortly after I returned home to resume my ministry, he called me into his office and asked me to be his secretary for that first year. I agreed. I worked as his secretary and also worked part-time in the tribunal because of my background in canon law. The following year he took over as the bishop of our diocese, and I moved to serve full-time in the tribunal as the adjutant judicial vicar.

During that year there were a lot of changes in pastoral assignments. In one of these rounds of changes, every parish slot was filled except for one. No one knew whom the bishop would come up with to assign as the pastor of Our Lady of Guadalupe parish in Calexico. Calexico is out in the Imperial Valley, about two hours east of San Diego, and sits right on the Mexican border. It is basically a suburb of Mexicali, the large city on the Mexican side of the border.

Around that time, Bishop Brom came to the parish where I was in residence to celebrate Confirmation. I remember it clearly: we were sitting in the living room after the Mass with his priest secretary and the pastor of the parish when at a certain point the two of them left the room, leaving the bishop and I alone. He said, "You know, we have all of the parishes covered, but can't find anyone to go to Calexico." Then he laughed and said, seemingly off-the-cuff, "How would you like to go to Calexico?" This was in 1991, and my goal at that point in my life was to become a pastor before the end of the millennium. So I immediately answered, "Sure, I would love to go there." The next day, he called me into his office and offered me the possibility of going to Calexico for real. He didn't order me to go, he offered, yet I jumped at the opportunity to become the pastor.

Those four years were influential in my life. If a priest's first assignment is formational in his priesthood, so is his first pastorate. I found the Hispanic culture of Calexico similar to the Sicilian culture I had grown up in, instantly making me feel like I was at home: family cohesion and family gatherings on a regular basis—especially on Sundays, when the entire extended family always got together. It was just like in my own family, except that in my family we ate spaghetti and meatballs, whereas in Calexico the families enjoyed *tacos de carne asada*.

Likewise, their culture incorporated many rich Catholic rituals and celebrations. There were novenas, Marian devotions, and celebrations of patron saint feast days that filled their homes and our parish. However, there were also some daunting challenges. Calexico was not an economically flourishing area. Most came from middle to lower-middle income level households. This economic hardship posed a burden for some families, and also a challenge in terms of meeting all of the parish expenses.

I had much work to do on the level of the physical facilities, as well as work in the areas of evangelization and education. Yet, I felt in my element. I was flourishing and had come into my own. At this point I became involved in other areas of ministry too, especially the Marriage Encounter movement, and I eventually became involved in its leadership on the national level. I sometimes felt overwhelmed with so much happening, but I had this feeling that, in God's plan, everything in my life was preparing me for this role: my parish experiences, my studies, my work for the bishop and for the diocese. It all made sense, and I felt it all culminated in that moment of my life, that this is what God was preparing me for.

I served in Calexico for about four years, and it had taken me about three of those years to address the immediate needs of the parish. At the beginning of my fourth year, I thought, *Now we can begin thinking long-term and really make some great strides.* I also served as the dean of the Imperial Valley deanery, which meant that I ran the regular meetings of the priests in the deanery and served as their representative at the monthly Presbyteral Council meetings in San Diego. Just as I was making great strides at my parish, the Lord had other plans.

The date is significant—December 12th, the feast day of Our Lady of Guadalupe. Another one of my duties as dean was to coordinate the deanery-wide Mass for Our Lady of Guadalupe, which the bishop would come to celebrate from San Diego on that day. I remember this moment very well. It was three-thirty in the afternoon, and I was leaving to set up for the Mass off-site. Before I left, I remembered I needed something from the sacristy of the church, and then also something from my room. When I entered my room, I saw that I had a voice-mail message on the answering machine of my private line. I thought, *I only left a minute ago. I wonder who that is.*

This was a traditional rectory with the office space and the living space next to each other. The message was from the parish secretary. She said Monsignor Raymond Burke from Rome was on the phone. Archbishop Burke was one of my professors in canon law and a visiting professor at the Gregorian University. We had become friends. He was at that time working at the Apostolic Signatura in Rome. I thought, *Oh, wow! This is exciting. I haven't spoken to him in quite a while.* I rushed out into the office area, and he was still on the phone.

After the usual niceties, he arrived at the point of his call. "I just received news that I've been named Bishop of Lacrosse." This was his home diocese here in the United States. This sounded really exciting to me, and I was very happy for him, for his diocese, and for the whole Church. I thought he was going to ask me to contact people and help him make arrangements, or something similar. Instead, he said, "We are short-handed here at the Signatura, and now with me leaving, we need yet another priest here who speaks English. How would you like to come work at the Apostolic Signatura?"

This threw me for a loop, since I was preparing to leave for the deanery Mass. I couldn't give him an immediate answer. "Let me call you tomorrow to discuss this further," he said. This created mixed feelings for me. I really loved this parish, and it was right at the point where I thought it was ready to flourish. I felt this was where God wanted me, but how could I say no to Raymond Burke, my friend for whom I have so much respect?

I didn't go into my priesthood with the thought of charting my own course. I thought, *If this is what is being asked of me, I suppose I should accept.* I also liked the idea of this rare opportunity. How many priests get the opportunity to work in the Roman Curia? There were other Americans working in various departments, plus another American priest whom I knew from my time in canon law studies working at the Signatura. I could adapt readily to this situation. I accepted the new job and returned to Rome.

It was by far the most difficult thing I have ever done in my priesthood. This might seem strange to the outside observer: to leave a large, demanding, economically struggling parish in the desert for a job in Rome with fixed office hours, the ability to go home and not worry about work, and to have the time and resources to enjoy all that Rome and traveling in Italy has to offer. Who wouldn't welcome that? While I certainly enjoyed these benefits, that didn't make it any easier. I knew, of course, that I would miss the people I left behind, but there was more to it than that. I had put my entire heart and soul into that parish. I felt myself identified with it, and so it was as if I'd left a piece of myself behind. I felt utterly displaced.

It took me a number of years to adjust. I did feel privileged and blessed to be Rome, and it influenced my formation greatly. I learned a lot more about canon law, but also a lot more *than* canon law. I was living and working with some really smart people and with brother priests who were wonderful examples of the priestly life. One of them was my immediate superior, who had been one of my professors when I was studying canon law. I always saw in him a kind spirit and a deep love for the Church, and great integrity and commitment in his service to the Church. He became instrumental in the way in which I developed in my ministry.

What happens at the Apostolic Signatura? It is a type of Supreme Court in the Church's court system. Among other responsibilities, it oversees and ensures the correct administration of justice in the Church. This area of competence is technically known as "vigilance over the administration of justice." My work was specific to this area and consisted of monitoring the work of tribunals throughout the world. This involved, among other things, reviewing the annual reports that tribunals throughout the world complete and submit to the Signatura with information about their personnel and the cases they've tried. In turn, I would write back to offer my observations and recommendations to help improve the tribunal's ministry of justice. It sometimes also required studying actual cases that tribunals had already tried, in order to offer more in-depth observations. The vast majority of these cases involved the nullity of marriage, but there are a few other types of cases that tribunals sometimes handled as well.

While the work was sometimes interesting, to be honest much of it was routine and monotonous. I appreciated learning more and becoming enriched. At times, however, I wondered if this was what God had planned for my priesthood. I acquired other jobs as well, including serving as a consultant on cases of priests requesting to be returned to the lay state, helping in a role of administration at the residence where I lived, and doing some pastoral ministry on the side too. I became reacquainted with old friends and made new ones.

After my sixth year in Rome, I felt settled in and comfortable with the idea that this must be God's calling for me. Well, that is what I thought until one of my yearly scheduled vacations home. I would always pay a courtesy call to Bishop Brom when I was home on vacation, and I called him on a Monday to set it up. He suggested getting together Friday morning at his residence for Mass, and then to visit over coffee afterwards. But on Wednesday he called my parents' house, where I was staying, and left a message that he wanted me to call him immediately. "I need to see you today," he told me when I called back. "It can't wait until Friday, so come in this afternoon. All I can tell you is that we got a phone call from the Nunciature." I went to see him and received news that I was appointed the Auxiliary Bishop of San Diego.

When a priest is appointed a bishop, he writes a letter of acceptance to the Holy Father. Although Bishop Brom had a computer in his residence where we met, it did not include a word processing program or a printer, so I had to type this letter on an electric typewriter, composing it as I typed.

It was a whirlwind of activity, another *fiat* moment, trusting in the Lord that somehow He was working out His plan in my life—even through me as an inadequate instrument, as Pope Benedict would say about himself. How much more would this apply to me!

It has been quite a ride as a bishop. It is a privilege to see the work of the Church active in so many different ways. I see a tremendous amount of good. Despite impressions some people may have, the Church is vibrant in many ways. The Magnificat women's ministry is one example.

As I look back on my journey through the priesthood, I can say that every change I passed through was met with mixed feelings, except for one—when I became a pastor. In those moments of transition, I liked where I was at the time, or thought it was God's will for me. I was finally beginning to make some progress, but He would then ask me to move on.

In retrospect, there are many times when I could have said no. I then wonder about my life. How would it have been different? I could have said no to the seminary. I could have said no to returning to Rome for graduate studies. No to becoming a pastor. No to Rome and the work at the Apostolic Signatura. But I realized God was unfolding His plan for me because I said yes. I gave my *fiat* at those times. And *fiat* continued to guide me as I embarked on one of the most extraordinary experiences of my life—helping to save marriage in California. This was even more extraordinary than being ordained a priest, being ordained a bishop, or those encounters with Pope John Paul II—at least in a certain way.

A group of lay people in San Diego was organizing a grass-roots effort to defend the definition of marriage in the law, and they reached out to me for my help. They were acting ahead of a California State Supreme Court ruling that they expected would overturn Proposition 22, thereby redefining marriage. Their goal was to get a state constitutional amendment on the ballot to protect marriage and essentially validate what the majority of California voters had already decided on and approved through Proposition 22. The new proposition became known as Proposition 8.

To get the proposition on the November ballot was no small feat. In order to file the proposition, we needed to collect 1.1 million signatures and raise $1.5 million for the paid signature gatherers in a short amount of time. I worked closely with them on this phase of the process by connecting people with different gifts, from those who could raise the money, to those who could educate people, to those who could motivate people about the sanctity of marriage, as well as helping to educate people myself about the importance of the issue. We eventually connected with Evangelical Christians, who share our deeply held beliefs on the sanctity of marriage and were trying to do the same thing. We worked closely together with them.

After obtaining the necessary signatures, the proposition qualified for the ballot. It was during this time that we also gained the support of the Latter-Day Saints Church, which proved indispensable for the passage of the proposition. It was our combined efforts that brought success, but I call it a "collateral blessing" that God brought His people together in a way we never could have imagined. All of us working closely together dispelled certain stereotypical misconceptions, and alliances were forged. The pastors I worked with truly became my brothers.

It is the correct understanding of marriage that gives us the opportunity to reclaim what I call the "sacramental world-view." The current culture in which we live sees the world in a purely materialistic way; it cannot see beyond the physical. The Evangelical Christians and the pastors I worked with understood the sacramental world-view of marriage as an image of the eternal marriage of Christ and the Church, even if they didn't use the word "sacrament." It is an outward sign of that greater reality. However, education of our own people is needed because so many have lost the sense of the sacred. Marriage is the key.

When I look back on all that transpired in my life, I believe this is a culmination of what God led me to accomplish. I was born in 1956, so I am old enough to be aware of how the world has changed in one generation. I remember President Kennedy's assassination, the Beatles' arrival in the United States, and the social upheavals of the 60s, which left me perplexed as I grew into a young man. I braced myself in August 2009 for the 40th anniversary celebration of Woodstock. I thought, *Is this really something to celebrate, this feast of self-indulgence and licentiousness?*

It demonstrates how much the world has changed in one generation. One generation of the past was defined by the icon of their generation, D-day. The next generation was defined by Woodstock. How did this happen? This gives me cause to be alarmed at the spiritual decay of our society throughout my life. I think this was my motivation to embrace the priesthood—an opportunity to evangelize and transform the culture to something healthy, something for Christ. I saw God calling me to do this through promoting the understanding of the true meaning of marriage.

That is what I see as the irony of God's plan for me. The hardest thing for me to give up in becoming a priest is what God called me to champion: my work in the tribunal to defend the integrity of marriage by fair judgments regarding the nullity of marriage; my work with Marriage Encounter; my work at the Apostolic Signatura; and then my work with my brother bishops and so many other priests on Proposition 8. God has set the course of my priesthood to be for championing the sanctity of marriage.

Although it might seem greatly inconvenient, it was really God's providence that at the peak of the campaign for Proposition 8, I had to honor a previous commitment I had made to the Filipino community in San Diego to accept their invitation to make a pilgrimage to their country on the occasion of the feast day of Our Lady of Peñafrancia. I had celebrated this feast day for them locally, but they wanted to bring me to the actual shrine in Naga, located in the Archdiocese of Caceres. The archbishop there invited me to preach at the Mass concluding the novena of celebration.

During my visit there, I was astonished to see the throngs of Filipino Catholics who attended the celebration to honor Our Lady. The incredible turnout was most visible during the procession, where an image of Our Lady of Peñafrancia was carried from their cathedral through the streets. Thousands upon thousands lined the streets to pray and to try to catch a glimpse of the image.

Participating in the feast day was providential in many ways because it showed me how faith can change a society's broken culture. If people with a postmodernist mentality looked at the faithful there, they would see the celebration of this feast day as a quaint folkloric custom. They might look at it with passing curiosity, but they wouldn't think it had anything to do with reality. But it is this same faith that brought down an unjust, brutal dictatorship years before in the Philippines. It is the same faith that transformed the culture. The experience gave me hope that this kind of transformation that I witnessed in Naga City was possible for us here in California as we fought to defend marriage.

We too are facing brutal dictatorships in our own world: as Pope Benedict famously put it, the "dictatorship of relativism." But the power of the faith I witnessed in the Philippines that toppled a dictatorship there can do the same for us and transform our culture.

My message to young people, then, is to be open and respond to God's call to heal the culture. The postmodernist mentality toward religion considers it boring, but religion is what gives spice to life. It is a life of spirituality—no matter your vocation—that enriches your life and makes you truly happy. You want boredom? Watch prime-time TV! The Church has 2,000 years of wisdom. It was founded by Christ! Life, truth, and happiness are found here.

Be open to God's call, even if you don't know what He has in store for you. You may not believe He is calling you to priesthood, to religious life, or any particular vocation. However, you may be surprised. My own life is an example of that. I believed my career was in the military. As it turns out, while God was calling me to be a warrior, it was as a warrior in the culture war over the fundamental values that define our society. I thought my vocation was marriage, to be a husband and a father. However, God was calling me to be a husband in the sense of another Christ for His bride, the Church. God called me to be the father to lots of spiritual children. I have many titles, but the only one that really means something to me is "father," when it is said sincerely.

The call of Peter is special to me. Pope John Paul II challenged us at the beginning of the third millennium with the words that Jesus spoke to Peter, "cast the nets out into the deep." The phrase in Latin is *duc in altum*.

The world needs fathers. Pope John Paul II was a father to millions of people. Some of the priests I lived with in Rome received and read his mail. They told me that people looked to him as a father. We are a fatherless culture. We need fathers to mentor our young people into maturity and to challenge them to cast their nets into the deep.

I love Peter's response. While it looked hopeless, he said, "At your command ..." The Latin version, *in verbo tuo*, is the more literal translation of the Greek: "I'll take you at your word." This is what I chose as my episcopal motto, because it is Peter's response to the challenge that Jesus gave him, and that Pope John Paul II has given us. Humanly speaking it looks hopeless. "But, Lord, I will take you at your word and do what you say."

That is my challenge to you. Take the Lord at His word and trust in Him. Cast your nets into deep water and you will be surprised at what you will catch.

Bio–

Salvatore Joseph Cordileone was born in San Diego in 1956. His roots run deep in San Diego. He attended Crawford High School, San Diego State University, the University of San Diego, and St. Francis Seminary in San Diego. He was ordained a priest of San Diego July 9, 1982. He was appointed Auxiliary Bishop of San Diego on July 5, 2002. He earned his Doctorate in Canon Law from the Pontifical Gregorian University in Rome. In 1995, he was called to Rome and served seven years as assistant at the Supreme Tribunal of the Apostolic Signatura, the Church's highest canonical court.

On March 23, 2009, Pope Benedict XVI appointed Bishop Cordileone as the fourth Bishop of Oakland. Three years later, on July 27, 2012, Pope Benedict XVI appointed him the Archbishop of San Francisco. He chairs the United States Conference of Catholic Bishops' Subcommittee for the Promotion and Defense of Marriage and sits on the Committee for Canonical Affairs. The archbishop is committed to the defense of life. He wrote "We need to be supporting and strengthening the institution of marriage for the sake of children, not redefining it or weakening it. Defining marriage as it has been understood for every society since the beginning of the human race is hardly the stuff of which unconstitutional laws consist."

Rev. Fr. Patrick Crowley, SS.CC.

What the world and the church need today are ... "heralds of the Gospel expert in humanity, profoundly knowing the heart of today's man, who share his joys and hopes, his fears and sorrows, and yet who are contemplatives in love with God."

~St. John Paul II

In sharing my testimony, I am very sensitive to the action of God's grace in my life. Please do not look upon it as an ego trip. Far from it. My life and vocation in general can be summed up in the words "total surprise." I was born in the west of Ireland and came from a family of six siblings—three boys and three girls. I was the oldest. My dad was a blacksmith by trade and a farmer. My mom served as postmistress for the country post office in my area. During those years, she shared the joys and sorrows of the local people. She perhaps heard more confessions than I will ever hear during my years of priestly ministry.

I was sent to the diocesan college (St. Flannan's) for my secondary education. It was there I befriended a young man who is at present a priest member in our congregation. He was older than I and graduated two years prior to my finishing college.

Before leaving, I asked him what he intended doing with his life. He told me he was joining the Congregation of the Sacred Hearts of Jesus and Mary. I later discovered that the great St. Damien of Molokai was one of its most illustrious members, together with Fr. Mateo Crawley-Boevey, SS.CC., the Apostle of the Enthronement of the Sacred Heart.

We each went our separate ways. Two years later, the vocation director from the Congregation of the Sacred Hearts came to visit me. He said, "I've been given your name."

"For what?" I asked.

"We would like you to come and see our Community."

I had never heard of the congregation before, except that my friend had mentioned the name in passing. The invitation was to "come and see." I came, and I stayed!

I made my novitiate in Cootehill, County Cavan, Ireland, and then came to the United States. I arrived in New York on September 21, 1957, as a young teenager together with fifteen members of my class. We were headed for the Queen of Peace Seminary in New Hampshire to begin our preparation for the priesthood.

The next time we had the opportunity of visiting our families was the occasion of our ordination to the priesthood. I was ordained a priest in Cootehill, County Cavan, Ireland, on June 23, 1963. The ordaining bishop was the Most Rev. Eugene O'Callaghan, Bishop of Clogher. It was a wonderful reunion for family and friends. My first Mass was offered at St. Joseph's Parish in Miltown-Malbay, County Clare, on June 24th. The parish priest, Canon O'Reilly served my first Mass in Latin.

In August 1963 I was assigned to teach at Damien High School in La Verne, California, with residency at our Community house in Glendora, California. I was given a number of freshmen and sophomore classes, which included teaching general science, English, and religion. As a young priest fresh out of the seminary, I did not like teaching. However, in retrospect, I have always attributed my three years of high school teaching as great preparation for my future ministry. It was both challenging and rewarding!

I received an assignment to our novitiate in Wareham, Massachusetts, in 1966. This served as a preparation for future novitiate work. I was assigned a year later to the novitiate in Cootehill, Ireland, which eventually led to pastoral work in England. Those five years overseas with the various situations and circumstances were the Lord's way of preparing me for something in the future.

I returned to California in 1971. The provincial assigned me to a state hospital in Pomona to care for exceptional children and adults. The assignment was for six months, yet it lasted four years. During those four years, the Lord began to do a tremendous work in my priesthood.

One day while in the chaplain's office at the hospital, a lady walked in and said, "We would like to have you as a spiritual director for our Sunday night prayer meeting." She didn't mention the prayer meeting was Charismatic.

On Sunday evening I arrived at a family residence in Diamond Bar, California, where I found a number of people sitting on the floor with Bibles. They were singing and praising God with uplifted hands.

My first reaction was, *What have I gotten myself into? This is unbelievable!* During the entire meeting I sat there stoic, emotionless, judgmental, and wondering repeatedly, *What have I gotten myself into?*

As strange as it seems, I went back the following week. I discovered that most of these wonderful souls were searching for something more meaningful and fulfilling in their lives. They had discovered what they called the Baptism in the Holy Spirit.

This terminology was totally foreign to me. They shared how they participated in the laying on of hands, and after the laying on of hands, some prayed in tongues. There were others who received the gift of prophecy. Their faith came alive, and they organized a weekly prayer meeting, which included sharing the Sacred Scriptures. They experienced the joy and strength of the Lord, and their lives took on a whole new meaning and purpose.

During the next two years, I went through what someone described as "the paralysis of analysis." My analysis centered around the Baptism in the Holy Spirit and the Charismatic Renewal in general.

One evening I found myself at the Sacred Heart Chapel on the Loyola Marymount University campus in Los Angeles. Fr. Tichenor, S.J. was leading the Eucharist celebration. About eight hundred people were in attendance, which included university students and men and women from various parishes in the Archdiocese of Los Angeles.

Sometime during the liturgy, there was singing and praising God in tongues. The atmosphere was electrifying. I remember saying to the Lord that night, *Lord, if heaven is like this, please let me in on it!*

And He did.

After Mass, I approached a nun, and she prayed over me for the Baptism in the Holy Spirit. Heaven did not open at that particular moment as I thought might happen. There were no sparks. No moments of experiencing a "spiritual high." The Lord met me exactly at my point of need and ministered to me very sensitively in keeping with my personality. By nature, I am shy and introverted.

I remember driving home on the Santa Monica Freeway—I felt joyous and like singing. It was eleven o'clock at night, and I said to myself, "Father Pat, keep your eyes on the road. Don't get too taken up with what is going on right now."

Eventually, I arrived home. Praise God! However, I had changed. I knew something had happened to me, something beyond my wildest dreams and imagination. The Spirit of God had touched me, and life would never again be the same.

For the next two years, I held a prayer meeting every Tuesday evening at Lanterman Hospital where I worked as chaplain. A small group from some of the local parishes came together for praise and worship. God began to do a mighty work touching lives and touching people who came to that meeting. I remember one lady in particular who got the giggles after she received the Baptism in the Spirit. She received the gift of laughter and couldn't stop.

When the prayer meeting ended, many from our group usually went to one of the nearby restaurants for coffee. This lady joined us. The waitress came to take her order. "Honey, what would you like to order tonight?"

The lady broke out into laughter, and she laughed and laughed. The poor waitress looked in utter shock, as if wondering what was going on. Was this woman drunk? Was she all there? Was she on drugs?

I eventually learned that the lady went home and woke her husband. She was still in hysterics, laughing. His first response was, "Where have you been tonight? Wherever you've been, that's the last night you are going out on your own." She could not convince him that she had gone to a prayer meeting. She exuded such joy.

I completed my assignment as chaplain of Lanterman Hospital in June of 1975 when I was elected provincial of the west coast province. This necessitated moving the prayer meetings to Holy Name of Mary parish in San Dimas, which was ministered to by our Community. Prior to coming to Holy Name of Mary, the members of the prayer community had gone into a time of prayer and fasting asking God for some new directions, especially in the areas of ministry. Little did we think that God had a "mighty work" in store for us.

On Tuesday evenings, the prayer meeting attracted two to three hundred people. People left work in the evening and came directly to the parish hall just to get a seat. It was during this time that the Charismatic gift of healing began to manifest. A number of people experienced spiritual, physical, and emotional healings without any imposition of hands or personal ministry. There was an intuition on my part (sometimes expressed through a "word" or "picture") that someone was being healed. In Charismatic terms, we refer to this as the "word of knowledge."

Some of these healings involved cancer cases, bone problems, healing of memories, depression, oppression, addictions of various kinds, and deliverance from evil spirits. These meetings had an evangelistic thrust—the preaching of the gospel with an opportunity to renew one's commitment to Christ.

During the course of thirty months, the leadership of the prayer community estimated that 5,000 people were profoundly touched by the Holy Spirit. In sharing the above information, I am very mindful of my brother priests in the presbyterate. Theirs too is a ministry of healing and reconciliation expressed in so many beautiful ways as the Spirit leads.

True charism does not flower without fraternal communion because the Author of this charism, the Spirit, operates within the mutual love and communion of the faithful. Therefore Paul, with the help of the image of the body, asserts the mutual dependence of these gifts. (1 Corin. 12:12–13)

(Antony D'Cruz, J. O. Praem, "The Role of Charisms in the Church," *Vidyajyoti Journal of Theological Reflection,* Volume 78, No. 8. August 2014.)

One evening, a friend took his mother to a healing service. She had been crippled from the waist down. Unfortunately, they were late, and the meeting had just finished. I asked the leadership to join me in praying for this woman. As I began to pray, first laying my hands on her, I sensed the warmth of God's healing touch on her head. Intuitively, not audibly, I heard the words, *"Tell her to get up, that she is now completely healed."*

My immediate reaction was, *Absolutely, not, Lord! My reputation is at stake.* Not only that, but I wasn't going to tell somebody "you are healed" when I didn't know if it was my voice or God's.

I continued to pray for her and there was tension within me. What could I do to save face? I eventually got around the situation by using words that were rather evasive. "I think that you are now healed."

Before the words left my mouth, she jumped up out of the wheelchair and began to dance around the floor with joy. Guess who was the most surprised person in the entire place? Yours truly!

It was during this time that I began to experience the purifying grace of the Holy Spirit. I grew up with many fears in my early childhood, especially fears picked up from going to Irish wakes and being encouraged to kiss the body of the deceased out of respect. I probably kissed more dead bodies in my homeland than I ever kissed in my life.

As a result, certain fears had left deep scars in my subconscious mind. Someone shared the name of Agnes Sanford, a pioneer in the healing ministry, with a wonderful gift for "healing of memories." I made an appointment to visit her.

Mrs. Sanford was born of American missionary parents in China. Her first encounter with the healing ministry was experienced through an Episcopal minister, who had an appointment with her husband one day. At the time, she was suffering from a heaviness of spirit.

Agnes Sanford describes his visit:

"How are the children?" the minster asked.

"Oh, the baby's sick," I replied. "He's been sick for six weeks."

"Well," said he in his pleasant voice, quite casually, "I'll go up and say a little prayer for him."

This surprised me greatly. I believed in a vague, general way that God answered prayer for healing when He felt like it—unless for some reason He preferred for a person to remain ill.

"Oh, the baby wouldn't understand. He's too little."

The minister went upstairs and prayed for the child. "Now, you shut your eyes and go to sleep," he said to the baby. "I'm going to ask God to come into your ears and make them well. And when you wake up, you'll be all right."

His prayer was very simple. "Please, Lord Jesus, send Your power right now into this baby's ears and take away all germs or infection and make them well. Thank You, Lord, for I believe that You are doing this, and I see these ears well as You made them to be."

When the child woke, his temperature was normal and his ears were well. (Notes taken from *Sealed Order* by Agnes Sanford, Logos International.1972)

At a later time, Agnes Sanford went to visit this minister. She had a powerful experience of the Holy Spirit and began to study healing. One time, a young man came to visit her who needed a healing of the memories. Agnes prayed for this young man a number of times, and yet there was no release. Eventually, she sought the Lord's guidance. She received the words, *Pray for the inner child in "him that is hurt."*

This was the beginning of Agnes's involvement in the healing of the memories. Agnes took the "inner child" with her to Mass, the Sunday Eucharist, and applied the full power of the death, burial, and resurrection of Jesus to his "inner child." He was completely set free after a few weeks.

I went to Agnes for prayer. The Lord used her mightily in ministering to my inner childhood fears. I was set free after a time. Since then, the Lord has used me in other ways to pray for people for inner healing and especially for fears and phobias experienced in early childhood.

One of my great missionary desires as a teenager was to go to Africa. During the years of my priesthood, I never had the opportunity to go to the foreign missions. I always seemed to minister to the local church. However, the desires of my heart were answered when I received an invitation to minister in Indonesia. In all, I have made five trips to Indonesia ministering in Java, Sumatra, Sulawesi, and Bali. The Lord was instrumental in opening doors for me.

In one service, we had 5,000 people present. A large group of Muslims were in attendance, all in need of God's touch. Keep in mind that Indonesia is 90% Muslim, but many had no inhibitions when it came to attending a healing service. The Lord blessed them beyond their wildest dreams and expectations.

For the new millennium, the Lord again surprised me with an invitation to minister in Singapore at the World Trade Center. There were over 1,000 people in attendance. What a special moment to evangelize and experience the healing touch of the Lord.

It has been a special privilege to share the Word of God over the years to various denominations. I believe that my stay in England helped prepare the way. It was an opportunity to interact with several ministers from various churches such as Methodists, Episcopalians, Seventh Day Adventists, Congregationalists, and non-denomination Christians. Subsequently, I have been open to conducting a healing service when invited to one of those churches.

As you read this today, I would remind you not to underestimate the power of the Holy Spirit. Don't underestimate the surprises the Lord has in store for you. I am a wounded healer very much aware of my own faults and failures but completely cognizant of God's infinite love and mercy.

You may wonder about some of my experiences. It is interesting to observe the diversification of the expressions of the Holy Spirit at work. In some healing services, the emphasis may be on inner healing, like the healing of memories—wounds of bitterness, alienation, unforgiveness, and depression. At other times, a person with little hope for survival due to cancer will receive a complete physical healing. Yet, at that same meeting there may be six different cases of cancer, and none are physically healed. This doesn't mean God is not doing something special in their lives. One of the greatest consolations is the healing of the soul, when someone requests the sacrament of Reconciliation and is reconciled with God after twenty or forty years away from the Church.

"We are a people who have largely defined ourselves outwardly. Within we feel out of control, denied, afraid, guilty, and on foreign soil. We try to compensate by self-help books and courses, by quick aphorisms, and falling back on the cultural and familial emotional responses. The result is that we are producing the greatest amount of material success along with the greatest amount of neurosis and interpersonal and spiritual failure in the very same group of people. We are educated for careers but not for the living of a full human life. Feelings are not 'educated' at all. In fact, most people do not seem to know that it is possible." (cf. Eddie Ensley, *Prayer That Heals Our Emotions*, Contemplative Books, Columbus, GA. 1986)

I am reminded of those beautiful words of Pope Francis, "Let ourselves be embraced by the mercy of God; let us trust in his patience, which always gives more time. Let us find the courage to return to his house, to dwell in his loving wounds, letting ourselves be loved by him. We will feel his tenderness, and we too will become more capable of mercy, patience, and forgiveness." (*A Year with Pope Francis—Daily Reflections from his Writings*. Edited by Alberto Rossda, CMF)

To the Sacred Hearts of Jesus and Mary … Honor and Glory!

Bio –

Fr. Pat Crowley is a priest from the Congregation of the Sacred Hearts of Jesus and Mary in the West Coast region of the United States province and was provincial superior for six years. He has been actively involved in the healing ministry and Charismatic Renewal since 1972. For five years he was spiritual director of the Light of the Valley Prayer Community in San Dimas, California. Father holds a Master's Degree in Applied Spirituality from the University of San Francisco. Presently, he resides in Hemet, California.

Rev. Msgr. Stephen Doktorczyk, J.C.D.

A s I reflect on my vocation story, which I term "the joy of the priesthood," I note that, while the substance remains intact, my analysis has changed over time. Events once not considered significant or given much thought have now emerged as worthy of reflection and appreciation. I suppose that as one grows in wisdom and has various experiences—along with the benefit of hindsight—a different perspective results.

I grew up in San Pedro, California, a city that—at least for several decades—could rightly be identified as one with a Catholic culture. I attended a Catholic school beginning in the seventh grade and graduated from Mary Star of the Sea High School. The school was ethnically diverse with a mix of Italians, Croatians, Mexicans, and some Portuguese.

As the oldest of four boys, I attended Mass on Sundays (or the Saturday vigil) and—when time permitted—on some weekdays before school. The parish was blessed with a stream of newly ordained priests, who brought with them a zeal for the faith. At least five dedicated priests regularly visited the classrooms, participated in retreats, played basketball, attended sports events, and were often found around the school and church. Confessions were offered on a regular basis and at various times. While I cannot recall anyone specifically encouraging me to consider the priesthood, witnessing the joy of the priests was good publicity that I have not forgotten to this day.

At the age of sixteen, I began working as a bag boy at the local Vons supermarket. The job continued through high school, college, and until I entered the seminary years later. After graduating from California State University Long Beach with a degree in business administration, I began working full-time in lower-level management. I soon expressed interest in attending a one-year Food Industry Management program offered through the University of Southern California.

Though I was not accepted, higher management took note of my interest and began promoting me through the ranks. Minor promotions (which usually meant the same hourly wage) involved transferring me to other locations, often with less than a week's notice. These positions often included a range of hours and shifts, from swing to graveyard and anything in-between. I had to be flexible, work hard, and not shrink from making sacrifices, which included busy periods such as Easter, Thanksgiving, and Christmas.

During this time, I continued to practice my faith, attending Mass on Sunday or Saturday evening. I never considered *not* going to Mass, but I was not particularly inspired to seek a deeper knowledge of Sacred Scripture or the teachings of the Roman Catholic Church.

At several of the stores where I was transferred, I can recall lively conversations with various "born-again" Christians. They openly shared their concerns with the Catholic Church, concerns of which I was hitherto unaware. These concerns included: the necessity of confessing one's sins to a priest; the Real Presence of Jesus—Body, Blood, Soul, and Divinity—in the species of the Holy Eucharist; the concept of purgatory; that Sacred Scripture alone contained everything one needed to be saved; that the Magisterium was an invention; the Immaculate Conception of the Blessed Virgin Mary; the practice of praying to saints; and the practice of praying for the dead.

The general consensus was that I would probably end up in hell unless I left the Catholic Church and accepted Jesus Christ as my Lord and Savior.

What was I to do? I did not panic, but I did come to the conclusion that I owed these well-meaning folks an explanation. Additionally, important to me was the woman I was dating. She was a Protestant with similar concerns.

Having practiced my faith for my entire life, I was not going to simply accept what these people presented to me. Yet I needed to articulate clearly what I believed and why I believed it. Upon reflection, I found it difficult to believe that the Catholic faith, which had been passed down from the beginning for centuries and centuries, was somehow defective.

I decided it was necessary to undertake some serious research.

It turns out that I was not the first person to be approached by someone questioning the Catholic faith. A number of books recently published addressed this issue. This was in the early 1990s, and the Internet as we know it today did not exist. I ended up meeting with one of the priests at the local parish. He recommended helpful reading material from converts Scott and Kimberly Hahn, as well as books by Catholic Answers.

Much of my free time was spent researching and taking notes. I slowly arrived at the point of feeling comfortable and confident—that I could adequately present the Catholic position, as well as offer an explanation for the reason why. The result: lively conversations with various born-again employees at 2 a.m. while stocking frozen peas and popsicles. The young lady I was dating was not keen on shifting her position. We conversed much about our beliefs, but in the end we could not arrive at an agreement. She remained Protestant, and I stayed Catholic.

I don't know if the conversations brought the others any closer to the Catholic faith, but the value of these encounters for me was quite high. Frankly, I think my work colleagues were surprised that someone would take the time to research and get back to them. They were not accustomed to seriously dialoging with those identifying themselves as Catholic.

The priest also recommended that I consider volunteering to teach religious education (CCD). I objected initially, retorting that if I was unable to respond to questions posed by Protestants, how could I explain the Catholic faith to children? He promised that the Lord would provide and added that when one has to teach a subject, he needs to know it well.

The priest was right on both accounts. I ended up teaching religious education for eight years before entering the seminary. Teaching requires preparation, study, and a certain dedication.

Yet I did not pursue the seminary. I went back to school to pursue a Master's Degree in Business Administration. I took part-time courses in the evenings and completed the program in two years. Because of this advanced degree I felt confident enough to apply for an office position in the human resources department for Vons. I was selected. The job required car travel, but it also included weekends off.

I began to attend daily Mass. The masstimes.com website was helpful in this regard. I could check when Masses were offered in various areas during a given week. In addition to helping me beat the traffic, attending morning Mass provided a certain rhythm and rigor that ensured that I would get to sleep at a decent hour and get up early in the morning.

I attended scores of parishes during the two and a half years I served as a human resources representative. I also agreed to fulfill the role of sponsor for a man who was in the RCIA program at the local parish. I did the same thing a second year. Along with teaching CCD, which required me to be prepared, accepting the role of sponsor demanded the same. Some of the questions posed did not have easy responses. The Lord worked through these various situations.

Two of my brothers and I lived together for several years. When they both got married eleven months apart, I was the only one remaining in the house. Soon afterward, I made the radical decision to cancel cable television. This resulted in not being able to access any television shows. I now had more time to read, pray, and listen to the Lord.

I used this newly found time wisely. I spent my free evenings reading the Bible or a spiritual book. It soon became clear that there was too much outside noise in my life. It was impeding my ears and heart from hearing the voice of the Lord. When one is busy with many things and does not want (or perhaps finds it difficult) to quiet down, truly discerning the Lord's will for one's life becomes a difficult and even arduous task. How long had the Lord been knocking but I was not listening, ignoring, or simply did not want to hear from Him, at least regarding His perfect will for my life?

When I reflect on Jesus' call of the twelve apostles, I can connect the dots. Oral tradition was passed down from generation to generation in their families. It would have been almost impossible for the apostles not to be aware of the prophecies Isaiah made seven to eight centuries before their time. It is not a stretch to conclude that their hearts were already prepared in some way for the call of Jesus.

Peter and Andrew, James and John—the sons of Zebedee—were fishermen. They likely had a fair bit of time to reflect on those same prophecies. When Jesus invited them to come and follow Him, they immediately dropped their nets and accepted the invitation.

However, those of us who find ourselves "busy with many things" do not have the same disposition as did the twelve. With the state of the electronic age today, I am concerned that young people might find it difficult to know what Jesus is asking of them, given the many possibilities available to involve themselves with activities that do little to foster quiet time or interaction with others.

The decision for me to move forward toward the priesthood came in 1998 during a retreat where I assisted. I enjoyed my involvement in the confirmation retreat, which was held in Big Bear (in the mountains of San Bernardino, California). Near the end of the retreat, I asked one of the other helpers what he planned to do once he finished his advanced degree. He mentioned that first he would need to better consider "this priest thing."

I believed the words coming out of his mouth were intended for me. I was the one who needed to consider "this priest thing," and without further delay. I could not continue to run from the Lord and delay giving an answer. Enough was enough. I soon took the proper steps—finding a good spiritual director and making an appointment with the director of vocations—before submitting my application to the seminary.

I began studies and formation in August 2000.

From the time I received word that I had been accepted to the seminary in April 2000, to the date it was made public that my service to the company (Vons) would end, at least four people suggested that I might want to become a priest. These were folks I worked with: a coworker, two store managers, and another person whose identity I cannot remember. Until this time, I had never mentioned to anyone that I was discerning priesthood. These conversations solidified that I was making the right choice and responding authentically to the Lord's call to follow Him in this way.

Someone suggested that instead of quitting my position at Vons, I request a one-year leave of absence. This way, if the seminary did not work out, I could return to work right away and not worry about searching for another job. I never entertained this advice. I was sure the Lord's will for me was to start fresh in the seminary. I believed God would provide, and that He would honor my decision to totally free myself for this new endeavor. From a practical standpoint, I knew enough people in the grocery industry that if for some reason I were to discern out of the seminary, I did not foresee major difficulties in reentering the work force.

I was content at St. John's Seminary in Camarillo, California, where I pursued my pre-theology studies. The program was designed for those who entered seminary with another degree besides philosophy or theology. This was a time of preparation in the academic world. My philosophy studies were not easy. I studied much, both on my own and in small groups. The environment was one of collaboration rather than competition.

Ten of us entered the pre-theology program in the Jubilee Year 2000. I made many new friends and planned to spend the entire six-year preparation—which included a pastoral year—at St. John's. (During a "pastoral year," a seminarian is assigned to live in a parish for two academic semesters. It is generally designed as a time of discernment, for the seminarian to learn more about parish and rectory life. His performance is reviewed by the pastor and a number of parishioners and staff members.)

Up until the end of the academic year I had no reason to believe I would not stay for the full six years. The grounds were beautiful, and the seminary in general was conducive to study, exercise, and prayer.

It was in May 2001—the evening before our class graduated from the pre-theology program—that the possibility of continuing theological studies in Rome was approached. The diocesan bishop, the Most Reverend Tod D. Brown, an alumnus of the Pontifical North American College in Rome, shortly after Pope Saint John Paul II named him Bishop of Orange in California, decided to begin sending some seminarians to Rome for their studies and formation. He sent the first two seminarians in 1999 and later expressed to the director of vocations for the diocese that he was open to sending more.

There were only two possible candidates to begin theological studies in Rome in 2001, since only one other candidate and I had entered the previous year. The other seminarian said yes, and it was for me to decide whether I wanted to switch seminaries or not.

Accepting this opportunity was not an easy decision. There were many unknowns, at least in my mind. I had never been to Rome, let alone to the North American College there. I did not know what to expect other than it would be necessary to learn another language. Moreover, I did not have an abundance of time to ponder the decision. The seminary in Rome expected an answer sooner rather than later.

I spoke further with the director of vocations and told him I was interested in going to Rome. After he spoke to the bishop, the vocations director informed me that the bishop was in agreement. I should begin taking the necessary steps to make the transition from one seminary and country to another. This involved a fair amount of work, including enrolling in a local Italian language course and arranging to ship my necessities to the seminary. I also took two independent studies courses through St. John's seminary that summer and was awarded a bachelor's degree in philosophy.

My time in the Eternal City was amazing. While many seminaries are "stand alone," since all the structured formation occurs there, others are set up for the seminarians to live, eat, pray, and have pastoral, spiritual, and human formation on site while attending a pontifical university for academic courses. The Pontifical North American College follows this latter model. After three years of theological studies and upon successful completion of the coursework, a student earns a bachelor's degree in Sacred Theology, or "STB."

In Rome, seminarians walk or take the bus each day to the university. This routine is fun, so long as the weather is not inclement. A practice of many seminarians to this day is to pray the Rosary on the way to school. During my time there, we received encouragement from Pope John Paul II to continue this pious practice. The seminary rector once announced to us that he had received a phone call from the pope's secretary, who informed the rector that the pope was edified by the reports he received about seminarians praying the Rosary publicly. He asked the rector to thank the seminarians and ask them to continue praying in this way.

This positive gesture on the part of the Vicar of Christ motivated us to continue this pious practice! Later, during one private Mass I was privileged to attend with the now-canonized pope, it seemed to me (and to others) that he was in ecstasy communing with the Lord. He did not let his advanced age or bodily pains prevent him from going deep with the Lord.

I undertook my theological studies at the Pontifical University of Saint Thomas Aquinas, also known as the Angelicum. The university is staffed mainly by the Order of Preachers (Dominicans), whose priests hail from various countries. We took courses in Sacred Scripture, Moral Theology, Liturgy, Ecclesiology, Eschatology, Canon Law, Church History, Mariology, Christology, and others. It was not uncommon for seminarians to discuss what we learned in class on the walk home from the university to the seminary. It reinforced the course material and provided opportunities for deeper reflection and clarification.

I took it as a positive sign from God that in general I enjoyed these courses. I remain grateful to this day for the opportunity to study and pray in such an environment.

With the arrival of our first Lent in Rome, we were encouraged to consider participating in the Station Church Pilgrimage. Even today at 7:00 a.m. daily during Lent outside of Sundays, an English Mass is offered in churches long since designated as the *statio* of the day.

It is a good practice to rise early to arrive in time for the station Mass. Some churches are nearly an hour away by foot. Most of the churches, on their designated day, will be adorned with numerous reliquaries containing bones or other body parts of saints, some of whom were unfamiliar to me. Other churches allowed us to visit parts of the church not normally open to the public, such as the crypt or the original church built several centuries prior. In addition to visiting these station churches, we sometimes stopped inside various churches to briefly pray and to appreciate the beauty.

While in my third of three years of theological studies, the bishop and I discussed possibilities for my second-cycle studies. The Program for Priestly Formation calls for four years of theological studies, so completing three years is not enough. There are a couple of options. One is to take classes for an additional year, pursuing a one-year master's degree or completing a license in sacred theology, canon law, philosophy, Sacred Scripture, and other areas. Another option is to pursue a license, which takes between two and four years to complete. A license is offered at Pontifical Universities. In the American system, this would fall between a master's degree and a doctorate.

Bishop Brown and I had already agreed before I transferred seminaries that I would stay and complete a second-cycle program, to be determined. It was decided that I would complete studies in canon law at the Pontifical Gregorian University at the beginning of my fourth year of studies at the seminary. By that time, however, the length of the program had been extended. Two years were no longer sufficient to finish the program. Three were required. I began the program four days after ordination to the transitional diaconate.

I had many positive experiences in Rome, but one stands out as the most profound. A few days after our class's ordination to the diaconate at St. Peter's Basilica, each newly ordained deacon received an invitation to submit his name for consideration to serve as a deacon for the Mass that would inaugurate the Year of the Eucharist. I expressed my desire to serve the Mass and was selected. The Mass took place on October 17, 2004, ten days after I was ordained a deacon. Five and a half months later, Pope John Paul II would pass to his eternal reward.

On the day of the Mass, the pope was not doing well physically. Shortly beforehand, it was decided he could not celebrate the entire Mass on his own and provisions must be made. While he was the principal celebrant, when it came time for the Liturgy of the Eucharist, the Secretary of State, Angelo Cardinal Sodano, took over. The Holy Father remained in his chair.

As one of the deacons of the Eucharist, it was my job to bring the chalice to the pope so that he could consume the Sacred Species. When we were about to make our way from the high altar to where the pope was sitting, I saw His Holiness making insistent hand gestures. It turned out that his assistants were arranging to have the kneeler in front of him removed. John Paul II made it known that he would receive the Body and Blood of Christ while kneeling.

He indeed was kneeling by the time we arrived, and he took his time consuming first the Body and then the Blood of the Lord. Perhaps he was in ecstasy. His profound respect for Jesus present—body, blood, soul, and divinity in the Sacred Species—was evident. No matter how much pain he endured while in the kneeling position, it was important that he give the Lord the reverence due Him.

I will never forget this experience. I pray that I might have the determination that John Paul II had, should I find myself in a position where it would be painful to give proper reverence to Jesus.

Life in Rome involves much more than attending papal liturgies. On the education front, I found canon law interesting. Never before had I known its breadth or importance. While I might be taking liberties to conclude that ignorance of canon law is ignorance of Christ (borrowing from St. Jerome's saying that "ignorance of Scripture is ignorance of Christ"), or that the Code of Canon Law contains all the things Jesus would have said if He'd had more time, still it is useful, practical, and necessary for the good ordering of the Church.

I completed my final two years of the program as a priest. I lived at the Casa Santa Maria, a house in Rome for priests pursuing further studies. A good number of priests residing there were also studying canon law. This provided opportunities to discuss matters outside of class and with priests who had more experience than I, both in priestly service and in the field of canon law.

To complete the program, it was necessary to write a mini-thesis (*tessina*). My topic covered the theme of the promotion of vocations to the priesthood. I enjoyed the research. Even better, my *tessina* could be submitted in English, which made writing it less cumbersome.

With canon law studies completed at the end of June 2007, I returned to the Diocese of Orange and was assigned as a parochial vicar in a parish that had more Spanish-speaking parishioners than English. I worked one day a week in the diocesan tribunal. This increased to two days a week in 2008.

My time in both assignments was wonderful. The parish was busy, providing me with many opportunities to visit the sick, prepare couples for marriage, baptize babies, visit the parish school and religious education classes, and celebrate Holy Mass. I began meeting potential future seminarians with some frequency. The parish had a large number of altar servers, a pool from which seminarians (and eventually priests) traditionally had been drawn. I hoped to capitalize on the situation.

The entire parish experience was truly a time of great joy and hard work, but these are not mutually exclusive. Those in search of a soft life should not pursue the priesthood. There are many needs, and a dedicated priest can bring many souls (back) to Christ. He must desire to serve the Lord without counting the cost.

I recall the words of Pope Francis in 2013, when he met with the clergy of Rome. A native Roman pastor informed the pope of the many demands upon him, and that he was often tired at the end of the day. One reason for the demands is that although the parish did not lack a quantity of priests, only the pastor was Italian. As a result, he received the brunt of parishioner requests for counseling, marriage preparation, funerals, and the like. The others may have been fine priests, but they came from other countries—some of them students in residence at the parish—and were unfamiliar with the Italian culture.

The Bishop of Rome responded that the priest should continue to serve his people with zeal. When one serves tirelessly in this way, indeed he will be tired at the end of the day. But he will experience a "good" tired, which is opposed to another kind of tired that occurs when one does not spend his time particularly well.

I remember Wednesday, December 8, 2010, as if it were yesterday. As an adjutant judicial vicar, I had regular meetings with the bishop to discuss various matters that were pending. At what I thought was the end of our meeting, the bishop asked, "Is there anything else?" I responded with no, there were no further matters of business that needed to be discussed. He then told me that a few days earlier he had received a letter from the Prefect of the Congregation for the Doctrine of the Faith, William Joseph Cardinal Levada. His Eminence had asked the bishop to release me for service to the Congregation for a period of five years, beginning the following summer. The cardinal had suggested to the bishop that there should be no reason why I could not concurrently pursue a Doctoral Degree in Canon Law.

The bishop was willing to let me go if I agreed. He did not try to sway me one way or the other. He was certainly open to honoring the request of the prefect, but the decision was mine to make. I was permitted to speak only with the Lord, as the matter was to be kept quiet.

It happened that Cardinal Levada came back to California that Christmas, and we met for lunch on New Year's Day, 2011. He encouraged me to accept the invitation but was not pushy. He explained that he too had to make such a decision back in the mid-1970s, when he was asked to work as an official at the same Congregation.

The cardinal's advice to me was sage. If the Church asks a priest to accept such an assignment, his response should be one of openness. It should include the word "yes" unless there is a grave reason why one would need to say no, such as in the case of an only child who has elderly parents in need of his assistance.

After our lunch meeting, I decided in peace that I would accept the cardinal's invitation. I arrived in Rome during the summer of 2011.

I believe the Blessed Mother was there to guide and protect me all along. Nearly every date associated with a step along the way of eventually going back to Rome fell on a Marian feast day. Even the announcement of my reassignment to the diocesan presbyterate was made on one such date—March 25th, the Solemnity of the Annunciation.

My time in Rome opened a world different from that of a seminarian or student priest. In this new assignment, I worked in an office and researched in my free time. I came to realize that I needed to have a plan in place in order to successfully juggle work, study, and other obligations. My normal day included working in the office during the assigned hours and researching and writing on free afternoons.

I was fortunate to be surrounded by top-notch theologians and canon lawyers. I learned so much over the five and a half years. My routine was in place for a good three and a half years. This strategy worked while I slowly but surely plowed through material. I was able to defend my dissertation four years after beginning the doctoral program.

In addition, shortly into my first academic semester after returning to Rome, the rector of the Pontifical North American College invited me to serve as a part-time adjunct spiritual director. I did not live at the seminary, but an office was provided for me to meet with seminarians on a regular basis. I enjoyed this aspect of priestly ministry and remain grateful for the opportunity to serve in this capacity. I regularly pray for former directees who are now priests, as well as for those whom I was not able to see to priesthood ordination due to my return home.

While in Rome this last time, I did not find much time to travel. However, I was part of a small group that went to the Holy Land in February 2013 for a retreat. A booklet I brought along to read had been given to me just a week or two earlier by an official at the Congregation for the Clergy. It was entitled *Eucharistic Adoration for the Sanctification of Priests and Spiritual Maternity*. I was impressed with the encouraging stories and testimonies contained in the fifty-two-page booklet.

The Prefect of the Congregation encourages ordinaries to promote "true and proper cenacles in which clerics, religious, and lay people may devote themselves to prayer, in the form of continuous Eucharistic adoration in a spirit of genuine and authentic reparation and purification," and "All those devoted to the Eucharistic Heart of Jesus" are also called to foster Eucharistic adoration to pray for the sanctification of priests.

Realizing the importance of this initiative and that people of good will might be assisted in learning ways of praying during holy hours, and having received encouragement from Prefect Mauro Cardinal Piacenza, author Kathleen Beckman and I founded the Foundation of Prayer for Priests. The website www.foundationforpriests.org was created with the helpful assistance of a savvy seminarian. It boasts many visitors, and a number of them submit prayer requests for themselves or for priests they know. I am encouraged when I learn that new cenacles are regularly being started in various parts of the world.

After working for nearly five and a half years in Rome, the bishop recalled me to the diocese for service as judicial vicar at the beginning of 2017. This too is an office job. I reside in a nearby parish and assist with the celebration of Masses and by hearing confessions.

I often find myself correcting others (kindly and gently) who comment that a priest involved in anything besides parish work is not exercising sacred orders to the full, and that such work is anything but "pastoral." I must disagree. Seeing the duties a priest performs as part of the bigger picture— that almost everything in one way or another has an effect on the faithful— is important. An organized priest secretary can help the bishop effectively carry out his duties. A talented and zealous professor at a seminary can help his students acquire a burning love for the subject matter.

Imagine a priest who loves the Sacred Scriptures and can impart his knowledge and zeal to the seminarians taking his courses. This will have a positive effect on parishioners throughout the diocese and even further due to future priests who learned under a devoted man. Is this not "pastoral"?

I am reminded of the importance of obedience, firstly obedience to our Lord Jesus Christ. A priest must not be so concerned about controlling every aspect of his life that he misses out on the opportunities the Lord wants him to experience.

There are various ways to serve the Lord outside of a parish setting. Some priests (especially those who hail from dioceses not suffering from a lack of vocations) spend years in a high school classroom. Others are sent for further studies, with an eye toward eventual placement in the seminary.

We don't know what the Lord has in store for us when we are obedient to His will. For seminarians, priests, and deacons, the Lord works through competent superiors. One who holds on too tightly to his own will and plans may miss out on many surprises from God. He might also shortchange the people of God and the Church due to his stinginess.

Looking back, I owe a debt of gratitude to my Protestant friends for challenging me. I found the environment different in Italy. At the present time, over 90% of the people are baptized Catholics, even if the percentage of those actually practicing the faith is substantially lower. I was rarely questioned about a tenet of my faith. There was either no interest, or the teachings of the Church were so evident and familiar to Italians that there was no need to pose an objection or doubt. Whereas in the United States—with its diversity of religions—such dialogue was not uncommon.

With so much familiarity in Italy and most likely in other European countries as well, the chances of regular encounters to speak about the faith are slim. If we don't challenge and encourage each other, the result might be stagnation, which can lead to apathy.

I remember a testimony given at a Magnificat breakfast in February 2009 by the then-auxiliary Bishop of San Diego, the Most Reverend Salvatore J. Cordileone. One theme woven into his testimony was that of a "vocation within a vocation." He was called to be a priest and said yes to the Lord's summons. Yet the various assignments he was given could also be considered types of vocations.

I agree fully with the good archbishop, even though I've been a priest for a much shorter time. Each assignment has been a vocation in itself within the larger context of a vocation to the priesthood. In my case, it was a vocation to be a parochial vicar, adjutant judicial vicar, official at the Holy See, spiritual director, student, and now judicial vicar while assisting in a parish.

I never dreamed of such a path when I was discerning whether to enter the seminary. For His part, the Lord had other plans. I will be forever grateful to Him for His goodness to me.

Bio–

Msgr. Stephen Doktorczyk attended the seminary at the North American College from 2001–2005. After ordination to the priesthood for the Diocese of Orange in California, he continued canon law studies at the Pontifical Gregorian University while residing at the Casa Santa Maria, earning a licentiate in 2007. During the following four years, he was assigned as a parochial vicar at St. Joachim Parish in Costa Mesa while also serving as adjutant judicial vicar in the Diocesan Tribunal. Msgr. Doktorczyk returned to Rome in the summer of 2011, assuming the role of Official in the Discipline Section of the Congregation for the Doctrine of the Faith. He worked as an adjunct spiritual director at the North American College and earned his Doctorate in Canon Law at the Gregorian University. On October 7, 2015, he successfully defended his dissertation: "Persistent Disobedience to Church Authority: History, Analysis and Application of Canon 1371, 2°." This work was published in 2016. Msgr. Doktorczyk currently serves as judicial vicar and is in residence at St. Polycarp Catholic Church in Stanton, California.

Rev. Fr. John H. Hampsch, C.M.F.

A s I relate my life story, I may write of miracles and marvels. Please regard these in view of the norm first formulated by Jesus in Matthew 5:16: "Let your light shine before others, that they may see your good deeds and glorify your Father in heaven."

Paul rephrases that norm for the Corinthians quite succinctly: "The person who boasts must boast in the Lord" (1 Corinthians 1:31).

Mary, in her one-sentence life testimony couched in her Magnificat canticle, exemplifies that guideline with similar brevity: "He who is mighty has done great things for me, and holy is His name" (Luke 1:49).

As you marvel at the heaven-planned events in my testimony, be sure to direct all honor and glory to God alone. Keep in mind that He's the potter—I'm the clay.

A teacher once asked her pupil, "What does the word *biography* mean?"

The little kid answered, "A biography is a story about a person's life."

"So, then what does *auto*biography mean?" she asked.

The boy's reply was quick and confident: "An *auto*biography is a story about the life of a car."

A spiritual autobiography is also known as a testimony—a life story shared for the benefit of others. Jesus urged the exorcised demoniac to "Tell others what God has done for you" (Luke 8:39). It is looking back over one's past as if through a rear-view mirror. It's not an over-the-shoulder looking back like Lot's wife (Genesis 19) who, because she disobediently looked back at Sodom's destruction, turned into a pillar of salt. (One kindergartner countered this by declaring, "That's nothing. When my mother was driving, she looked back, and she turned into a telephone pole!")

As you look back with me, let me begin with a two-sentence geographical overview of my life. I was born in 1925 in Nashville, Tennessee, and spent my childhood and my youth in a Chicago suburb (Oak Park). Aside from global travel in fifty-eight countries and every state in the U.S., most of my priestly ministry was exercised in California, Texas, and Arizona.

Everyone's life story begins with one's mother. My mother was a remarkable person. Her formal schooling ceased at the fifth grade.

This freed her for child farm labor to help support the family, while she concurrently became self-educated. After learning to write shorthand, she snared a job as a lawyer's secretary.

My mother's real yearning was to become a newspaper reporter, a job she finally landed. She later came to be recognized as the first woman newspaper reporter in the United States. This was in 1915, when women in America were not allowed to vote or seek an electoral office. Any woman working in a typical "man's job" was often belittled by the narrow anti-feminism of that time.

Because of her deep Catholic piety, the Lord graced my mother with an extraordinary charism of evangelization—an uncanny ability to make converts to Catholicism. That charism of the Holy Spirit began to flourish when she converted her fiancé before she married him. He later became the devoted father of our family—my sister, my brother, and myself.

With no theological training except the Baltimore Catechism, my mother managed to make between thirty and forty converts (and occasionally "reverts") to Catholicism in a most unique way—by inviting her many non-Catholic women friends into a chatty type of sewing club that she founded. At the weekly gatherings, she often interjected into the midst of the gossipy chitchat a few enthusiastic remarks about her spiritual joy and fulfillment in the Catholic sacraments, devotions, and practices. Or she would share a clever quote gleaned from a recent Sunday's homily.

The chatty sewing club in which her charism thrived was called the Stitch-and-Snitch Club. (In view of her persuasive conversion charism, I accused her of religious piracy and facetiously referred to her group as the Snatch-and-Patch Club.)

Before marriage, her first assignment as a newspaper reporter was to interview the pastor of St. Boniface Church in Evansville, Indiana, who was celebrating his 50th anniversary as a priest. He was an old German priest, Fr. John Henry Hillebrand. His apparently gruff demeanor terrified my mother, who soon realized—as his deep spirituality began to show through—that he was crusty on the outside but tender and compassionate on the inside. Actually, he was a Spirit-filled Charismatic long before the word "Charismatic" came to flourish in common parlance.

Mother persuaded Fr. John to become her personal spiritual director. During one of their monthly counseling sessions, after deep prayer, he said, presumably with a charism of prophecy, "You are going to get married soon. You will have three children who will live, and two others who will die in childbirth. Your oldest boy will become a priest.

"I want to be the godfather of that future priest," he went on. "On this, my 50th anniversary, I received a beautiful chalice refurbished in Germany, with an artistically hand-engraved life of Christ around the base of the chalice. I want to give you that chalice to keep for your future son. When he becomes a priest, I want him to use this chalice."

Mother almost flipped out. She took the chalice home and put it in a safety deposit vault. Every year or so during my childhood, we took the chalice out, looked at it, and marveled at the engraved images of events in the life of Christ decorating the chalice base. I used this magnificent chalice for my first Mass in 1952 as a priest. I used it for my 25th anniversary, and again for my 50th and 60th anniversaries.

I marvel that Father Hillebrand correctly prophesied that I would become a priest. That chalice is now more than a century old. I am amazed that I became the owner of that chalice *ten years before I was born!*

Ours was a deeply Catholic family. We all attended Mass daily, with my younger brother and I usually acting as altar servers. Every Saturday our entire family lined up outside the confessional. My mother legislated that we must be "clean in your body and clean in your spirit." The result was that every Saturday we were cleansed by both a bath and confession. (I don't think showers had been invented at that time.)

Mamma was careful to keep an empty chair at the dinner table "for Jesus, our daily dinner Guest." Any time we kids were making a ruckus she would point to the chair and employ her usual threatening restraint: "Jesus is sitting here watching you kids argue. Be quiet."

The family Rosary, or at least a decade of it when we were very young, was part of our daily routine. As I review my childhood environment, I can see clearly how my vocation as a priest was formed. Our home atmosphere provided an ideal matrix from which my vocation sprang.

A missionary who conducted a parish mission visited our school to foster religious and priestly vocations. In his talk he asked, "How many boys want to become priests?" Half the boys raised their hands. The other half said they wanted to be firemen.

When we got home, my younger brother and I related this survey to our mother.

My mother asked me, "Did you raise your hand, John, when he asked if you wanted to be a priest?"

"Sure."

Mamma knew I had wanted to be a priest since I was six years old. I planned to paddle my canoe across the Atlantic and convert all the heathen in Africa.

She then questioned my brother. "How about you, George? Did you raise your hand?"

"Nah, I didn't raise my hand."

"Why not?"

"Well," he replied, "he didn't ask who wanted to be pope." He did take a step in that direction later by becoming a Trappist monk.

My sister chose the married life and raised eight kids—four boys and four girls. All four boys entered the same seminary I attended.

Shortly before I was ordained, my mother said, "I can hardly wait until I can call you 'Father John.' I want to be your first confessional penitent." And she was! She spent a full month on a private retreat to prepare for that "general" confession covering her entire life.

The Lord assigned for me an extraordinary guardian angel. I kept him busy, for I had many close brushes with death—sometimes by doing foolish things like playing "chicken" with my brother to see who could keep a foot on the track the longest while facing an oncoming train. I almost lost a foot that way. Only one foot—otherwise it would have been a "feat." (Sorry about the pun. I couldn't resist.)

One near-death episode occurred at the Chicago World's Fair in 1933. I was eight years old and wanted to take my first plane ride. My brother and sister also wanted to try. My father agreed, but he planned for us to fly later that day before leaving the fair.

The sightseeing plane was a seaplane with pontoons. It floated on the lake between each fifteen-minute sightseeing flight at a cost of a dollar per passenger. I could hardly wait for my first ride in a real "aeroplane," as it was called.

While perusing the fair's exhibits, just before returning to the plane's takeoff dock, my mother watched a demonstration of a new invention, a pressure cooker. She persuaded my dad to buy one for her.

When we arrived at the plane's takeoff dock, Dad realized that purchasing the pressure cooker had left him with not quite enough money to buy three one-dollar plane tickets. "Sorry, kids," he said. "No plane ride for now. But plan on it for next week, when we visit the fair again."

I cried my heart out in disappointment, yearning to be on that plane floating on its pontoons right in front of me. I tearfully watched it take off and soar skyward. Then the motor sputtered. The plane crashed into the lake right in front of our eyes, killing the pilot and every passenger on board.

That shocking event was a God-designed lesson in my life. It taught me something that even as a child I could grasp—that disappointments in life are often blessings in disguise when seen from the perspective of God's will implemented by His loving providence. Perhaps God preserved me to convey that truth to someone today, almost eighty years later.

Sometime ago I was flying over Chicago en route to Detroit, looking out of the plane's window. Since I was familiar with the topography of the navy pier areas at Lake Michigan, I could determine the exact spot where that seaplane had crashed. It occurred to me that I would be viewing the location of my childhood death if my mother hadn't bought that pressure cooker. Or if it hadn't yet been invented or demonstrated. Or if my father had another dollar in his wallet, etc. The loving providence of God is breathtakingly awesome!

I survived many harrowing experiences in my travels through fifty-eight countries, some with demonized Satanists. There are far too many episodes to relate in detail in this brief testimony, but a few include surviving typhoons, waking to find a snake in my shoe, as well as other unnerving episodes, of which quite a few were on air flights.

For instance, I have been in a plane with a cabin fire while airborne. I was in a plane that was almost hijacked. The culprit in the seat behind me was arrested just before takeoff.

One frightful airplane experience occurred while flying in a 747 over the Rocky Mountains during a terrifying thunderstorm. Lightening somehow got inside the plane—"ball lightening"—one of several rare types of lightening. It looked like a basketball of fire floating down the aisle. It burned a hole in the lavatory, crossed under the center seats to the other aisle next to my seat, and then dissolved, leaving a pungent, sulfurous odor.

I have been close to death many times and in so many ways. Each harrowing event has left me with a strong conviction that God wants to keep me around for a while longer in spite of my bumbling ways.

At a priests' retreat one time, I dashed into the dining area to get a quick cup of coffee before my next conference. I put some instant coffee in a Styrofoam cup, filled it up from an urn labeled "hot water," and quickly gulped down the mixture.

The urn did not contain hot water. It held hot acid being used to clean the inside of the urn.

I thought my throat was on fire. I staggered into the kitchen and asked the cook what was in the urn. She showed me a container labeled "Deadly poison. Fatal if swallowed."

She called the local poison control center and reported the chemical ingredients listed on the container. The doctors said the effect could be fatal, or at least leave permanent damage to the throat and vocal chords. A lengthy round trip for an ambulance would delay treatment, so it was suggested that I be driven directly from the retreat house to the hospital.

The medical team was waiting for me in the emergency room.

While waiting for the car, the Lord spoke to me interiorly. *My Word. Turn to My Word.*

I had never quoted Scripture under stress before, but in the face of possible death, my faith was more caffeinated than the poisoned coffee, so I croaked out the prayer, "I claim Your Word, Lord, Mark 16:18: 'Those who believe in me, even if they drink deadly poison, it will do them no harm.'"

Within a minute or so, I was completely pain-free and normal. I guess they're still waiting for me at the emergency room.

God has used each alarming, near-death event to remind me to be grateful for the gift of life and to renew my promise to make my life as faith-filled as possible. Instead of relating more near-death episodes, I will regale you with a few lessons I've learned the hard way—through several adversities I have survived by God's grace.

My call to the priesthood crystallized at the ripe old age of thirteen as I launched into the life of a seminarian. (In the 1930s, vocation recruiters were called "cradle snatchers.") Propelled by a five-year scholarship, I was accepted into the Chicago diocesan minor seminary. However, it was with obvious reluctance by the seminary's board of directors when they became aware of my severe speech defect of stuttering. This was a serious impairment with which I had been afflicted since early childhood.

I was expelled after two years, and the remainder of my scholarship was confiscated. They bluntly informed me that I should give up all hope of ever being a priest. Such a severe impediment would render preaching impossible.

In spite of this indictment, I applied to the Maryknoll Fathers. They soon expelled me with the same reprobation: "You cannot be a priest. You can't communicate." I then went to the Divine Word Fathers' seminary and had hardly applied when I was shown the door for the same reason. I tried the Salvadorian Fathers and was met with the same rejection. Finally, I went to the Claretian Missionaries. They were so hard up for vocations that they took me in … and now they're stuck with me.

After trying five seminaries and being rejected by four of them, I was finally professed as a Claretian Missionary in 1944, during the war. After my priestly ordination in 1952, I spent eighteen years teaching mostly philosophy in seminaries and several universities (campus chaplain and Scripture professor in one of them). I preached retreats on weekends—stuttering all the way. The patient congregations were too tense to sleep through my sermons, except for one walkout, whose wife claimed he was a sleepwalker.

I spent a full summer at a speech correction school in Indianapolis, with no improvement whatsoever. By reading countless books about speech defects, visiting many speech therapists, attending speech correction schools, psychiatrists, hypnotherapists, and even rendered unconscious over fifty times under carbon dioxide inhalation therapy, I became an expert in speech therapy.

I can now teach anyone how to stutter.

It was eighteen years after I was ordained that God heard my prayer and healed me overnight. That is a major part of my life story, which I will explain in the coming pages.

Before that miracle, my speech problem became worse. I did manage to accomplish some things in my widening ministry, however, including a three-year term as associate pastor in a parish in Texas. I became a professor of philosophy and psychology at several universities and seminaries. While doing post-graduate studies and teaching, I became the psychological consultant for NBC, a contributing editor of the country's largest Catholic magazine, and director of suicide prevention programs in two states.

But the stammering, stuttering, and cluttering continued. I dreaded answering the phone or meeting people. I occasionally put the last syllable first. Instead of saying "hello," I would say, "Oh, hell!"

The "academic bug" kept biting me. I dreamed of acquiring more degrees than a thermometer but finally settled for a brief teaching position in a fellowship arrangement at Notre Dame University. I gained much-needed pastoral experience when assigned as an associate pastor in Fort Worth, Texas, then as Cursillo director in Arizona. After that, I was assigned as rector of an adult vocation seminary in San Francisco. Then I took up itinerant preaching, traveling around the U.S. and later in many other countries, preaching wherever I obtained requests to preach, amazed at the tolerance of my audiences.

My speech impediment continued until eighteen years after I was ordained. It was only at that late date that I received the miraculous healing for which I yearned.

My desire was to preach the Word, and I did much of it as Cursillo director in Phoenix. There I learned about the Catholic Pentecostal movement, as it was called back then. (After four name changes, it is now simply called the Renewal, or the Catholic Charismatic Renewal.) That movement provided the matrix for God's healing power to finally reach me in my speech handicap.

I had witnessed miraculous events through the Cursillo movement, the Antioch movement, the *Encuentro* movement, and other such spiritual, group-centered movements. There were at that time forty or fifty different types of movements designed to change peoples' lives overnight.

Having worked in the Cursillo movement, I was familiar with God's power to change human lives in a weekend. It became a launching pad for me to engage in the newer Catholic Pentecostal movement, which I was eager to explore after reading about the amazing healing miracles and life transformations taking place.

I had witnessed prostitutes become daily communicants after our Cursillo weekends. One Cursillo attendee was a hit man for the Mafia. He had killed hundreds of people. I brought him in front of the Blessed Sacrament, had him put his hand on the tabernacle, and prayed with him.

Tears flowed down his face when he exclaimed, "Oh, Father, you have changed my life completely!" He pulled out a big wad of money. "I have to give you $25,000 for changing my life."

"You have to give that money back to the people you embezzled it from," I said.

His conscience, of course, had not yet matured, so he needed firm guidance. But it was amazing to see human lives transformed in a matter of hours on a weekend. Changes were often spiritually spectacular.

I learned that similar events were taking place in the Catholic Pentecostal movement. In my statewide travel eliciting Cursillo candidates, I searched for—but couldn't find—any Catholic Charismatic meetings in the whole state of Arizona in the early days of that movement.

Finally, I attended an interdenominational prayer meeting of several hundred people, held after business hours in a Roy Rogers restaurant. I wanted to see what a Pentecostal (Charismatic) prayer meeting was like. Before I went, I prayed, "Lord, let me see the gift of tongues used in a way that proves it to be truly authentic in our modern times and is right for me."

I knew the theology of tongues, and Paul's references to the four ways of using tongues: praying in tongues, singing in tongues, speaking in tongues (to be used with interpretation of tongues), and fourthly, tongues as a sign to the unsaved—as a tool to convert 3,000 in one day at the first Pentecost (Acts 2). In that form of the gift, persons are amazed to hear you speak their native language without having ever learned it.

Besides those scripturally cited forms, I had also studied the four modalities of that gift: paralinguistic (non-language utterance), linguistic, jubilant, and ecstatic utterance. I knew about saints having reached the heights of holiness through the more advanced modalities of this gift.

Now, in this restaurant prayer meeting, I was witnessing first-hand what I had learned academically. A lady next to me began praying in tongues. It sounded articulate, linguistic, inflectional, and emotionally modulated—all the characteristics of a language. But I didn't know what language she was speaking.

Another lady on the other side of me came around behind me. She went over to her and asked, "Do you know what you are saying?"

"No," she answered. "Paul says, 'If I pray in a foreign language, my spirit prays but my mind is not productive'" (1 Corinthians 14:14).

The inquiring lady remarked, "You don't know what you're saying? Well, I know what you are saying. You're speaking the Hopi Indian language. I was raised with Hopi Indians in northern Arizona, and I clearly understand your prayer of praise in my Hopi language."

It was just as the Pentecost witnesses in Acts 2 heard in their own languages the gift first used by the apostles and the 120 disciples. The first lady had the basic gift—speaking fluently without understanding—while the second lady experienced its fruition in affirming it by understanding.

In overhearing this remarkable conversation, I realized I was receiving an answer to my prayer for the authenticity of that gift of the Spirit. Since then I have witnessed hundreds of cases of miraculous events related to the use of this sublime gift. I wish I had space to share some of the things I have seen in San Francisco, Israel, and many other places, where truly remarkable events occurred related to the gift of tongues.

I learned why it is referred to as the "entry gift," since it opens the person to receive some of the other twenty-five Charismatic gifts mentioned in the New Testament—especially the nine "classical" Charismatic gifts mentioned in 1 Corinthians 12, and even some of the "sanctifying gifts of the Spirit" mentioned in Isaiah 11:2–3.

That restaurant event launched me into a search for more prayer groups, both Catholic and interdenominational. I found in each group a wondrous flourishing of love, joy, and peace that I had almost never witnessed in non-Charismatic, ritualistic forms of Catholic liturgies, in spite of the awesome—though seldom-appreciated—real Eucharistic presence of Jesus in the Mass and Communion.

I started celebrating Charismatic Masses without disrupting the liturgical structure of the Mass, but linked with prayer meetings and healing services. I was heartened to see love, joy, and peace begin to flourish in Catholic prayer groups. Some Catholic parishes—previously labeled as "God's frozen people"—began to melt into a comfortable conviviality and peaceful fervor.

It was when I was invited to preach on this matter in both Catholic and non-Catholic churches that I began to feel, with a sense of true ecumenism, like a pioneer of what the Spirit has now guided into fruition by Vatican II, and what has been applauded by the last several popes.

Some of the spontaneity and exuberance I witnessed in the Cursillo movement began to manifest itself in Charismatic Masses. For instance, people were "raising up holy hands in prayer," as Paul urged in 1 Timothy 2:8—the *orans* position of prayer used by all priests at Mass and by all early Christians as portrayed in ancient religious art. I realized then that we have not been conditioned to pray with true, Bible-based spontaneity in group prayer.

I also began to realize that I, myself, had not yet received much of what Jesus promised in his pre-Ascension farewell: Pentecostal power (Acts 1:8). I felt a burning desire to receive the Baptism in the Holy Spirit with its primary characteristic—power, in its many forms—"to be effective witnesses" as Jesus promised. I hadn't received that promised power in an appreciable degree.

While stationed in San Francisco as an adult vocation seminary rector, I attended a wide variety of prayer groups—even one on skid row. Disguised in my sporty, bright Hawaiian shirt, I ventured into a storefront church in the seedy Tenderloin district. It was furnished with folding chairs and a welcome sign that read: "First Church of Christ—Under New Management."

Leading a small congregation of perhaps fifty people was an obese, sweaty minister pacing back and forth while shouting, "Praise the Lord! Praise the Lord! Hal-le-lu-jah! Praise the Lord!" There was no teaching, no preaching—just stentorian shouts of "Praise the Lord."

I wondered if perhaps the Lord, in His condescending sense of humor, might want me to receive the Baptism in the Spirit here in this bizarre environment. I walked up to the minister and said, "I'm a Catholic priest, and I want to receive the Baptism in the Holy Spirit."

The congregants went crazy.

"Hey, we have a really big fish here," the minister shouted. "Come on! We gotta pray over him!"

I knelt as the group crowded around. They all reached to place their hands on my head, while singing and shouting hallelujahs and ferociously pressing down on my head until I thought my nose would unbuckle my belt. They kept shouting, "Speak in tongues, speak in tongues! Come on, speak in tongues!"

I tried, but no syllable passed my lips—just grunts as I writhed under relentless pressure.

"We don't have enough prayer power," screamed the minister. So, some men went out into the street and brought in a few smelly, drooling drunks to provide "sufficient prayer power."

I wish I had a picture of that first attempt to become baptized in the Holy Spirit.

After that raucous failure, I asked myself what I was doing wrong—or not doing right—to become a Charismatic. I kept seeking out various prayer meetings, begging to become "Charismaticized," but to no avail.

I think the Lord was preparing me for the future, so that I could empathize with persons similarly obtunded in their efforts to receive the initial gift of tongues—which is normally the sign of success in attaining the Baptism in the Spirit. Not everyone finds it as easy as did the twelve Ephesians mentioned in Acts 19. This gift normally (but not always) affirms not only the indwelling (*inhabitatio*)—state of grace Spirit-presence, but also the infilling (*infusio*)—Spirit-filled state of being baptized in the Spirit.

Jesus told His apostles in John 14:17 that they were not yet Charismatic, but in the pre-Charismatic state ("the Spirit *with* you now" before Pentecost). Later they would be in the Charismatic state ("the Spirit *within* you" post-Pentecost). The nine-day interval from Ascension Thursday to the Pentecost vigil was the first *novena*, and also the first "Life in the Spirit Seminar"—a preparation for the Pentecostal experience. "Stay here in the city until you have been clothed with power from on high" (Luke 24:49).

Like those apostles, I hadn't yet completed the individually designed preparation time for my baptism, with its promised sign of spiritual power. That awesome experience came a year later and was reaffirmed by my miraculous healing. It happened in Pecos, New Mexico.

It started while I was conducting a women's retreat. A lady approached me and said, "I want to commit suicide, but I decided to sign up for this retreat before I take my own life, to give God another chance to see whether He'll solve my many problems—if there *is* a God!"

This lady wouldn't come near the altar during Mass when I invited the retreatants to do so. I assumed that she stayed in the back pew to observe but not participate. Somehow, though, at the consecration moment during that Mass, the reality of the living presence of Christ in the Eucharist impacted her soul: "This is My Body, this is My Blood." She recognized that the Eucharist was real and not symbolic of His presence. The Holy Spirit almost explosively inspired her of this truth.

She came to the sacristy after Mass and said, "Father, I want to tell you something. First of all, I hate Catholics, and I especially hate Catholic priests."

I said, "Well, that's interesting."

She continued, "Now—and I don't know why I am saying this—I want to become a Catholic."

I thought of my mother and her charism of letting God work through her to convert many people. To see God work that miraculously by His awesome mercy was a staggering experience for me as a young priest. I had to do a lot of canonical research to arrange for this lady's marriage to be con-validated. That is a long story, especially after her husband returned to the Catholic Church.

At my suggestion, they both attended a Life in the Spirit Seminar, and together they received the Baptism in the Holy Spirit, even though I hadn't yet received it. At a healing service, she was miraculously cured of alcoholism, nicotine addiction, and advanced cancer.

She came back for another retreat where, in the middle of the night, she kept hearing a voice saying, *"Give this message to Fr. Hampsch, the retreat master."* She said, "God—if you are God speaking—I am just a new convert to Catholicism, and You're asking me to give a message to the priest?" The voice replied, *"Yes, give him this quotation from Scripture."*

She approached me the next morning and asked, "Is there a first book of Samuel?"

"Yes," I replied.

She then said, "I think God spoke to me last night with a scripture to give you from that book of the Bible, so I got out of bed and wrote it down. This is the third night He woke me up saying the same thing, but I questioned the validity of the first two times and didn't tell you it occurred. I wrote on this scrap of paper what the Lord told me."

We looked up the passage in 1 Samuel 10:6, which said, in essence: "You will see a group of seven prophets coming down a hill playing musical instruments, and at that time the Spirit will come upon you, and you will be changed in a mighty way."

I thought, *Wow, changed in a mighty way by the Spirit sounds like the Baptism in the Spirit that I've been seeking.*

Suddenly she said, "Father, the Lord is telling me that you should go to Pecos, New Mexico."

"Where in the Bible does it say that?"

"I just feel God wants you to do this," she said.

"I have no reason to go there."

"Well," she said. "I feel God wants you to go there."

When I got home from the retreat, I found a box full of mail that had accumulated in my absence. After trashing most of it, I glanced at the wastebasket and noticed a flyer that said, "Retreat House—Pecos, New Mexico—Charismatic Retreat for Priests and Deacons." It was to be held a week or two later.

I recalled what the converted lady had mentioned about Pecos, and I thought, *Maybe God does want me to go there.* I asked my superior to provide my airfare to New Mexico, which he gladly did. Miraculously, my preaching schedule had two cancellations during the period of my planned retreat, thus providentially freeing me to attend.

The monk who picked me up at the airport mentioned that the Community expected a visit from a group of seven young people—five boys and two girls—all of whom had been converted and miraculously healed of heroin addiction when they received the Baptism in the Spirit and with it the Charismatic gift of prophecy. They had gotten together and formed a music group called "The Trees" and traveled in a refurbished school bus with their sleeping bags around a built-in wood stove. Their income came from presenting a Life of Christ program in music, using a weird collection of old instruments.

During that retreat, while watching a snowfall and listening to talks about the Charismatic Renewal, I saw this rickety old school bus coming down the hill. Seven teenagers leaned out the windows, announcing their arrival by playing their weird collection of musical instruments.

Seven prophets coming down the hill playing musical instruments!

That was the very prophecy the lady from the previous week at the retreat house in California had given me. That biblical prophecy being fulfilled before my eyes gave me the chills.

The teens presented their two-hour program for us priest-retreatants. With all the available Bible translations, I found that the list of their instruments—including a lyre, a flute, and a harp—matched the list in the biblical prophecy from the first book of Samuel conveyed to me by the lady at the California retreat. With this prophecy unfolding before my eyes, I became excited. I expected the fulfillment of the rest of the prophecy about my becoming radically changed by the power of the Spirit.

There is a lot more to that story, but I will put that aside for now. But I must mention that when the retreat master prayed over me for the Baptism in the Spirit, my life-long speech impairment disappeared.

I praise God in recounting and reliving that moment now! I have never felt so free as at that memorable time when that bondage was lifted. That miracle occurred eighteen years after I was ordained. I couldn't help thinking of the crippled woman healed by Jesus, whom Satan had kept bound in her affliction, also for eighteen years (Luke 13:16).

That experience of the Baptism in the Holy Spirit changed my life completely. My prayer life changed radically overnight. My preaching changed overnight. Everything changed completely in my life, especially my fervent desire for a deeper spiritual life. As the charisms began to be manifested, my love and understanding of Scripture blossomed amazingly with the Holy Spirit's gift of understanding (Is. 11:2), like the "spiritual wisdom and understanding" that Paul prayed would grace the Colossians (1:9).

After my speech healing, Psalm 103 became profoundly meaningful: "Praise the Lord; he heals us of our ailments and crowns us with His loving compassion." I deeply experienced the loving compassion of God.

The Lord began to act in my ministry in surprising ways. I sometimes found myself reminding confessional penitents of sins they had deliberately concealed because of shame. This left them overwhelmed by their own hypocrisy and the evil of a sacrilegious confession. I pleaded with God to stop that charism. I didn't want to read souls or invade the privacy of anyone's conscience—unless, of course, it would help souls to be saved or sanctified. I asked the Lord to instead give such souls a self-correcting grace of humility.

Thankfully, the Lord heard my prayer and released me of that burden.

I was privileged to receive two invitations from the Vatican's dicastery of the Pontifical Council of the Laity to participate in a colloquium of shared experiences and theological insights, since recent popes have urged a deeper theological exploring of the Charismatic Renewal.

Early on, when I started retreat preaching, I had a new opportunity to lay hands on people for healing and developed a healing program, the Healing of Memories. Since that time, I have written six different healing books and programs: *Healing through Scripture, Healing through the Power of the Eucharist, Healing of Memories, Healing through Compassion,* and the most popular one, *Healing of the Family Tree* (on CD).

In its published form, *Healing of the Family Tree* is a 300-page question-and-answer book on the family tree healing program. It came to be regarded as a pioneer study in that particular area of healing. Since then I have authored twenty other books, over 100 booklets, and an extensive repertoire of CDs and DVDs for TV and the Internet. The income from these is used to help the poor of our Claretian missions.

The first $50,000 that I made selling my materials through the Claretian Teaching Ministry that I founded was used to construct a seminary in Nigeria to replace the primitive one that had no floors—only open dirt floors—and only a few shared text books in the entire seminary.

Can you imagine training future priests with almost no books? That rebuilt seminary is now flourishing. Its first graduates were forty newly ordained priests now working in the missions of Nigeria and in many other countries.

As I continued to practice my ministry, spiritual gifts began to operate in my life. I feel I have only two fairly pronounced charisms out of the many charisms mentioned in Scripture: teaching, and to some extent, healing. Some physical healings occur occasionally when I pray over persons, but most have been psychological healings or deliverance healings from pervasive forces of evil, often when praying with a prayer team, especially in deliverance prayer (sometimes called "minor exorcism" prayer).

I have had the privilege of seeing thirteen people cured of blindness. Some of them took several hours. Others took several weeks, but six of the blindness cures were instantaneous. It is a dramatic thing to see a person cured of blindness.

I have witnessed several people cured of terminal cancer and several married couples on the verge of divorce, whose marriages turned into a second honeymoon overnight. I would often say to myself, "God, You are alive. You really are! You're working miracles today as you did twenty centuries ago in the dusty streets of Galilee. You are not 'hiding in Argentina.' You're alive and truly present to us—and showing Your incredible love for each of us."

When you see miracles happening, your faith is stimulated. You may believe because of the miracle. However, it is one thing to believe *because* of the miracle, and it is quite another thing to believe with a faith that *causes* the miracle ("prior faith" and "posterior faith"). My faith began to grow prior to and after each miracle I witnessed in my own life and in the lives of others.

Most of my life I'd lived my faith on the lower level of posterior faith—faith aroused *after* (posterior to) witnessing the miraculous. Then God turned up the flow of grace and began to activate within me a prior faith—a faith that produced miracles—a faith that is operative *before* (prior to) the miracle, which causes it to happen by eliciting divine power. This is especially amazing in healings of body, mind, or spirit, or healings of interpersonal relationships like healing of marriages.

When I found people being healed as I prayed over them, it was a little easier to accept the words of Jesus in John 14:12: "The person who trusts me will not only do what I'm doing, but even greater things, because I, on my way to the Father, am giving you the same work to do that I've been doing."

Those last words really hit me between the eyes. I came to realize that I was being called to the preaching-teaching-healing ministry, especially after I received some Charismatic gifts when I was baptized in the Spirit and became Charismatic. From that period of my life, much of my ministry has become focused on the Charismatic dimension of Christian spirituality.

I started a writing ministry. Formerly I'd thought, *How can a priest, especially an itinerant retreat preacher, find time to write books?* But somehow, especially after the invention of computers, I started to write. God also provided time for me to produce CDs and videos and to conduct my own TV program, all while preaching and traveling globally.

I put my ministry into a more structured form by founding an enterprise called the Claretian Tape Ministry through which I've sold my writings and recordings to help the poor of our Claretian missions overseas. This outreach developed to a point that at one time I needed to hire eight office workers.

Some of my writings have been translated into thirteen languages. I do a lot of international counseling by email, especially with seminarians in Africa and other places. By today's modern technology, God has provided an amazing array of outlets for talents and charisms. I try to use such modern tools as much as my limited knowledge allows.

I don't know how much longer God is going to keep me around, but I am eager to get to heaven. Death is the most perfect healing there is. I can't see why people are afraid of death. I have to say, like St. Paul, "I desire to be dissolved and to be with Christ" (Philippians 1:23). But until the Lord brings me into the next life, I'll do my best to fulfill His will for me. Please pray that I fulfill that goal with persevering faith and love.

Through a widespread ministry, I learned how marvelously the Lord uses hopelessly weak instruments. Why would He pick me, a stutterer, to be an itinerant preacher and to eventually have my own television program? Why does He "use the weak things of the world to confound the strong?" (1 Corinthians 1:27).

God likes to work with poor instruments—even sinful ones—like the first pope who denied Christ three times, but who ended up working many miracles and even writing two epistles as inspired biblical masterpieces. Often God chooses a sin-blackened soul in preference to a snow-white soul to display His mercy, just as a diamond displayed on black velvet has more appeal than one displayed on a sheet of white paper.

Here is an overview of what the Lord has done in my life. He took a speech defect with emotional impairment, a psychological disorder that led me into the study of psychology, which in turn led me to the psychology of tongues. The psychology of tongues led me to the study of the Baptism in the Holy Spirit. The Baptism in the Spirit led me to the Spirit's gifts, including the gift of healing.

The gift of healing led me into the program of the Healing of Memories and its recording and selling, which led to the founding of a tape ministry, which provided an outlet for my writings that hopefully enrich the lives of many people but also supports our Claretian missions.

With the first $50,000 from sales of my books, tapes, preaching honoraria, etc. we built a seminary in Nigeria to train hundreds of priests now serving the Church worldwide, while the follow-up income feeds thousands of physically and spiritually hungry souls served by those same priests.

That chain of connected events all started with my speech defect. It ended up blessing souls globally through hundreds of priests trained in that seminary, some of whom we subsidized in their training because they could not afford their seminary tuition. Isn't God marvelous in His loving providence?

That concatenated series of events is only *my* life journey. Each person reading this has his or her own series of events in their divinely customized life journey. From heaven's viewpoint, each person's life journey, whether broadcast or hidden, is a magnificent marvel. For that reason, it should culminate ultimately in glorifying the Lord only and not oneself.

Please pray for me that I might become holy someday. God bless you always and in all ways!

Bio –

The Rev. John H. Hampsch, C.M.F., ordained as a Catholic priest in 1952, is a member of the Claretian Missionaries. He has served as parish priest, seminary professor and rector, college professor, lecturer, magazine and newspaper columnist, editor, retreat master, director of suicide prevention programs, and Cursillo. He has also served as a hospital, prison, and campus chaplain. He earned degrees in philosophy, and in ascetical and mystical theology. Widely traveled, Father calls himself an "itinerant preacher-teacher" with special emphasis on teaching and healing services.

Fr. Hampsch has experienced and witnessed countless miracles. His primary interest is in bringing Jesus to the hearts of people through the mass media with his two TV series, *Send Forth Your Spirit* and *Glad You Asked*. As director of the Claretian Teaching Ministry, his audio and video recordings constitute one of today's largest Catholic communications ministries. He has authored twenty books and 100 booklets, which are often used as discussion material for study and small faith-sharing groups. He has been active in the Charismatic Renewal for over forty-two years and has been a speaker at the Southern California Renewal Conference since its inception. Father is now semi-retired while recovering from a stroke at the age of ninety. He is actively writing books, articles, and video scripts for his Internet ministry.

Bishop Emeritus Sam Jacobs

I grew up in a Catholic family that rooted me in my faith. It was in this context that I discerned God's calling to be a priest. During my seminary formation, I sought to grow in holiness and understanding. I was ordained a priest for the Diocese of Lafayette, Louisiana, on June 6, 1964, and was appointed a parochial vicar in St. Joseph Parish, Rayne, Louisiana.

It was during the fifth year of this assignment that I became aware that something was missing at the core of my heart. I was popular and effective as a priest. I was a good preacher. However, I realized that if I did not discover what was missing, I could become an angry, critical, negative, unhappy priest, which I did not want.

In my desperation, I cried to the Lord to reveal to me what was missing. In His mercy, He answered me in time—not directly, but through the experience of a friend, a religious sister. She was enrolled in summer courses at Boston College. While there, she attended a Catholic Charismatic prayer meeting and experienced a new spiritual awakening in her life. She wrote me about her experience and said she had more to share when she returned at the end of the summer.

True to her word, she returned to her job at the parish school. Although busy, she shared briefly not only about her experiences but also about her invitation to a priest on his way to his monastery in New Mexico. She asked me for permission to gather a small group of about fifteen people to meet with the priest when he came. I agreed.

When the priest arrived a few weeks later, we all went to a camp to listen, and he spoke to us for about two hours. What he said touched that hole in my heart. I knew he was speaking directly to me. The two things that resonated was the need for Jesus to be the Lord of one's life and the need to follow the leading of the Holy Spirit in all we do. These were the very two things that were missing in my personal life and in my priestly ministry.

That night I made the decision to totally surrender to the Lordship of Jesus, to give Him everything and to hold nothing back. At the same time, I invited the Holy Spirit to come into my life in a fresh, new way and to stir up the gifts He had given me in the sacraments of Baptism, Confirmation, and Ordination.

There were no bells and whistles as a result, but a conviction that my life would be different from that moment. It was, and it has been. I began to pray to the Holy Spirit before each homily for His anointing, and I often experienced the anointing of the Holy Spirit in my preaching.

It was not a feeling but a conviction that God was working through me. Often this would be confirmed by people after Mass who said, "Father, thank you for saying such-and-such in your homily. I needed to hear that." I chuckled inside because I knew I had not said that in my homily, but God took my words and spoke His message into the person's heart.

The gift of counseling became more evident in my ministry. As the person spoke, I would hear the beginning of what the Lord wanted me to say in response. Many times it was right on the mark, exactly what the person needed to hear.

I became freer to pray with people for their physical and spiritual healing. God, in His mercy, occasionally allowed me to witness the healing. I knew the Lord was healing whether I personally witnessed the results or not.

After the initial evening with Fr. David, Sister and I decided to begin weekly meetings with those of the group who wanted to continue praying together. We were neophytes in the Spirit. Our gatherings were spent in praise and worship, in song, in sharing Scripture readings and praying with one another. We were open to the gifts of the Spirit and tried to freely move in them.

A few months after that evening with Fr. David, I had the opportunity to go to New Orleans with a few of the men, part of that same gathering. We learned of a monthly prayer gathering held at Loyola University and were interested in participating. After the afternoon and evening sessions, someone said that anyone desiring individual prayer should come to the prayer room.

Each of us went separately. Fr. Harold Cohen prayed over me, and I felt a fresh outpouring of the Holy Spirit that brought me a deeper inner peace and joy.

Providentially, I had no idea about the future and the journey God would place before me because of His anointing love. A few months later, the bishop called to reassign me as the pastor and campus minister for McNeese State University in Lake Charles. At the time, I didn't understand God's plan. Being a university parish pastor was not something I wanted to do, nor did I believe I was qualified for the position with only six years under my belt.

It soon became clear that one of the things God wanted me to do was start a Charismatic prayer group meeting in Lake Charles—first in a private home and then at the campus ministry center. Our numbers grew quickly.

God wanted more than a prayer meeting. He wanted a spiritual renewal retreat that would open those attending to a personal encounter with Him, openness to the Person of the Holy Spirit and the fuller release of the Spirit's power. Thus, the Awakening Retreat developed. It has transformed the lives of thousands of young adults at universities around the country. During this time, I saw many signs and wonders brought about by the Lordship of Jesus and the working of the Holy Spirit.

Two specific healings come to mind.

My dentist was diagnosed with a grapefruit-sized tumor on his brain. The prognosis was dim. Depending on the extent of the spread of the cancer in his brain, he would either not survive the operation or he would end up in a vegetative state. The family called for the Anointing of the Sick, and I prayed with him in the hospital the night before his surgery. I asked a few people to join me to pray. I anointed him. We prayed over him with faith expectancy and laid hands on his head. We stayed in the room no more than ten minutes.

Returning to the rectory, I went into the chapel to continue to pray and intercede. The next morning when the doctors operated, they found a pea-sized tumor that had not even penetrated his brain. They removed it, and my dentist has full use of all his faculties to this day. The doctors had looked at the x-ray and seen a massive tumor, but what they found during the actual operation baffled them. God revealed His glory!

Another miracle involved a little girl who suffered from a rare eye disease. Whenever she went out into the sunlight, she experienced severe pain in her eyes. The doctors were not aware of any cure. They recommended she wear sunglasses outside to lessen the pain. The mother asked me to pray over her little girl after Mass one Sunday. Together with the mother, I laid hands over the child's eyes and prayed that God in His mercy would heal this girl from the disease.

I lost contact with the mother for several years. When I saw her again, I asked about her daughter. She said that shortly after we prayed, she took her daughter to the doctor for another examination. The doctor was amazed! He found no trace of the disease in the girl's eyes. She could be in the sunlight without any pain. Praise God!

My involvement in the Charismatic Renewal expanded after a few years. I went from being part of the leadership group for our local prayer community to a diocesan role after the diocesan director for the Charismatic

Renewal for the Diocese of Lafayette decided to resign. The priests involved in this renewal were called together to pray for the priest who should take his place. I went to the meeting, but I did not expect that I would be asked to step into those shoes.

My first task came in June—to prepare for the annual diocesan Charismatic Conference in November. To date, no preparations had taken place, no site chosen, no committed speakers. I pulled together a small committee from past committee members, and together we tackled the task. Getting speakers did not prove to be an enormous task, but finding the site was difficult. None of the previous venues were available.

The only site we could find was the local horse-racing track in Lafayette. At first I rejected this possibility on the grounds of appearances— "Welcome to the Charismatic Conference at a race track"—but it became our only option.

Once the decision was made to select this place, spiritual warfare began in earnest. It came about in surprising ways, even during the conference itself. We had to build a covered stage away from the site then haul and install it the morning of the conference. It rained, so we had to wait for the state police to authorize transportation on the highway to the site. I don't know how many people interceded, but we received the permit at noon. The conference started at six p.m..

We held the event outdoors on the track because the clubhouse was too small. On Saturday afternoon, a cold front came through with torrential rain, yet there was great joy and celebration. The attendees danced and sang in the rain. That night the temperature dropped to the low thirties, making it unbearable to continue outside the next day—Sunday. We moved 2,000 chairs indoors for the morning session and Mass. We were wall-to-wall and shoulder-to-shoulder, with very little breathing space.

Yet in spite of all the evil one's darts, the Lord's power and glory prevailed. What a memorable weekend!

As the diocesan director for the Charismatic Renewal, the Charismatic Conference in New Orleans asked me to become a member of their conference-steering committee. Another expansion of my tent pegs by God! This position lasted for several years.

Then I was invited to become a member of the advisory committee for the National Service Committee of the Charismatic Renewal for the United States. I felt honored but felt like the proverbial fish out of water. I attended the annual meetings for two years but said very little. A close religious sister friend who also was on the committee said, "I doubt if you said more than ten words during the entire time."

The stretching of my tent pegs was not nearly over. God had more. I was asked to serve as a member of the National Service Committee itself. Once again, I felt out of my league. Here were the leaders, some of whom were there at the beginning of the Charismatic Renewal. These were the people I had admired from afar.

My first experience was challenging. I felt like I was in the early Christian community of Corinth. There were different visions being shared which made it difficult to move forward as one group. Eventually it was suggested to divide the various assets between the two major groups that had evolved within the community.

Three of us were not connected with either group and could not go along with the decision to split up the assets. However, God, in His mercy, intervened and showed us a way out of what seemed impossible. The *impossible* was resolved when one group left to pursue other endeavors while the remaining community chose to stay with the three of us and continue the work of the National Service Committee. Out of what could have been a shambles came new life.

God opened doors for me during this time to begin speaking at various Charismatic conferences around the country and eventually around the world. This gave me a broader view of the Church, and in particular the Charismatic Renewal movement worldwide. From a tiny mustard seed that was planted and gave birth at The Ark and The Dove Retreat Center outside of Pittsburg, where a handful of students experienced a New Pentecost, a large tree has blossomed with many branches, in many languages, and with more fruit than I could imagine.

All the praise and glory goes to God!

Bio −

Born in Greenwood, Mississippi, on March 4, 1938, Bishop Sam G. Jacobs was reared in Lake Charles, Louisiana. He studied at Immaculata Seminary in Lafayette from 1951−57 and Catholic University of America in Washington, D.C., from 1957−64. He was ordained to the priesthood for the Diocese of Lafayette in 1964. Bishop Jacobs served as pastor, chaplain, and associate pastor of several parishes in the Diocese of Lafayette and the Diocese of Lake Charles. He served as the chairman of the National Service Committee for the Charismatic Renewal and diocesan director of Vocations and Seminarians for the Diocese of Lake Charles. He formerly served as a board member for Cross Catholic Outreach and is now an advisor. Notably, Bishop Jacobs was appointed the tenth Bishop of Alexandria in 1989 and was installed as the third Bishop of Houma-Thibodaux in 2003. He served as the Spiritual Advisor for two Magnificat chapters: Thibodaux and Alexandria, Louisiana, in 2013. Bishop Jacobs formally retired and is now Bishop Emeritus of Houma-Thibodaux. In 2014, Bishop Jacobs celebrated two significant anniversaries: fifty years of priesthood on June 6, and twenty-five years of Episcopacy (Bishop) on August 24.

Deacon Alex Jones

M y journey into the Catholic Church is a story I will attempt to unfold. Before I do, I want to point out that the real heroes in this journey are the people who came alongside me. I clearly saw what God wanted me to see. Others didn't see it as clearly, yet they believed. They believed what I taught them and endured the ridicule and all of the problems that are inherent in changing faiths. They endured because they believed that what I said and taught was truth. They believed in me and what the Lord was doing in our collective lives.

They are the heroes of my story. This is *our* story.

The question people most frequently ask is "why." Why did I endure the hardships to become Catholic? Why did I leave a strong, vibrant faith that birthed me into the kingdom of God? Why did I change to a faith I knew nothing about, one that neither my father nor my ancestors were familiar with or understood?

As far as I know, I am the first in my family and extended family to become Catholic. Why did I take this course of action? For all practical purposes it destroyed the church I pastored and caused it to cease to exist. Why did I make a decision that would alienate my friends, members of my family, and those I loved? *Why?*

My answer? I had no choice. How could I tell God no? How could I look into the face of truth and say, "That's nice, but it will cause me problems"? How could I look into the face of a loving Savior—who loved me so much that He died so that I might be with Him—and say no?

Instead, I said yes. That "yes" cost me dearly, but I feel something like the Apostle Paul. I have suffered loss, but not of everything. I still have a lovely wife, and we went through this journey together.

To understand the why, return with me to 1958. I was in an inner-city church in Detroit. It was 10:30 on a hot summer's night when I came face to face with our Lord. It was a profound experience that has shaped my life ever since.

I am not perfect. I have failed many times and have the witnesses to bear proof. But never in my life since that night have I considered turning away from my Lord. In an instant I knew that God existed. I can't explain how I knew—I sensed His presence in a way that no words can describe.

He filled my soul with joy, peace, and love. In an instant my whole life changed by the presence of the resurrected Lord. Ever since then I experienced a hunger to know Him more. I wanted to know Him like St. Paul knew Him. I wanted to know the Lord that forgave me. I wanted to know the God who set me free. He set me free from hatred, anger, and fear. He gave me a destiny.

I began to seek after God with all my heart. There was a hunger in me to know *truth*. I wanted to know truth, not something that would make me feel good, but real truth. I don't mean to imply that the previous years were wasted years, or that it was a time of drought or a time of emptiness.

During those forty years of seeking to know God better, I learned how to pray. I learned how to believe God. I didn't have the sacraments. I had no knowledge of the Blessed Mother or other things Catholic. But I incorporated what I did have into my life.

I learned to walk by faith. I learned how to lean on the Lord in tough times. I learned the Bible. I read it and reread it until it became a part of me. So much so that, like the prophet Jeremiah, "Thy words were found and I did eat of them, and thy words were the rejoicing of my heart" (Jer. 15:16).

Oh, how I ate the Word! I ate it until it was like a fire shut up in my bones. Every time I speak of God, I am on fire. During those years, I learned to walk with the Lord.

However, in 1998 the ultimate stretch and test of my faith began. To understand how much of a stretch, one must appreciate a Pentecostal, Charismatic, Evangelical's view of the Catholic Church. I wasn't anti-Catholic at the time, just indifferent. There are people who say they love God and do what others may consider weird things, such as talking about signs or healing. However, in 1998 the Lord began what I term the process of deformation.

It began when I asked my congregation an unconventional question one Wednesday night while studying Paul's first letter to Timothy. In the second chapter he talks about worship. I felt it was time to be innovative and creative, so I asked my congregation, "Would you like a New Testament worship service?" They answered, "Yes."

"Give me thirty days," I told them. "We will set a date and have a New Testament worship service. We will do it the way the early Christians did." I was prepared to recreate as much as possible the same experience of the early Christian worship.

During those thirty days of reading and searching, my whole life was transformed. It was not that I was unhappy with our current worship services. I was very happy, but I became aware of how much we were missing. There was so much more.

As I began to read the church fathers—St. Ignatius of Antioch, Justin Martyr, Clement of Rome, and Bishop Polycarp—I saw a different Christianity. It was not the way I worshiped on Sunday with my congregation. The early church was very different.

First of all, the early church was liturgical. In other words, they had a system—a way of worship—that was prescribed and followed by all. It was uniform and universal. They had prayers. Pentecostals don't say prayers. They *pray*. Sometimes it is difficult to say prayers because we are calling on the Lord with our hearts, and have done so for many years.

But the early church was liturgical. Great preaching was not at the center of the service. The moving of the Holy Spirit wasn't the center. The center of their worship service was the Eucharist, the blessed Eucharist.

How strange it is for pastors like me—who are enamored with the importance of great preaching—to learn that preaching was not the center of worship during the time of the early church fathers. It was the blessed Eucharist. They spoke of it as being His body and His blood.

I had always thought that the belief of transubstantiation came into being during the Middle Ages. The early fathers did not call it transubstantiation as it is called today, but Ignatius said of the heretics, "They do not partake of the Eucharist because they do not believe it is the body and blood of our Lord."

That stood out as very interesting to me. It was not a memorial. It was a sacrifice. I thought, *Oh! The door is opening now. It is opening wider. Eucharist centered. Eucharist, a sacrifice.* The Scriptures began to fall into place. God began to reform what I had previously known—in an imperfect way—and put it all together again.

I began to see that if I was going to have a New Testament worship service, I was headed for trouble. The early church was not only liturgical, but it was also hierarchical. Ignatius of Antioch said, "Take care to do all things in harmony with God; with the bishop presiding in the place of God, and with the presbyters in the place of the counsel of the apostles, and with the deacons who are most dear to me."

These three offices—bishop, presbyters, and deacons—were in place around the turn of the first century. I couldn't believe it! What a shock! Being a non-denominational pastor, I didn't have a bishop.

Ignatius goes on to say, "Where the bishop is there is the Catholic Church."

We have a problem here, I thought. *I have a church, but I don't have a bishop.*

What I found the most telling aspect in the reading of the church fathers was that the spirit of the apostolic and post-apostolic church was totally different from the Christianity I saw around me.

Everyone wants to be blessed. Everyone wants to receive. Everyone wants God to do something for them. Bless me, Lord. Shine on me, Lord. Rain on me, Lord. Give me, Lord. Give me the house on the hill. Give me a car. Give me a good job. Give me, give me, give me, give me.

I didn't see that kind of thing going on in the early apostolic church. Instead, I saw a desire to serve Christ to the point of giving up one's life. I saw a call to holiness. I saw a dedication to holiness and holy living. When St. Ignatius wrote to the Roman Church he said, "Don't do me any favors by trying to save me from the lion's teeth. But I am the wheat of God. Let me be ground in the teeth of the lions as an offering to my God."

This is so different from what we hear today. Christianity then was a taste of something vibrant and alive.

I discovered that many things I had previously believed were not true. First of all, there is no such thing as *sola Scriptura,* the belief of "Scripture alone." This widely held Protestant belief is not found in Scripture. It is not true or from God. There are scriptures about reading the precious Word of God, the living Word of God, but nowhere did I read that the Scriptures were the sole authority.

Instead, teaching about apostolic tradition kept coming up. I had always been taught that tradition was written, not spoken. After all, didn't Jesus condemn tradition? Paul, however, tells the Thessalonians to be careful to "follow the traditions you have received from us whether oral or written" (2 Thessalonians 2:15).

Very interesting!

In the third chapter, Paul warns the church to "avoid those people who do not follow the traditions you have received from us" (2 Thess. 3:6).

What is this apostolic tradition? I had never heard of it. But as I read and researched I began to see the meaning, and it made sense. The Bible wasn't the only authority of the "pillar in the ground of the truth" (1 Timothy 3:15). Paul tells Timothy that the Church is "the pillar in the ground of the truth." It was becoming clear to me that the authority of the Church could not be found in Scripture alone. The authority of the Church is Scripture *and* tradition—together.

I also discovered that men are not born again by simply professing faith in Christ. They must be born of water. As an Evangelical, Charismatic, and Pentecostal all rolled into one, to be "born of the water" meant to be "born of the Word." This was a convenient interpretation of the Word for many pastors, but there was one problem. None of the church fathers said "the Word." They said "water."

I also found 1 Peter 3:18 troublesome. Baptism in water *does* save us. That was a difficult scripture to interpret, but if you put it alongside what the fathers taught the early church, then this made perfect sense. Jesus said "water." What did He mean? He meant *water*. That was a new revelation for me.

At this point I realized I had a decision to make. I was learning these wonderful things, and I was excited—so excited! I was learning so much. Everything was falling into place. After all my searching and struggling, God was putting me back together again.

Everything was clear to me. It looked wonderful, except for one problem. I was a pastor, and I had a church. If it was only me, I could easily go to the nearest Catholic Church and join the class to become Catholic— the RCIA (Rite of Christian Initiation of Adults). However, this was not an option for me. I had a congregation of about 200 people. What a dilemma! What should I do?

One scenario looked like this: I could walk into my church and say, "You know, I have found the most wonderful truth—the greatest revelation of my life. I know you will not accept it, so here is my resignation. Make do the best you can. I am out of here."

But how could I in good conscience say that to people I loved? How could I leave them shepherd-less just because I believed I had found a greater truth? How could I not share that truth?

I decided I would take the chance of rejection. I realized my teachings would be rejected by many, if not by all. If they asked me to leave, I would go. However, I had to give my flock the opportunity to hear what I had learned. I loved them and wanted to lead them into the truth. I could not let them stay where they were without ever learning about this great revelation.

Since I could not in good conscience up and leave my flock, I decided to turn my church into one that worshiped like the early Christians.

So I began to teach. The first thing I did was incorporate a communion service into every Sunday. This did not go unnoticed. "When you were a Pentecostal, you had communion twice a year," someone said. "When you started this church, you changed it to every month. Now you are doing this every Sunday?"

It hurt me deeply when the communion service began and people stood up and walked out. They did not understand.

The second change involved dividing the service into the Liturgy of the Word and the Liturgy of the Eucharist. More people left. I began to preach that we are saved through baptism. It is as simple as water. God uses water. I wanted to say, "Hey, wake up! Don't you remember Naaman the leper?" (2 Kings 5)

One of the greatest arguments occurred right after a sermon I preached one Sunday. Two of my elders confronted me in my office. "Do you mean we are saved by being baptized in water?"

"Yes," I replied.

"Do you believe we are saved by faith alone?" one elder asked.

"No, sir," I told him. "The Bible says to 'work out your salvation with fear and trembling' (Phil. 2:12). It also says we must all stand before God and give an account. The only place in the Bible where it mentions faith alone is together with faith and works, which is found in the letter of James."

Can a man be saved by faith alone? I believed the answer was no. More people left.

One by one they all walked away. I was accused of becoming Catholic. I was asked, "Are you headed to the Catholic Church?" Not necessarily. It was my attempt to resurrect the Christianity I saw lived and taught by the early church fathers. I wanted to shout, "This is it! This is the faith of the apostles!"

What finally convinced me to join the Catholic Church? During the course of my studies and readings, I learned two irrefutable truths. First, "Thou art Peter and upon this rock I will build my church, and the gates of Hades will not overthrow it" (Matthew 16:18). Hades will not destroy it or corrupt it because it is His church. Christ is giving the Church perpetuity. In other words, there will never be a time when the Church is not.

So I began to look for this Church.

I could date the beginning of the Protestant churches after the 16th century. Where were they before that? Our Lord was saying that the Church He began in the upper room and breathed on, and said, "Receive ye the Holy Spirit," is the Church. If you can trace that Church from the upper room to present day, it seemed to me that one should give this Church serious consideration and thought.

The second truth was the promise of Jesus. He was going away, but He said "I will not leave you orphans" (John 14:18). "And I will ask the Father, and he will give you another Advocate to be with you always" (John 14:16). This Advocate would lead and guide them into *some* truth? No! *All* truth (John 16:13).

When the Lord opened my eyes to the truth that "the Holy Spirit will lead and guide you into all truth," I realized what this meant. The Church our Lord initiated in the upper room will never become corrupted. I had been taught that the Catholic Church was good for a couple hundred years, but then they fell off the edge of the earth.

That is not what our Lord said. He said, "The Holy Spirit will be with you forever." Not just until the apostles died, but forever. God is in the Church—guiding it, teaching it, and unfolding the mysteries of truth. God is taking the things I have said to you, opening you up to understand, and showing you the real truth. If the Church has perpetuity and the Church has incorruptibility, that means there must be a clear line from the upper room until now.

I mentioned earlier an experience that transformed my life. I felt there was no price too high to pay for the truth, even if it cost me my life. I can hear these words in my heart and mind to this day: "The Catholic Church is *the* Church." It seems as if the Holy Spirit branded that in my mind and heart.

If you believe in the devil, perhaps you no longer believe in spiritual warfare and think it is a myth. I wrestled with evil early in the morning. The devil would wake me up and say, *I want to talk to you.* I would wake up as fresh as if it was afternoon instead of two-thirty in the morning. He would start asking questions. *Are you crazy? Have you lost your mind? You are destroying your church. You are wishy-washy. You are going into error.*

In my experience when Satan begins to talk, he also brings along his environment—depression. At two or three in the morning I went from my living room back to my bed fighting spiritually. I'd hear, *You know you have really lost it this time. You are out of the box.*

After I wrestled for a long time, I would recall the words of Ignatius, "Where the bishop is, there is the Catholic Church." The Catholic Church is *the* Church. Then I'd believe it—it is the Church! I would suddenly feel the negative environment lift, and I was able to go back to sleep resting in this truth. I found His Church.

I found His Church!

It may not seem significant to you, but it is to someone who had been searching for a long time. I have found His Church!

It cost me my friends. It cost me brothers I had walked with for forty years and whom I love dearly to this day, brothers with whom I would lay out and pray. When I say "lay out and pray," I mean prostrate on our faces before God, and we often fasted and prayed.

However, this teaching I had found was too much of a stretch for them to believe. "Pastor, we love you," they said. "But we can't walk with you."

That was the most painful event in this journey, to watch good people walk away. I'm not talking about heathens and demons. I am talking about good, praying people. One by one they began to walk away.

That was the price I paid. Only three Christian pastors stayed, and they are still my friends to this day. These three pastors talked about me as their little "Catholic brother" and allowed me to eat lunch with them every Monday.

How would I live? I had been in public education for twenty-eight years before pastoring my church, but I could not return to the classroom at this late date. I fell on my knees. "Lord, please! How will we eat?"

My wife was worried too. "What will you do for a living?"

"I don't know," I answered. "I really don't know."

How was I going to pay the bills? That was a genuine concern.

I did not know what I was going to do when I arrived in the Catholic Church, but I did know Who sent me. He has proved Himself more than faithful. In the end He not only came through, but He also blessed me so I could pay off my bills—every last one of them. He provided an income for three to four years so I could go to school full time.

I did not come to the Church empty-handed. However, I came humbly. The Lord gave me the ministry I had as a Pentecostal pastor and blessed me. Then He asked for it back.

I eventually became a permanent deacon in the Archdiocese of Detroit. In addition, fourteen members of my family and fifty-four members of my previous congregation joined me in the Catholic Church. Deep down in my heart I have a passion for our Lord. Deep in my soul I have a love for His Church.

I love the Church—that sweet, holy, sanctified Bride of Christ. I love everything about it. I love the priests. I love the nuns. I love the smell and the bells. I love it all because I have discovered it.

It has cost me much, but thank God, I am home at last.

Bio–

Deacon Alex Jones was an on-fire Pentecostal pastor in Detroit. He spent the better part of twenty-five years as a preacher and pastor of two prominent Detroit churches, Zion Church of Christ Congregational Church (1975–82) and Maranatha Christian Church (1982–2000), before discovering a calling to the Catholic Church. In light of that discovery, he, his wife, Donna, and their family began an incredible journey that culminated with entering the Catholic Church on April 1, 2001. He was ordained a permanent deacon in the Archdiocese of Detroit in 2005, where he also worked as the evangelization coordinator until he retired in 2007. Deacon Alex Jones, described by some as a "giant in evangelization," died on January 14, 2017, at the age of seventy-five.

Rev. Fr. George T. Montague, S.M., S.Th.D.

―――――∘∞∘◇∘∞∘―――――

Father Montague's Note: What follows is from the first chapter of my book *Riding the Wind*, published in 1974 and reprinted for a new generation twenty years later as *Still Riding the Wind*. Though the forty-three years since writing it have enriched and matured me in many ways, the grace of those first hours still empowers my life. It is my joy to share it with you, with only minor retouches for clarity or emphasis and an update note at the end.

I was born on a Texas ranch in the summer of 1929. The stock market crashed shortly thereafter. This sequence of events has always amused me, and I later reminded my mother that my birth was so important that after it the whole country went into a postnatal depression.

That Texas ranch would shape my roots. I learned to love the moist mornings and the smell of the fields at harvest time. On summer days when I was not rounding up livestock or squirrel-hunting with my dog in the river bottom, I found nothing more fascinating than lying in the shade of an oak tree and letting myself be mesmerized by the endless armada of cumulus clouds that floated through the skies. Sometimes I would be distracted by swirling specks I knew to be a flock of buzzards riding tireless circles on the high winds.

Coming home with my father at the end of the day, I learned to pause before a symphony of color as the sun set ablaze the western sky before dipping out of sight behind the distant hills. At night I never tired of drinking in the sky full of brilliant stars. I never bothered to learn their names. I just let them create in me a sense of wonder and awe.

But often my contact with nature produced not exhilaration but a mysterious melancholy and nostalgia. This feeling puzzled me then, as it does even now. Perhaps it was the "otherness" of the universe I felt, an otherness that I could never fathom nor possess. The stars and the clouds had been there for millions of years before me, and they would continue their timeless journeying when I was no longer there. They did not appear to notice me when I came to admire them, nor did they say good-bye when I had to leave. They seemed to be pursuing some elusive goal with relentless and undivided attention, like the shoemaker I once stopped to watch through a window. He took no notice of my presence, nor did he seem diminished by my absence when I left. So perhaps the greatest lesson I learned from nature was that my heart was made for something more.

My life story has been the search for that something more. Part of that more was my family. My father was a man full of life in every ounce of his six-foot, two-hundred-and-eighty pound frame. He filled any room he entered. When he stood on Main Street in front of the O.S.T. Café, as he often did, he was the biggest man in town. Part of my periodic growth-measuring was to see how much closer I could come to getting my arms around his fifty-five-inch waist. I don't remember if I ever made it. Little wonder that in later years his grandchildren would call him Big Daddy. We called him Papa.

"Papa" meant working with the cattle or a drive to town sitting on his lap and pretending to help him drive the car. Papa meant meeting and entertaining new people every day, for he reveled in hospitality. Papa meant an hour or two of yarns and jokes to extend the Thanksgiving or Christmas Day meal until he would join us in yawning at his own stories. Above all, Papa meant the thrill of hunting deer and wild turkey in the late fall.

But Papa also meant business. More than once I learned that the fifty-five-inch belt had another function than simply holding up Papa's pants. Strangely, as I grew into my teens, I began to develop a fear of him, a fear that made it impossible for me to talk to him about the deeper things on my mind and heart. He was a very emotive man and tremendously tender at heart, but sometimes it seemed he felt the only outlet worthy of himself was his volcanic temper. I feared to cross him. If our opinions differed, I did not talk about them.

It was not for Papa's lack of goodness. On one occasion, as we were preparing to sit down to dinner, I feigned the courtesy of pulling out the chair for Aunt Margaret. I did not push it back under her, letting her almost hit the floor before I caught her. Papa's anger blazed. His right hand slapped my left cheek like the flash of a striking rattler.

I was dazed and ashamed of myself. As I toyed with my food I became more ashamed because Aunt Margaret, who couldn't believe I would do something like that, came to my defense and said, "He was only trying to help me."

Papa grunted unintelligibly, and the meal went on in unbearable silence until I could escape to my bedroom upstairs. The weight of the whole event smothered me. Then I heard Papa's heavy footsteps on the stairs. One of the wooden steps always creaked, and under Papa's boot it groaned louder than usual, speaking the panic I had in my heart. I froze as his mighty frame blocked the faint light of the doorway.

He came over to me and knelt down at my bed. "I'm sorry, George, that I slapped you," he said. "Will you forgive me?"

If I could have sunk through the earth to China, I would have, so stunned was I at this big man shrinking to a kneeling penitent and asking forgiveness for what he had come to believe was his misinterpretation of what I had done.

My father was indeed a *big* man. What was I to say? "That's all right," was all I could offer. He kissed me on the forehead and said good-night. Lingering fear in me blocked what should have been a mutual confession.

I was born with a foot that turned in, and even after much therapy I walked pigeon-toed. This seemed to irritate Papa. He used every occasion to tell me to walk straight, even when strangers were around.

When we worked cattle in the pens on a cold winter morning, he would not allow me to put my hands in my pockets. They should be kept free, he said, in case a steer charged and I needed to reach for the fence. I couldn't see what difference the breadth of cloth made in speed, especially since it would keep my hands warm, limber, and agile. His judgment, I felt, was simple tyranny. But I didn't dare say so.

The fact is—I see it now—my father idolized me. He wanted me to become everything he was—powerful, self-disciplined, manly—and everything he wasn't. Sometimes, especially as he saw me growing away from him, he wanted it too much.

Much of my later life was shaped by my image of my father, even my idea of God. Like my father, He was the Mighty One to please, the One not to cross. He was not the One in whose presence I could relax and pour out my soul. Much in my memory of my father would need healing. The medicine would be a mixture of the memory of my father's goodness, the discovery in myself of all the things I hated in him, and the Lord's grace.

With my mother, on the other hand, I could share my greatest excitements. She was strict. I think I got more spankings from her than from Papa. But something about her made me want to share everything that excited me. I began to write at an early age. At the age of eleven I was printing a monthly tabloid that eventually numbered some six hundred subscribers. Mama was the one with whom I could hardly wait to share everything I wrote. It was probably because she saw not its imperfections but its promise.

My three brothers were five to eight years older than I. They were close enough in age with one another to do things together: riding, working, rodeos, and hunting trips. They formed a musical trio of violin, guitar, and mandolin. I was too far behind in age to keep up with them, so I had to learn how to survive on my own. Writing and publishing and the kinds of things I could do by myself were the primary outlets. I developed a great sense of independence even from my peers at school.

Those years were not without religious experience. Papa was a strict Catholic of Irish descent, and Mama was a convert. Sunday morning was always a routine of rounding up the family and driving the five miles to St. Stanislaus Church in Bandera. Though the population of the town was less than a thousand—and the Catholic population was a minority of that— there was a Catholic grade school attached to the church and staffed by the Sisters of Charity of the Incarnate Word.

It was here I began school at the age of six. I remember very little about that first year, but one scene made a deep impression on me. Standing before the class with a crucifix in her hand, Sister described the sufferings of Jesus in the Passion and spoke of His great love. I was moved to the point of numbness.

Papa was so committed to giving us a religious education that the next year when my older brothers were of high-school age, he moved the whole family to San Antonio, where we could be placed in Catholic schools. Adapting to city life, even for only five days a week, had its hilarious moments. It meant that my education from then on would be a unique combination of country life, city life, and religious influence.

On New Year's Eve during my sophomore year, word came that my brother Charlie had been killed in the battle of Tarawa in the South Sea Islands. I was too young to understand fully what this loss meant, but I could see the effect it had on the rest of the family. The cultural Catholicism that had been our heritage was inadequate to cope with this experience, which shattered the very heart of our family.

What we needed was naked faith, and Charlie's death showed how little of that we had. Papa lost one of the sons he idolized, and he seemed to withdraw like Job to the dung heap to scrape his wound in bitter silence. It was as if he could not forgive the Lord for this, "If it is not he, who then is it?" (Job 9:24). The rest of us tried the alternative of forgetting. We applied a local anesthetic to a portion of our memory so that we could go on living. But the wound we had suffered was not healed.

The Lord began a healing, but it was in taking another son of the family away—me. During a retreat at school I experienced a sudden crystallization of awareness that I could call conversion. There was a good deal of fear and negative father-image about the way I received the Lord into my life at that time. However, as a result of the experience, I began to attend Mass daily, sometimes making the effort to get up at five-thirty in the morning.

One day, after receiving the sacrament of Penance, I was kneeling in prayer and staring at the tabernacle. I suddenly felt a kind of tug inside me that almost took my breath away. It was a mixture of fear and delight, like the times my older brother had picked up my little frame and tossed me into the air and caught me in his arms. I can say no more except that I knew the experience was from the Lord. I hardly dared to think that it might mean He was calling me to cast all else aside and follow Him, but as the days passed, that is what it came to mean. In the spring I announced my intention to enter the Society of Mary.

All Mama said was, "If that is what you want," though it was with tears. Papa wanted me to wait another year, but he said he wouldn't refuse to let me go sooner. The day I was to leave on the train for St. Louis, he made up an "important business" excuse that required his saying good-bye at the ranch. I walked with him to the green Chevrolet pickup. He said a few words then shook my hand and jumped into the pick-up and gunned it in an attempt to get out of my sight before I could see him bawling like a baby.

Fifteen years later, when I gave him my first priestly blessing, I saw how he had been healed even of the loss of Charlie. Somehow, in the whirlwind of his Jobian faith, he had come to see that letting go to the Lord was not to lose but to get back a hundredfold. When I anointed him on his deathbed three years later, he took my hand and moved it gently back and forth in the best embrace he could manage.

Maryhurst in Missouri was quite different from the ranch in Texas— colder weather, taller trees, soccer instead of horses, and the dark, endless tunnels they call hallways in the motherhouse. It was one of the happiest years of my life. I rejoiced in newfound friends—though I still knew how to keep a bit aloof—and the lives of the saints became a passion with me. Of the many I read, the life of Teresa of Avila made the deepest impression. I was excited by these heroes and I wanted to be like them … right then and there.

The next year of novitiate began a curious development in my life. I was taught that the conquest of sanctity is a science and an art, extremely intricate and organized. I'm sure I derived benefit from this organized approach, but it put me on the road of seeking perfection more as a work than as an opening to grace. It reinforced my tendency toward isolation and independence. Close friendships are dangerous things, I was told. So I began to view the friendships that I had enjoyed so much the year before as potentially harmful and learned to keep a cool and distrustful distance. It was more important to excel than to enjoy putting the other first.

From then on, through the years of college formation, the experience of Paul was mine. "I advanced beyond many of my own age, so extremely zealous was I for the traditions of my fathers" (Galatians 1:14). How well the Lord was preparing me, even in my experience of those years, for understanding the Paul I would one day write about in books!

I was a self-made Pharisee, logging my achievements but really a slave. My *experience* of the Lord still lacked the freedom of sonship. I was out to prove to myself to others, and to God, that I was perfect. If I had to admit I wasn't there yet, it should at least have been obvious that I was perfectly programmed. Sanctity was a race, and passing up others was so much assurance I would be first to the goal.

Little wonder that I had trouble truly receiving others' love. They wanted to love me as I was, defects and all, but I would have none of that. I wanted to be perfect so that others would have to love me. They would have no choice!

As I recall the days of the seminary in Fribourg, Switzerland, where I was ordained and where I did my doctoral studies, I remember vividly a bike hike I took through the mountains with four or five of my peers. I distinctly remember the passion I felt to lead the pack, even though one of my brothers was having trouble with his bicycle. I let someone else worry with him. To be first to the foot of the mountain and first on top—that's all that interested me.

This scene is symbolic of where I was spiritually, of how important it had become for me to excel rather than to put others first. It was more important to get to the mountain first than it was to share the ride with my brothers.

It was not until a year after my ordination to the priesthood when the Lord hit me between the eyes with the inadequacy of this approach. I was making a Better World retreat in Segovia, Spain. Sitting under a big tree in the open air, surrounded by retreatants, I heard the retreat master speak of those who pursue even charity as their charity and delight in taking daily thermometer readings on the intensity of *their charity.*

I felt as if I had been hit by a two-by-four. Yes, *my* charity! What a contradiction in terms when put that way! For if there is any passion, human or divine that does not seek its own, it is love (1 Corinthians 12:5). But what a perfect picture of the contradiction I was trying to live, even under the guise of Christian holiness.

I returned to Fribourg to finish my doctorate in Saint Paul. Even as I pursued my research, I was exploring the implications of my new discovery about love. After six years abroad, I returned to the States. My first assignment involved teaching at my old alma mater, Central Catholic High School, in San Antonio. I was in the theological clouds, and I still wonder how those teenagers managed to put up with this Doctor of Theology who was so impressed with the salvific power of his theological distinctions.

At the end of the next year I made a Cursillo. Sitting in the sweltering June heat, I listened to blue-collar workers from Kelly Field, some of whom had hardly finished grade school, talk about Jesus as a personal experience in their lives, what a difference Jesus made to them, and how their lives had never since been the same. Then and there I saw that the good news is fundamentally a personal experience of Jesus so powerful that one is excited about it to the point of non-containment.

These men had the kind of personal Christ-wisdom I had studied about in Paul without deeply experiencing. I began to see holiness in others. I felt a compelling desire to have that kind of faith, so inadequately developed in my theological head-trip of the previous years.

And yet, in the Lord's plan my theological preparation had destined me to teach theology. I was appointed not only to teach at St. Mary's University in San Antonio but also to head up the graduate program in theology. I was a success on both the undergraduate and the graduate levels. But I still had much to learn about the ways of the Lord, and He arranged events in my life to bring about a new growth.

During the Christmas holidays of 1966–67, I managed to drive a thorn into my knee while mountain climbing. Resisting detection by x-ray, it stayed lodged there for over a year, disabling me from any serious participation in physical recreation. To amuse myself I took up the guitar.

The next summer I began to make up guitar ballads on the prophets I was teaching. The songs had a country twang, which did nothing to conceal my Texas roots. I never intended them for anything more than recreation. The guitar seemed a bit incompatible with a professor's image. But there's nothing wrong with singing in your study, is there?

It did not occur to me that singing the message was really much closer to the prophetic experience than talking about the prophets academically. It meant a greater commitment of my whole person to the message the Lord obviously meant to go beyond a professor's lectern. It had been that way for the prophets themselves. There is evidence that Ezekiel was a balladeer (Ezekiel 33:32).

The time would soon come when the desire to sing would fade. "By the streams of Babylon we sat and wept … On the willows there we hung up our harps … How can we sing a song of the Lord in a foreign land?" (Ps. 137:1–4).

Not long after the singing success I entered a spiritual and emotional exile, where the guitar gathered dust and my tongue stuck to the roof of my mouth. The securities that had supported me to this point in my life began to erode. For one thing, the stable church I had known began to fall apart. When Pope John XXIII and Vatican II relaxed the tight controls, the repressed adolescence of thousands created household chaos.

But more than that, in my personal life I began to feel the horrible limitations of my own strengths. My aloofness, independence, and self-sufficiency had not brought me oneness with others, and I began to painfully feel my alienation. I noticed how preoccupied I was with my self-image and reputation, how many tasks I had taken on precisely to prove (to myself primarily) how good I was—and therefore how worthy of being loved! In the words of an advertisement I saw recently, I was feeling "the awesome responsibility of being the very best."

And it was killing me.

Not realizing the root of my trouble at first, I tried to react in the only way I knew how—to seize even greater control. I was approaching the age of forty. Perhaps I was feeling the kind of middle-age depression my cousin doctor tells me is quite common—realizing that one's life is about to crest with most of one's life dreams unrealized.

In the summer of 1968, still impressed with my ability to do everything, I took on the preaching of six week-long retreats, besides the regular summer session at the university. In the middle of July, after a succession of sleepless nights, I went to my doctor.

"Drop everything at once," he told me. "Go to the ranch and take a six-week rest." The diagnosis: emotional exhaustion.

It was true. Interiorly I was wound up tighter than a tourniquet. I dreaded facing people. The rest and the great outdoors of my boyhood brought physical strength, but I knew the deeper root of my problem was unhealed. I felt like a spectator at the dance of life—not like one so involved in the dancing as to forget myself. I wasn't even sure life was a dance. The dancers, I suspected, were the phonies. But I wasn't eager to affirm that my spectator position was real, either.

About this time, a few people began to gather weekly at our scholasticate residence on St. Mary's campus to pray. I did not attend, but I heard a lot of talk about the Holy Spirit, about tongues and prophecy and such things that made me suspicious about the mental balance of some of the people who attended.

Some of the members of my Community went to the meetings, however, and I became impressed with the change I saw come over them. I saw greater love, joy, peace, and patience in them, and these I could identify as Paul's fruits of the spirit (Galatians 5:22). I was particularly impressed with the spontaneity and enthusiasm with which they were willing to take up the dull and monotonous chores in the Community—doing the dishes, cleaning the house, serving at table—*putting others first!* I sometimes did those chores when I felt they were expected of me, but I certainly didn't enjoy them very much.

I began to see they had something I lacked, something I needed, something I wanted. I decided to go and find out what turned them on so much. I went to a prayer meeting. By now the prayer group had grown to a regular attendance of fifty to sixty persons.

My first feeling was great discomfort. There was an exuberance and a freedom of outward expression that was alien to my way of praying. There seemed to be a hypnotic preoccupation with praise of the Lord. This bothered me, for I did not feel there was that much in my life to be praising the Lord for. Job's laments seemed to fit my experience better. And yet, precisely at this time, I had been writing a commentary on some of the Old Testament prayers and psalms in which I underscored precisely the absorption in praise, a repetitive praising of the Lord that defied rational analysis and could only be explained by the exaltation of a spirit chanting almost ecstatically.

My prayer until then had begun with bringing all of my problems to the Lord, complaining about them, then rising enough to ask Him to do something about them "if you can" (Mark 9:22), but then concluding with the burden of the anxieties slumping back upon me again. This is what I now call "lower-parabola" prayer.

The prayer I was finding so strange was just the opposite in its movement. These people began with praise. It was as if the praises sent up were seeding the clouds. Then came a flood of wonders with more praises resulting. It certainly was different. It's what I call "upper-parabola" prayer. My lower-parabola trajectory of prayer (beginning and ending with woe) had collided with their upper-parabola (beginning and ending with praise), and it was unsettling.

I secretly wanted what I saw, but I was scared to death at the price that might be asked. Here I sat in intellectual control (or so I viewed myself) of all my experience, even of my experience of the Lord. I must check out at the gate of rationality whatever I experience. That, after all, is what a theologian, a professor, a wise and respected scholar is supposed to do. The only problem that I hated like hell to admit was that I was having less and less life-giving experience to check out! I began to perceive that the chief experience I was really having was precisely the increasingly frustrating passion to "check out" everything and everyone, yes, I must admit it now, even the Lord.

Some power was moving the prayer meeting, and it was converting people, changing them. Some spoke of conversion from lives of great sin like alcoholism, sex, and drugs. My ministerial eagerness first responded, "This Charismatic stuff looks like the best missionary technique I've seen yet."

Then I began in some way to feel the Lord look at me—spectator, bystander, judge. Here Jesus was banqueting with Levi and Zacchaeus and Magdalene and asking me where I stood. I could not help but feel myself among the Pharisees standing outside the door and trying to check all of this out through my academic categories. I then realized it was not sinners with whom Jesus failed. It was the "good" people, whose "goodness" was so sufficient they could not hear the good news of the better life to which Jesus called them.

So it had become with me. My Christianity had become professionalism, and behind that professionalism was not the sinner or even the little child of the Gospels. It was the self-righteous Pharisee.

I could hardly suspect, in the nervous sweat of my discomfort at the prayer meeting, that there was already a stream of life deep within me waiting to be tapped. The release of it would amply compensate for the pain of crushing the rock holding it back. I little realized the force of that river, for I had kept it well covered for years with layers of protective stone. It was an old river, in a sense, for it had been there in some way since my youth. I would later call it the gift of the Holy Spirit.

What I did not realize was how much the release of that gift would mean the release of pent-up energies within that would utterly stupefy me with their power. What frightened me for the moment, I suppose, was the realization that all my defensive reaction, "But I've had the Holy Spirit since my baptism!" however theologically exact, also covered over the fact that though I may have had the Holy Spirit, *He* was far from having *me*. The crazy "Baptism in the Holy Spirit" of which the Charismatics spoke, and of which the outward gesture would be nothing more than kneeling and asking to be prayed over, might be just the thing I needed—and feared— the most: the gift of *being given* to the Lord in a new way, a way in which I would let *Him* take over the controls.

Whatever moved me, I don't know, but on Christmas Eve 1970, I stepped forward and asked to be prayed over. Some of the people who prayed over me I admired greatly, but some were persons whose psychological stability I questioned. To accept their prayer as efficacious for me was another way of losing control. Jesus never promised He would channel His life to us through a perfect church. But to experience the life He offers, I must not despise the channel He chooses.

I did not know exactly what I was asking for. I asked for an infilling of the Holy Spirit. I did not ask for specific gifts, and I especially remember not asking for tongues. I didn't know what tongues meant (I still had to understand!), and after all, it was the least of the gifts. If the Lord wanted to give it to me, fine, but I felt sure I really didn't need it. I would just as soon He gave it to somebody who did.

As I knelt there hearing the voices of those praying over me, many of them babbling in tongues, I felt a warmth and a tapping entry into the rock within me. I began to feel a bubbling inside. Yes, that is the best image I have for it—bubbling. It was just there, and I didn't know what to do with this feeling.

One of the ways in which I sought to release it was by finishing the last three chapters of a book I was writing, and I did it in less than three days. But the bubbling was still there. On New Year's Day as I drove to the ranch to visit my family, I felt moved to relax and let the bubbling come out however it would. It came out in a melody without words. Three days later words came to fit the melody. "The Spirit of the Lord has touched my soul ..." (Little did I suspect that a new album had begun then and there.) The melody came to me on New Year's Day—the words on the feast of the Epiphany of our Lord—but the bubbling from which it flowed was the Lord's Christmas gift to me a week before.

Far from being spent by the song, the bubbling was still there. It seemed to go beyond what I could put in either melody or words. Could this be the gift of tongues? *O Lord, please not that!* I then spoke with one of my own theology students about his experience with tongues, a man I had trained in the Scriptures. I became more attracted, though still afraid. I began to study the New Testament passages with a passion and an interest I never had before. I concluded that tongues was not an experience of being zapped suddenly with a new language spoken somewhere on the face of the earth (at least not directly), and that unless I actually moved my lips and started babbling praise, nothing would happen.

The gift, then, was the courage to be that foolish for the Lord—and that free. To the last resistance of my pride the Lord seemed to say, "Will you have the humility to ask for the least of the gifts? Will you step forth and let go, trusting that I will carry you?" I was still afraid to let go in the presence of my former student. Frankly, the whole prospect frightened me to death. What would it do to my professional image?

I went to my room, closed my door, knelt … and let go. I stopped a couple of times, looked at myself in the mirror, and reflected at how stupid this sounded. Then I tried to ignore that, realizing I felt the same way when I first tried to dance. I began to focus on the Lord, and it was easier to let go. More and more came. I was singing God knows what, but I felt the awkward yet liberating freedom of not having to know or care what syllable or note would come next.

Then I began to feel, for the first time in my life perhaps, like the buzzards I had as a child watched gliding in the sky for hours without flapping their wings. They let the wind carry them. (Sorry about mentioning the buzzard when you were expecting something more aesthetic like dove or seagull or eagle, but I'm from Texas. It's the wind, not the bird that gets the credit. In Texas the most repulsive bird is the most graceful flier, and it's all because he lets the wind do the work.)

So that's tongues! Gliding on the wind of the Holy Spirit! Praising God by letting the Spirit do it in you, for you, with you! And not caring what syllable or tone comes next! *All right, Lord, but not in public, please!*

The Lord had His hour for that too. I was invited to celebrate an afternoon Mass at the convent of the Sisters of Divine Providence in Castroville for a regional meeting being held. They sang my new Spirit song at the end of Mass. Sister Charlene invited me to stay for supper and then for a prayer meeting.

Contrary to my plans, I accepted. During the prayer meeting one of the young sisters said she had been very burdened and wanted to be prayed over. Naturally, with my compulsion to preside, I was one of the first to step forward to pray over her. Nice, rational prayers (I was very practiced in that kind of praying), and then a dead silence fell over all, a moment of intensely quiet prayer. I felt a nudge that said, "*Now.*"

I said, *Lord, You're kidding.*

"*Now!*"

But this is stupid!

"*Now!*"

I plunged and began to sing in tongues. Several others, to my amazement, joined in. The spirit of the whole prayer meeting seemed to be lifted like a jet plane climbing above the clouds.

That night I drove home singing the Lord's praise at the top of my voice. I am surprised I was not stopped by a patrol car for driving while intoxicated. I don't know what answer I would have given other than telling the patrolman, "That's what they thought on Pentecost morning too!"

My life since then has been so different, so rich, and so full of inexplicable events that I cannot begin to relate them. I have come to realize that the gifts of the Spirit are not toys but tools made for the building of the kingdom. On one occasion, a nun of Native American descent, whose father had just been murdered on the reservation precisely because he had tried to help a delinquent boy, came to me to ask for prayers. After praying over her for a few minutes I began to sing in tongues.

When I finished, she stood up with tears in her eyes. "I have, in faith, experienced the resurrection of my father. And some of your words I recognized as words of the Sioux dialect my grandmother used to speak. One of them was *waka*, which means Great Spirit."

I had nothing to do with that except to surrender to the Lord as best I could while praying.

I have witnessed physical healing, like that of Gus whose hearing—lost for twenty-five years—came back completely when the community of believers at Biscayne College in Miami asked the Lord for it. Most of all, I have witnessed the powerful inner healings of soul and spirit—the healing of marriages and families, the healing of long-festering hatreds, and deliverance from evil spirits. To me, the rebirth of love and forgiveness is the surest sign that this is the Lord's work.

My greatest witness to the Lord's deep healing is myself. I have found a new strength and vitality, a greater willingness to risk for the Lord, a greater ability to cope with stress and chaos. Many of my early, painful memories have been healed. I have been able to say, "Praise God" for the whole of my own past, that of which I have written and that which remains unsaid. The Lord has put the dispersed energies together more and more too, especially as He helped me accept my uniqueness with its grandeur and its limitations and shown me how to love even myself, with less and less need for the kinds of reassurance I used to seek.

The reality of my healing is matched only by the realization of how far I have yet to go. The Lord has at least given me to see that life is not a race to be first to the mountain but a daily yielding to His Spirit, wherever and however He leads. It is not a question of beating my wings but of learning how to lend them to the Wind.

Post Script

When I wrote about my father forty-three years ago—a story I was asked to share on National Public Radio—I focused on the wounds I had suffered from him and how this skewed my relation with God the Father. In my elder years I have become painfully aware of the ways I hurt him as I morphed into an adult. If only I could kneel at his bed and say, "Papa, I'm sorry!" But now I am able to do that only in prayer. Even so, I have fallen in an unspeakable, tearful love of Papa and a burning desire to know his embrace in heaven. Or maybe his kiss on my forehead.

Bio–

Author of more than twenty books in biblical and pastoral theology, Fr. George Montague received his Doctorate in Sacred Theology at the University of Fribourg, Switzerland. Former president of the Catholic Biblical Association of America and editor of the *Catholic Biblical Quarterly*, he has been a speaker on six continents. He served as seminary rector in the U. S. and Canada and was director of novices for six years in Kathmandu, Nepal. He did a summer study in Israel with Hebrew Union College and participated in the excavation of Tel Gezer in 1966 under Dr. William Dever.

In 1997, with Fr. Bob Hogan, he began a new religious community in the Marianist family, the Brothers of the Beloved Disciple. Fr. George also teaches Scripture at St. Mary's University in San Antonio, Texas. With Father Marshall, he was given permission by his Marianist superiors to work with the new community of the Brothers of the Beloved Disciple.

Rev. Fr. Sy Nguyen, J.C.L.

———◇◇◇◇———

It is always a delight to share about the greatness of our God and the wonderful, countless things He has done in my life. As you read this, my hope is that you look at your own life and see what God has done for you. The greatest blessing I have received from God is the priesthood. It is a marvelous gift, and I cannot give God enough thanks and praise for calling me to His priesthood. I ask that you pray for me that I may be faithful to this gift all the days of my life.

The blessings of God throughout my life led me to this beautiful gift of the priesthood. I was born in Vietnam in 1964 during the Vietnam War. My father was an army officer, and my mother worked as a clerk at the radio station. This was the only radio station in South Vietnam. I have a younger sister, and the two of us were baptized when we were born because both of my parents came from a long line of traditional Vietnamese Catholics.

North Vietnam made an offensive attack against the South in 1968, known as the Tet Offensive. It was during this attack that they bombed many places in South Vietnam. One of the first was the communications centers, which included the radio station where my mother worked. A bomb placed in a taxi parked at the gate contained explosives that destroyed the building and killed my mother. I was four years old at the time, and my sister was two.

I don't remember much about my mother since I was so young when she died. However, I was told that when I first began to talk, Mother taught me how to say the *Our Father* in Vietnamese. This is a story I cherish about my mother and her faith. Everywhere she took me, she wanted to show off her child. She did this by saying, "Listen, he can say the *Our Father*." Children at that age don't always speak in sentences, but Mother was very proud of the fact that I could pray.

This is a reminder to all of us who are mothers, fathers, grandmothers, grandfathers, women and men everywhere to realize how important it is to teach children the little things. Sometimes we become wrapped up in the "big concepts" and lose heart. We try to get the big concepts across to our children, but they may not understand.

Remember that it starts with the little things. For me it was the *Our Father* that my mother was so proud to teach me and to show off her little boy. That one event has stayed with me for my entire life. It is especially precious because it is the one thing I know about my mom.

My dad raised the two of us for two years. Then he remarried. His new wife practiced the Buddhist faith, and she became my stepmother. In Vietnam, only about seven percent of the population are Catholic. Most Vietnamese are Buddhists or practice ancestor worship. When she married my dad, she became a Catholic, and they later had two daughters.

My family consisted of one sister and two half-sisters. When my two half-sisters were born, they were baptized. These were the happiest years of my family life. I remember attending church together and worshiping with both my stepmother and my dad.

When I was nine years old, my dad—still in the army—was ambushed and killed. He was a captain at the time and had been assigned to be the mayor of a little town. During the war, the mayor had to be in the military to protect the people. Soldiers also protected the people, and Dad was assigned the task of leading them and taking care of this fishing town. This too is a precious memory. My dad was a wonderful man whom I will not forget.

When Dad was first assigned as mayor of that small town, the people were accustomed to bribing the officers. The government officials were known as being corrupt. During wartime in Vietnam, if you expected to visit and move from one town to another, you had to have the correct paperwork. The people would go to the office and ask for written permission to visit their relatives, or to conduct business in different cities or towns in the country. Usually, they had to bribe the officials for the paperwork. It was considered a normal practice that everyone expected.

When Dad took over as mayor, he refused to take bribes. The people would ask, "What can we give you?" He responded with, "Nothing. I am just doing my job."

The people were so impressed by my father, and they loved him so much.

We lived outside the village in the city of Saigon, and our house had a front yard with a fence. We woke up early to go to school and waded through many fish that had been thrown over our fence during the night. The men were so appreciative that after night fishing, they would dump the extra fish in our front yard. It was their way of saying "thank you" because my dad wouldn't take bribes.

As a young boy this impressed me, especially when wading through piles of fish in my yard. It impressed me even more when I learned why this happened. It increased my respect for Dad. He was a just man, and that was the legacy he left for me. It affected my life in such a way that it made me the person I am today.

It saddens me to see that today many fathers are not mindful of the legacy they leave behind for their children. I don't believe many men or women think about their actions as an example or leaving a legacy to their children, but they should. I pray that sharing my story and the effect it had on my life will help others recognize the importance and desire to live virtuous lives by the grace of God.

Another effect on me and part of my life was my step-grandmother. My stepmother also had a stepmother. When my father died, my stepmother had to work, so we were taken care of by her stepmother, whom we called "grandmother," but there was no blood relation.

This lady was one of the meanest women I would ever know. She was *very* mean. Very, *very* mean. She abused us physically and verbally. She would whip us, hit us, and expect us to do all the chores around the house. I was around ten at the time.

My little sister and I were in charge of making sure the house was clean, along with other jobs. "Grandmother" treated us like servants. My stepmother had to work to support the four of us children. She wasn't home, and when she did come home she was tired, ate, and was off to work again the next day.

Grandmother was very hard on us. She said things such as, "You are nothing. You do not deserve to live because your own parents left you. You are so worthless because your mother and your father died. You are so lucky to live in this house, but you don't deserve to eat good food."

When it was time to eat, my sister and I were not allowed to touch the good food on the table. My stepmother did not know about this. All it took was Grandmother giving us "the look," and we knew not to eat the food. She told us repeatedly, "You are nothing. You are less than the worms." This was very hard on young children, and naturally we cried together. Many times we missed our mother and father. But the Lord taught me so much through this experience.

When I was older I recalled these events after knowing Christ and reflecting upon my life. I realized that my grandmother, God rest her soul— and as mean as she was and as horrible to remember what she said to us— ultimately and unintentionally taught me something about the reality of who I am: that before God *I am nothing.*

Amazingly, I learned this from a Buddhist, the meanest woman in the world. She kept pounding into our heads "You are nothing, you are nothing, you are nothing," and I realized that God was teaching me through this woman that before God I *am* nothing and not worth anything. Anything that I am is because of what God does and gives me. This is an important insight that I gained from an abusive situation. Our amazing God taught me a wonderful spiritual insight and humility before God. As His creature I am nothing without Him.

My stepmother raised the four of us alone for two years. After this she married a widower with nine children from his first marriage. All were Buddhist. When my stepmother married my stepfather, she returned to the Buddhist faith and no longer practiced Catholicism.

Now I was part of a family of thirteen children—nine Buddhist and four of us baptized Catholics. I was eleven years old, but the wonderful fact became the actions of my step-mom. She continued to raise us as Catholics.

In those days, when a non-Catholic married a Catholic they promised to raise the children Catholic. My stepmother remembered and honored that promise. She allowed us to attend Catholic school and church every Sunday. As an eleven-year-old, I recall walking to church with my sister. The two youngest girls stayed home because they were too young to go with us. My sister and I would walk to church, but many times we wouldn't go inside for Mass but would play outside the church. After Mass was over we walked home, and my stepmother thought we'd gone to Mass.

This was our family life when I was about twelve. My step-grandfather, who had Parkinson's disease, could no longer walk by himself, and he needed someone to walk with him. Parkinson's caused him to lose his balance and he needed assistance, so my job was to help my grandfather throughout the day. I went to school, but as soon as I came home I would take care of him.

Grandfather was an astrologer. He made charts of all the stars for each person in the family, so of course he made a chart for me as well. He predicted everyone's future according to these stars. "When you grow up you are going to have two wives and four kids," he told me.

Obviously his prediction was incorrect. I use this account as a warning not to waste your money on astrologers!

Grandfather had to walk every day. The doctors explained that if he didn't walk, his muscles would tighten up until he would be unable to walk at all. This meant he had to walk as much as possible. We walked around the block—around and around—and during those walks we talked.

This Buddhist astrologer would pose questions to me such as, "What about the virgin birth? How can you explain that? How can she remain a virgin?" These were not normal questions to ask a twelve-year old boy, and if left on my own I wouldn't have thought of the "why" behind my faith.

But here I was in a situation that God placed me in where I had to answer these questions. I told my grandfather, "Let me look it up, and I will tell you later." Grandfather and I had a relationship built upon learning from each other what our religions taught. I learned so much from him about Buddhism, and he learned from me about Catholicism—or at least what I knew as a twelve-year-old.

This relationship made me understand my faith, or at least forced me to learn about my faith at a young age. I have no doubt that the conviction I have about my faith today started back then. As I look back over my life, I see God in every moment. Even during the difficult times, the times of suffering, the times of abuse, the fact that we were orphans, God had something in mind for me and was preparing me for His will.

The relationship with my grandfather helped me focus in a way I never would have on my own as a young boy, to learn my faith and to find the answers to his questions. I was like any other twelve-year-old who wanted to run outside and play. Instead, I was stuck in the house or walking with a very old man. This was a tough situation, but I was once again learning and being prepared by God. This time in my life was an education in the sacrificial, disciplinary life.

When I look back as an adult, I'm amazed that in helping my grandfather with Parkinson's disease I was learning firsthand how difficult it is to suffer as an elderly person. As a young boy I was learning how to sacrifice my own time. The Lord trained me and prepared me for the priesthood, and only in retrospect did I understand this importance.

The communists took over South Vietnam in 1975.

We had been stuck in Vietnam, living with the communist regime for four years, when my stepmother arranged for us to escape. The corruption escalated during communist control, and the government would look the other way if you gave them money. However, it was up to you to find your own escape route, and you had to find a boat to board at night, unseen. Once out on the ocean, you would not be shot since it was already considered risky to your life.

We had to come up with a lot of money, and they charged people by gold. As Asians we bought gold and did not put our money in the bank. Gold was in the form of jewelry. They expected us to pay five pieces of gold for each person. This was huge, a tremendous amount of money for my family. Our family was divided in half. My stepfather would take his children on a different trip. My stepmother would take us separately. There were just too many to go together.

My mother borrowed money from her sister, who was married to a Chinese-Vietnamese. These tend to be wealthy people, and her husband was a wealthy man. He loaned my mom the money to buy gold, which paid for our escape.

We were on the boat for five days and four nights and very lucky to be alive. We were city people. I had been to the beach only a couple of times. Finding ourselves on a little boat stuffed full with over 200 people was very difficult. People were below deck and on the top deck of the boat. We had never been out in the open sea, and this overfilled boat made it additionally risky. After five days and four nights we landed on an island in Indonesia. We were put in a camp to wait for a country to accept us as refugees.

An event occurred during my stay in the camp that deepened my faith, specifically in regards to the Eucharist. I was about fourteen at the time. Every day more boats arrived with Vietnamese refugees escaping Communism. The refugees went out daily to look for incoming boats and help them land safely.

One day, one of these smaller boats that held about forty people came in with only two survivors: a father, and a daughter about six or seven years old. They brought in the two, barely alive, and rushed them to the hospital. Everybody noticed that the father's arms were messed up. They looked so bad people didn't even recognize them as arms. The two eventually joined us at the camp a few months later, waiting for a country to sponsor them.

"What happened to your boat?" the people asked. "What happened to you?"

The father told us an incredible story. There were about forty people on the boat who had died from hunger and the lack of water. The only two people who survived were the father and his daughter. "There was no food nor water on the boat," he told us. "What I did was cut my arm and gave my blood to my daughter." He was convinced this saved his little daughter, and she survived when everybody else died. I don't know if this is medically feasible, but this father truly believed his daughter survived because he had given her his blood.

This incredible account made an impact on my life at the age of fourteen. Mass was celebrated at the camp, and I always questioned—like many people do—the authenticity of the Eucharist. *How can it be that God gives His Body and His Blood?* It sounds gruesome. It sounds weird, and many struggle with this concept. How is it that God accomplishes this, or why would God want to do this feat or have us believe it is His Body and His Blood?

This near-death event of father and daughter touched me and

deepened my belief and my understanding of the miracle of the Eucharist. I was struck by the thought and realized, *"Wow! That is what God is doing!"* We as His children are lost in this world. We cannot survive, just like that little girl could not have survived if her father did not give her his blood to sustain her.

That is in essence what God does for all of us.

God knows that life is like an ocean, and we cannot survive without Him—and so He gives us His blood. That is what the Eucharist is all about. It gives us life. This moment in my life taught me a deeper truth about the Eucharist, which I continue to share over and over again with Catholics. This is only one of the great truths and meaning of the Holy Eucharist—how God the Father gives His children sustenance so that we can survive in the sea of life.

We were very lucky to remain in the camp for only five months, and this was due to my father having been an officer in the army. When they checked his record, we were prioritized to go to another country, and the United States agreed to accept us.

Many Catholic and non-Catholic churches were sponsoring refugees in 1979. St. Hedwig in Los Alamitos was the parish that sponsored my family. When we arrived in Orange County I didn't speak a word of English, nor did anyone else in my family speak much English, other than my stepmother—who spoke a little.

As a refugee family in an internment camp we could have been sent anywhere. It was up to the country that agreed to receive us. It could have been England, France, or anywhere else in the world, but to me the fact that my family ended up in the United States in Orange County, California, means it is God's will. Not only that, but it seems He also wanted me to be a priest in Orange County. I see God's hand in every step of my life.

The church arranged for us to live in an apartment in Santa Ana. Everything was so strange. We arrived in the United States at the end of May or the beginning of June. The kids were still in school, walking past our house going to and from school. We looked out the window with our noses pressed against the glass watching them walk by. The entire family—from my mom to the children—all of us watched! The reason? None of us had ever seen yellow hair, blue eyes, or brown hair and green eyes. This was a spectacle to us. "Wow, look! There is red hair!" we said. It was truly a culture shock.

After living in that first apartment for about a month, we moved into an apartment in Los Alamitos. During that summer we attended English as a Second Language classes (ESL). We learned English to the best of our ability, and after the summer my mother found a job working as a cook at a convalescent home. We children began school in September. I attended Los Alamitos High School, entering the tenth grade. I eventually graduated from this school.

I am an introvert—an extreme introvert—and not speaking the language fluently only added to my shyness. I was self-conscious of my inadequacies, and while in high school I rarely spoke to other people. I was so shy I couldn't carry on a normal conversation.

During my high school years, I began to hear God calling me to be a priest.

This thought to become a priest really began in the eleventh grade in high school. I met Jesus in person when I became involved with the youth group, and the only reason I was involved was because of a girl named Loraine Duacsek. I am indebted to Loraine, who is now married and has two beautiful children. She was the daughter of the family that sponsored our family. She was two years older than I was, and she would drive us to church because my parents didn't attend. She taught me how to drive.

Loraine spoke to me when I didn't want to speak to anyone, and she was patient in helping me with my English. She also invited me to the youth group. No one else could have made me attend. I knew there would be other kids talking and socializing, which was something I couldn't do. I couldn't talk. I only went because Loraine was my friend, helped me in every way, and out of respect to her I went to her youth group. At youth group we prayed, sang, and learned about the Bible.

During Lent we had a retreat. The youth minister turned off the light and simply told the story of the Passion. That was when I met Jesus. I cried uncontrollably because for the first time in my life I understood that Jesus had suffered and died for *me*. Not just for the whole world, but for me personally. He had suffered and died for me. It hit me hard. This helped me to grow deeper in my faith and this calling to the priesthood. My vocation came due to the kindness and friendship of this girl Loraine, who cared enough to invite me.

It is important to never underestimate the little things you do for others. Invitations such as "Let's go to a prayer meeting" or "Let's go to a Magnificat talk." There are so many missed opportunities. Simple things such as these can change a person's life for the better.

When I heard the call I told God, "You are making a mistake. Being a priest means I have to stand up in front of people and give talks. There is no way! No way I can do this as I am." That was a variation of my conversations with God during this time.

But God didn't give up. He kept tugging and pulling on me, saying, *"I want you to be a priest."*

It remained in my thoughts constantly, but I kept fighting and denying this calling. I graduated from high school and decided to become an engineer. One of the reasons was that as an Asian I was good at math. The second reason was that as an engineer I could focus on a project in my own cubicle and not deal with people. I went to Long Beach State and signed up to be an electrical engineer, which I studied for two years.

During that time the Lord continued to tug and pull. He wouldn't let go of me. I kept asking Him, "Why? Why are You doing this? I cannot even carry on a normal conversation with people. Why would You want me to be Your priest? I will not be able to do it."

But God didn't stop pulling and tugging. Finally, after two years of study, I realized I was unhappy. I was doing well in school, and everything was going well academically. I told my stepmom and stepdad that once I became an engineer and made money, I would buy a home. I invited them to live with me. I wanted to be a good son!

My parents, of course, loved the idea. My father had nine grown children who had their own families and lived far away. My stepmom and father had one daughter together, and now there were five children living with them. My parents were very happy to have a son who was willing to take care of them in their old age.

However, after two years of studying I reluctantly gave in to the Lord's calling. I just couldn't fight the urge any longer. The thought would not leave me. "Okay, I am going to give You one chance," I told God. "I'm going to the seminary to give it a try, but if I don't like it, I will leave, and that's it!" In my thoughts I truly believed I would not make it. I knew the seminary would kick me out. I lacked the necessary social skills to even do the *normal* things. *How can I be a priest?* But I felt I had to give Jesus a chance.

I had decided to give God a chance, but there were many obstacles. The first obstacle was how to tell my mom and dad. They were still Buddhists and expected me to take care of them. I didn't know what to do. I seriously didn't believe they would give me permission to go to seminary.

The Asian culture is very respectful of parents' wishes. I decided to pray to the Lord. "This is Your idea, and if You want me to be a priest, You will need to take care of this issue. There is no way my parents will say yes. They are not even Catholics and won't understand what it means to become a priest and go to the seminary." I prayed and waited, then waited until the very last minute to tell them. School began in September, and I waited until August to gather up enough courage to talk to my mom.

When I finally sat down with her, I said, "Mom, I think I need to go to the seminary to become a priest." I held my breath, wondering what she was going to say.

"I thought you would never ask!" she answered. "I thought you would never ask."

I was shocked. "What?" That ruined my plan. I was hoping she would say, "Forget it!"

"What are you talking about?" I asked.

"When your dad was still alive he told me that if Sy grows up and asks to be a priest and go to the seminary, I was to let you go," she said.

She went on to explain the reason. I was born prematurely, and in 1964 during the war, the medical technology was very bad in Vietnam. My entire internal system didn't work. I couldn't eat anything, nor could I keep down any food. The doctor told my birth mother that I was going to die.

My stepmother continued to relate the story. My mother took me to the church and prayed, "My son is going to die, but if he lives, he's Yours."

As I listened to my stepmother, I now understood. I understood that this tugging and pulling by the Lord to grow closer to Him was real. I was called to be a priest. That was my life's purpose.

I said, "Thank you." I was so shocked, so surprised. It was the first time I had heard the account. "Why didn't you tell me this story before?"

"Because I don't want you to be a priest," she said. "I want you to become an engineer to take care of us. But now I have to tell you because you are asking me to go to the seminary."

So I went to the seminary and never looked back. I loved the seminary and knew this was where I belonged. I learned and grew so much deeper in my faith. I learned about the Church and came out of my shell. I was ordained in 1991.

My first assignment was the mission in San Juan Capistrano. As a young priest, I always went over the time limit. Because I preached so long the people complained, and the pastor complained. Imagine this from a guy who could not talk! I became a priest and could not stop talking. In fact, Bea, a lady at San Juan Capistrano who loved me told me jokingly, "Well, Father Sy, the way you preach less is by standing on one leg. When your leg gets tired then it is time to stop."

I took her advice, but it didn't work. The reason? At the time I was training to run a marathon, and my legs were in pretty good shape. Even if I stood on one leg I didn't get very tired, and I kept going and going. But thank God I have learned to limit myself.

I share this to once again demonstrate the power of God, the transforming power of God in my own life. If any of the kids who attended high school with me saw me today as a priest they would not believe it. Somehow by God's grace and God's power to change a person, He called a man to become a priest who now cannot stop talking about Christ, about my love for the Church and for the priesthood.

Where does this come from? I'm absolutely certain it is not from me. I am absolutely sure it is from the One Who calls me, Who chose me, and Who ordained me as His priest. This is the absolute truth. I share this so you can realize the power God has in your own life if you are open. God can change your life, your children's lives. You may have a son, a daughter, a grandchild you worry about. While it is good to be concerned, don't forget to entrust them to the transforming power of God. No matter how bad or how lost they seem to be, no matter how anti-religious they seem to be, God has the power to change their hearts.

Another important impact on my life has to do with the Blessed Mother. Earlier I shared that my birth mother died when I was four years old. I didn't have a mother, and when my father remarried, my stepmother became the woman I call "Mom" today. Yet, there is no one like your own mother. Growing up, I really missed those special times when I saw a mother holding her child, or a mother talking to her child in a loving way. I wondered what a hug from my mom would feel like. I wondered what her voice would sound like. I didn't remember, and I felt that loneliness, that hunger for my mother's love and my mother's presence that I didn't have in my life.

It was from this loneliness that I became close to the Blessed Mother. She has become my spiritual mother; the mother I did not have on earth. I am certain she is the mother that my own birth mother begged to take care of me for her. I found in the Virgin Mary that consolation, that strength of a mother. I find this when I go to her in prayer and in times of loneliness.

Another aspect of our spiritual life has to do with the saints. One of my favorite saints is St. Thérèse of Lisieux. In the seminary, we sometimes go through times of crises, when you question your vocation; question your calling. I went through that period during my last year of the seminary, not knowing for certain if that was truly what God wanted for me. I didn't know if this was truly what I wanted to do with the rest of my life either, and I questioned. It was during that period of confusion, which most seminarians go through, that I prayed to St. Thérèse for intercession.

St. Thérèse has a promise to send you "roses" from heaven. So I prayed, "Saint Thérèse, if it is God's will for me to be a priest, please send me some roses." Being in the seminary it was highly unlikely that I would receive roses. Yet I prayed, "St. Thérèse, send me some roses to show that God wants me to be a priest, because I am confused."

During holidays the seminary is closed, and the seminarians can go home. I didn't want to go home. I loved the seminary, and I was one of the few men who remained there during that time. It was very quiet, and I was saying my Rosary as I took a walk. Truthfully, I had forgotten my prayer asking St. Thérèse for the roses, when here came a florist's car pulling into the seminary parking lot. *Wow,* I thought. *What is this?* The florist delivery man came out with a dozen roses and said, "Excuse me. Somebody ordered a dozen roses to be put in the chapel. Where is the chapel?"

Wow! I thought. *What is the likelihood of this happening?*

I took the man into the chapel. He went straight to the image of St. Thérèse and put the roses right down in front. I was certain then that this was the sign St. Thérèse gave to me.

This account is to help you become confident in your relationship with the saints. Be sure to develop that friendship with the saints that seek you out and want to be your help and your guide in your life on earth. It goes without saying that they always point you to God.

Another event happened when I was nine years old concerning the Blessed Mother. My stepmother had done everything she could to help heal me of an ulcer, which was horrible and painful. About two years after being ordained a priest, I was suffering once again from this ulcer. I was in pain and I prayed to God. "I am going to need some help here. I don't know how long I am going to last as a priest in this condition if I keep suffering this way."

That summer I went on vacation with another priest to France, and we went to Lourdes. At Lourdes I took the bath in the spring. I prayed, drank the water, and came home. The ulcer is gone! I know it is gone because now I can eat chili and anything hot and spicy that I love. I attribute my healing to God and the intercession of Our Lady of Lourdes. I am forever grateful for the many miracles I have received in my life, but for this one specifically from the intercession of Our Lady.

I pray that as you read about what God has done in my life, it will help you look at your own life. God is close to us. God is near us. He wants to help us. He wants to save us. We only need to open ourselves to this God Who is always present. If we open ourselves to Him, we will be filled with tremendous grace and blessings. I thank God, and I praise God that He gave me the opportunity to share my story and His wonderful work in my life. I thank and praise God today that in one way or another we will be touched by His transforming grace, His mercy, and His love.

Please pray that I may be faithful for the rest of my life to this wonderful, marvelous blessing of the priesthood that God has given me. I always tell people—and this is from my heart—that my goal is to be a saint.

That should be the goal of every Christian—to be a saint. I work at it every day. Even though times are bad, even though the Church is going through a tough time, even though the priesthood is under tremendous attack, marriage is under tremendous attack, families are under tremendous attack, and many of us suffer from it, I hope to leave you with a sense of confidence that the Lord is more powerful than anything the devil can throw at you.

This is a time when God raises up many saints in His church. This is our chance, my brothers and sisters, to be great, to be holy, to be God's saints.

Let's do it together.

Bio –

Fr. Sy Nguyen is known for his powerful charism in preaching the gospel of life and speaking the truth in love. He came to the United States as a refugee with his family in 1979, graduated from Los Alamitos High School, and attended Long Beach University for two years before entering St. John's Seminary in 1984. He was ordained to the priesthood for the Orange Diocese in 1991. At the request of Bishop Todd Brown, he studied canon law in Rome for the Office of Canonical Services at Marywood Center in 2001. Father's testimony is a powerful example of the mercy of God in the life of a person called to the priesthood. He overcame many challenges in his young life that led to his complete surrender and gift of self to following Christ crucified, died, and risen. His inspiring witness will leave you with hope and gratitude.

Rev. Fr. Kevin Scallon, C.M.

O nce at dinner in a hotel on the shores of Lough Erne, Northern Ireland, my brother reminded me during the course of the meal that during World War II the hotel had been a residence for U.S. army officers. The mention of American soldiers reminded me of my earliest attendance at Mass in our parish church. The GIs lined up outside the church and marched into Sunday Mass to the front pews, which had been reserved for them. I have often wondered since then how many of these young men wound up on the beaches of Normandy, never to see their loved ones again.

My earliest memories of the priesthood were warm, positive, and had a profound influence on my life. My father and my mother had a great love for priests and often invited them to our home. I recall one of the chaplains from the U.S. Army base coming to dinner. I was intrigued by his American accent, his rimless glasses, and his suntan. Suntans were rare in Ireland in those days. My father had a boyhood friend who became a Passionist priest. Over the years, many Passionists and other orders of priests visited our home. They made a great impression upon me and my brothers and sisters.

We grew up on a farm, and even during the war when there was a great scarcity of everything, we always had plenty to eat and acres of space in which to roam and play. Our parish priest was a distinguished old man who had spent many of his early years of priesthood in the United States. He was affectionately known by his fellow priests as Chicago Jack. Each time he spoke about the love of the Sacred Heart, his voice cracked, and he would stop. I wondered why. Later, I learned that he was deeply moved in the Spirit by the thought of Christ's love for us.

During my growing-up years, my family lived in an atmosphere of prayer. We often said the family Rosary, and I was accustomed to seeing my mother constantly fingering her rosary beads and my father reading his prayer book. On the first Friday of each month, we piled into the car and drove to Confession at the Passionist monastery. Seeing my father and mother leading us in prayer, observing them regularly attend Confession, and witnessing their love for the Eucharist and their fidelity in attending Mass, I did not need many sermons to convince me of the importance of these things. Faith, prayer, and sacramental living were something I breathed in the very air.

It was not just the influence of my parents, but also the witness of my older brothers and sisters, who lived exemplary lives as young men and women. In this atmosphere, my vocation took root. Around the time of my first Holy Communion, I began to sense a real call to become a priest.

Vocation is not a man-made thing. It is given by God and often given early in life. Even then, the Eucharist had a special and profound meaning for me. I felt drawn to it and to Christ, whom I believed was present. I was taught in school by lay teachers, who also gave me a sincere witness of their deep faith.

For my high school education, I was sent to boarding school. Secondary high schools in those days were boarding schools run almost exclusively by the Catholic Church. In God's providence, I attended a school run by the Vincentian Fathers.

Boarding school is not an ideal way to educate children, but the Vincentians who taught me were real men of God, dedicated to their work and clearly at home in the priestly ministry. I believe my priestly vocation became clear in the sacrament of Reconciliation with one of these priests. Until then I had never met anyone who so reflected the gentleness of Christ as those good Vincentians.

An incident occurred while I was in high school that had a certain mystical influence on me. On one of our many compulsory walks, I saw a poor man to whom my attention was drawn in a strange way. I looked at him and saw him looking back at me. I was puzzled by the encounter at the time, but later I became convinced that I had met Jesus.

From then on, the call to a priestly vocation seemed to crystallize in my spirit. Over the period of my boyhood, I had considered various occupations. I fancied myself as a pilot, an architect, or a great singer. These were childhood fantasies compared to the force that now drew me in the direction of the priesthood.

Vocation is a very personal thing, a unique mystery of God's grace. I often wondered why, out of all my brothers, the Lord chose me to be the priest. There is something about the way God draws men to the priesthood that puts everything else in second place. The decision to become a priest at an age when a young man's thoughts turn in the direction of girls seems strange. Yet, somehow you know that the price to be paid, especially celibacy, is small compared to the prize that is the priesthood. Youth is the time when people choose to do great things. The priesthood is the greatest of all. The cost of discipleship, thank goodness, is hidden from us. We learn that later.

Ray McAnalley, an Irish actor, had once studied for the priesthood. He gave a good description of what a vocation is: "A vocation is where you begin to suspect that you are about to be called." You enter the seminary with this strong suspicion. After a year or two, you start to realize that this is either for you or not for you.

In those days in Ireland, there was not much talk about celibacy. It was one of those things you took for granted if you wanted to become a priest. When I went into the seminary, I knew that embracing celibacy was going to be a real sacrifice. Physical, sexual attraction does not need to be taught. Looking back, I now realize that celibacy was poorly understood and badly taught.

It was to be expected that—having received so much from the Vincentians—I would want to join them, which is what I did. I was received into the Community on the Feast of the Holy Rosary in 1953. My first year was one of spiritual formation. I learned about everything Vincentian and was steeped in the life and lore of St. Vincent de Paul.

Our life was robustly masculine. We played plenty of football, rugby, and soccer. On the seminary farm, we looked after pigs, poultry, and cattle. We milked cows, fed chickens, and lived a Spartan existence of prayer, study, work, and asceticism. The priest in charge of our formation had been educated by the Trappists, and much of what influenced him in his youth he passed on to us. We were on our honor to behave at all times. There were no deans to monitor our behavior.

All in all, we received a well-rounded, traditional college and theological education in those pre-Vatican II times. Looking back now, it did not appear very relevant. Times were different. Some features of our Vincentian life were derived from the French school of spirituality. For example, we were not allowed to vacation with our families. We spent our vacation at one of our high schools in Dublin. We were not permitted to read the daily newspapers or go to movies. Watching television was not a problem. There was no television in Ireland in the 1950s.

This detachment from family and the outside world meant that we led something of a monastic existence. This is fine for monks, but not, I think, for young men preparing for a busy pastoral ministry. Like so many other things, this all seems so obvious now with the hindsight of Vatican II and what has followed. Back then, it seemed normal and even reasonable. It was part of the renewal which Pope Saint John XXIII saw was so clearly needed in the Church. The problem with being cut off like this is that it tended to arrest psychological development and create a detachment that was probably not very healthy.

After eight years of study, seven others and I were ordained to the priesthood at Holy Cross College in Dublin on May 27, 1961. The ceremony was not an impressive liturgical event. We were told to appear on time for the eight-thirty Mass presided over by John Charles McQuaid, Archbishop of Dublin. He was a man of extreme liturgical and ritual propriety. When he ordained me to the priesthood, I knew I was "a priest forever according to the order of Melchizedek" (Hebrews 7:17).

Afterward, we were treated to a breakfast of tea, toast, and a boiled egg in the seminary dining room. Then we met our parents and family members to impart our first priestly blessing. It was like a dream. To finally be a priest now was something incredible and wonderful. Somehow, I felt transformed and different. I knew that the sacrament of Holy Orders, the laying on of hands, and the prayer of the Church had changed me forever.

Shortly after ordination I met with my provincial, who appointed me as an assistant priest in a Vincentian parish in Sheffield. Sheffield was a heavily industrialized steel town in Yorkshire, England. The Vincentians had administered a parish there for over one hundred years.

I arrived in Sheffield on a rainy October evening in 1961. The phrase "culture shock" was unknown to me at the time, but it was what I experienced. Imagine being lifted from the gentle rolling hills of County Wicklow and put down in the "dark, satanic mills" of the industrial north of England, where you could eat the air pollution with a spoon. One of my confrères remarked wryly, "Wouldn't it be awful to live in Sheffield all your life and then go to hell when you die?"

At the time, Sheffield was going through an extensive urban renewal. The narrow streets and housing of the Industrial Revolution were being swept away, only to be replaced by even more hideous high-rise flats, which have since been demolished. It was into this social and demographic upheaval that I was launched into the pastoral ministry.

One of my tasks was chaplain to a large hospital. My abiding memory of this place was assisting a man at the moment of his death while listening to Elvis sing "Viva Las Vegas" from a loud-playing radio at the other end of the ward. *Lord,* I thought to myself. *I like Elvis, but when I go, please let it be an operatic tenor singing "Ave Maria" and not Elvis who serenades me to the gates of paradise.*

I liked the people of Yorkshire. They loved the priests and had a real sense of loyalty to the parish. They were a warm-hearted, good-humored people who lived hard lives working in the steelworks and the coal mines. I made friendships there that have lasted to this day.

My parish priest at the time was a wise man who was aware of my naiveté and youthful inexperience. He taught me many pastoral skills and ways of dealing with people, which helped me enormously. He used to say, "Don't imitate me. Always be yourself. If you do that, you will be a good pastor."

To escape the air pollution of the city from time to time, I drove my Volkswagen out onto the Yorkshire moors and walked for an hour or two before returning to the parish. It became clear that much of what I had learned in the seminary—while being good from a theological point of view—was not of much practical use when it came to preaching. At that time, preaching was at an all-time low in the Church. The study of Scripture and Homiletics, which should have been given priority in the seminary program, was almost forgotten. This resulted in an impoverished style of preaching that everyone found unsatisfactory, especially the poor people who had to listen to us.

In my second year at Sheffield, Pope Saint John XXIII called for the Second Vatican Council, and I can recall how excited I felt when I first heard the news. I told people at Mass one Sunday about this upcoming council and uttered a little prophetic word to the effect that I thought the Church would never be the same again.

Little did I know.

With the coming of Vatican II and the issue of the successive documents, I felt that the Holy Spirit was beginning a great work in the Church and in the world. I read the first document, "The Constitution on the Sacred Liturgy," when it appeared. It was a beautiful and powerful revelation, truly the work of the Holy Spirit.

After that reading, I couldn't wait for each of the council documents to be issued, and I devoured them when they arrived. I thanked God that I was living my priesthood at this moment in the history of the Church and witnessing things coming to pass that so many people had hoped for.

Pope Saint John XXIII died in 1963. He was succeeded by Pope Blessed Paul VI, who could not have been a bigger contrast to his predecessor. Pope Paul presided over the remainder of the Council and brought a wealth of experience and deep spirituality to his Petrine ministry.

After three years in Sheffield, I received a letter from my provincial. He expressed his delight and confidence in me and said he was appointing me to our mission in Nigeria. I would take up my post in October of 1964.

My first experience was language school—in a place quite a distance from our mission. During this course, I came down with my first bout of malaria. It was severe and took a great deal out of me. I went through something of a "dark night of the soul" and felt very sorry for myself. However, it all passed, and when I recovered, I began my work of giving retreats.

My few years in Nigeria were a wonderful priesthood experience. There was none of the clericalism that governed life back home. There was a camaraderie amongst all of us who ministered there. In those days in Nigeria, there were only poor people and, as I know now, the poor blessed us with the privilege of ministering to them.

During this time in Nigeria, there was a great deal of political upheaval, which ultimately ended in a civil war and a declaration of the Republic of Biafra. I found myself in the rebel area, while some of my Vincentian confrères were in the federal part. The war of independence that ensued was mostly one of attrition. The federal government blockaded the Biafrans into their own small area and proceeded to starve them into submission. The real reason they were not allowed to secede was that the Biafran area contained vast oil reserves, which everybody wanted.

Some of my most formative experiences as a priest happened during this time. I was appointed as pastor of a parish in the heart of Igboland. As well as caring for the local people, I also cared for the thousands of refugees pouring in from the south. Because of the blockade set up by the federal armies, the only food supplies into Biafra were flown illegally from an airport in Sao Tome. The supplies were distributed to each parish and were then given to the poor by people like myself.

There was never enough of anything. I remember a young, very pregnant woman. She asked me to give her some food to help her through her pregnancy. I told her to come every Saturday morning, and I would give her whatever I could. One Saturday she arrived carrying a large, flat basket containing her beautiful newborn twins. She said, "Father, now I do not need any food for myself, but if you could give me some baby food for my twins, I would be most grateful."

My ministry in those days had many facets. Most of my time was focused on caring for the sick, the poor, the dying, and the starving. In addition, I attended to my pastoral duties. But my part in all of this was small compared with the efforts of the others.

One of the great lessons I learned about being a priest came to me during this period, and it came from the most unlikely of teachers. One Sunday after saying several Masses around my parish, I returned to my mission house expecting it to be surrounded—as usual—by dozens of starving people. To my surprise, no one was there. I felt relieved, thinking I would go in and have my breakfast of boiled eggs, toast, and instant coffee.

Just as I was going in the door, a young woman came around the corner of the house leaning heavily on a staff. She looked at me and said, "Good morning, Father."

"What do you want?" I replied irritably.

She smiled. "Good morning, Father."

"Good morning. What do you want?"

"Please, Father," she said. "Let me tell you my story."

I groaned inwardly. I had heard so many stories, and I was not in the mood for another one. But I said, "Please, tell me your story."

She told me how she was driven from her home many kilometers south of here. Her husband, herself, and her four children had been forced to leave because of the retreating armies. She recounted how her husband and four children had died of hepatitis along the way.

I was not inclined to disbelieve her. I knew how many people were dying of this disease. The wonder was that we did not *all* succumb.

"Please Father," she said. "Give me something to keep my body and soul together until this war is over."

I asked the catechist to bring the woman some food, clothing, a blanket, and a few other things. Salt was a commodity everyone needed. When she received them from the hands of the catechist, she put them on the ground and began to sing and dance in a circle around them.

Still thinking of my boiled eggs and instant coffee, I asked the catechist what on earth she was doing.

"Oh, Father, she is thanking God for you."

By now, the sun was high in the sky and the heat was overpowering. I went over to her and said, "So, you believe in God, do you?"

She looked at me with a kind of astonished disbelief. "Yes, Father, I believe in God."

I think she had it on the tip of her tongue to ask me, "Do you believe in God?" but in her charity, she refrained.

"Do you believe in Jesus Christ?" I asked next.

To this, she made no reply. She went over and picked up the things we had given her. Gathering them in her frail arms, she came and stood directly in front of me. "Father, you are asking me whether I believe in Jesus Christ. For me today, you are Jesus Christ."

This word from the lips of a simple, illiterate woman hit me like a thunderbolt. The truth of it pierced my heart. I felt chastised and blessed at the same moment. In one sentence, this frail woman had summed up for me the essence of what it means to be a priest, even though I had not made any attempt to be Christ-like to her.

I have often wondered if God does not send angels to us in the form of poor people to remind us of the important things in life. Her word has lodged in my heart all of these years and has provided me with powerful inspiration in the midst of all the controversies, changes, and scandals that have beset the priesthood.

Another lesson I learned during that time was in relation to the Holy Eucharist. The morning after I arrived in my parish, a man came to my door and asked me to follow him to his village. An old man was dying. When I arrived, I found him curled around a pungent, smoky fire in his little mud house.

"You know, Father," the dying man said. "There has been no priest in this parish for over three years. I prayed that you would come. I prayed every day to St. Joseph that I would not die without seeing a priest." He also said, "My own name is Joseph, and I am so glad that you have come because today I am going to die."

I was moved by the simple faith of this fine old man. Having ministered to him all the comfort that the Church brings to dying people through the sacraments and the Apostolic Blessing, he looked up at me with a beautiful smile on his face and breathed his last.

I came out from his house and was met by about a hundred people from the village. Their appearance shocked me. They were dressed in filthy rags and severely emaciated. Most of them were covered with awful, suppurating sores.

The man who had brought me here said, "Father, let me tell you about this village. The government rounded up all the lepers in this area and told us to come and live here. They promised they would send us food and medicine, but they have never sent us anything."

"Are you all suffering from leprosy?" I asked.

"All of us, even the children."

I was moved with pity for these people and told them I would return some hours later to help them. Back at my mission, I loaded up my old Volkswagen with all the food, medicine, bandages, blankets, and clothing I could find and drove back to their village.

The village headman met me. He received all that I offered with disinterested detachment. My pride was hurt. I thought that even St. Vincent de Paul on one of his better days did not do as well as I had done. And these people did not even thank me!

Such was my vanity and egotism. I have learned since that it is *I* who should have thanked *them* for the privilege of ministering to Christ in them. I asked the headman if he would like me to come and say Mass in their village.

Reflecting the deep depression that was in the heart of everyone there, he said, "Oh, all right. If you want to." He showed little enthusiasm at my suggestion.

As I stood there, still wounded in my pride, I sensed an inner voice say, *"Do not worry. You have done all that you can do. But come and celebrate the Eucharist for them and allow Me to do what I alone can do."*

The following Tuesday I celebrated the Eucharist in a large lean-to hut that they used for their meetings. *Lord,* I prayed, *do not allow the atmosphere inside this hut to affect me. I do not want to embarrass these poor folks in any way.*

I spoke to them about the Our Father—The Lord's Prayer—and the love and care the Father shows for His children. *Why am I saying this to these poor people who have experienced so little of the Father's love or care?* I thought. *Not only are they starving and suffering from leprosy, but they are liable to be bombed or killed in this terrible civil war.*

After Mass, I came out into the sunlight and stood there with the catechist. For a long time, no one came out of the hut, which was strange. Eventually, after about a quarter of an hour, the villagers began to emerge. One by one they came toward me, starting with the children. They performed a strange little ritual uncharacteristic of Africans. They came over, took my hands, and kissed them. Finally, when all of them had done this, the headman stood in front of me. Tears ran down his face.

Hardly able to speak, he said, "Father, I thank you on behalf of all of our people. Today you have brought Jesus amongst us once again."

I suddenly realized that the dark cloud of depression that hung over them had lifted. The women were talking, the men were laughing, and the children were playing in the sunlight. I recalled the earlier words I had heard in my heart: *"Come celebrate the Eucharist, and allow Me to do what I alone can do."*

I always believed deeply in the power of the Eucharist to transform people's lives, but I had never witnessed it so graphically displayed as I did amongst those poor, suffering people on that hot afternoon. Normally, they *attended* the Eucharist. Today they were *living* it.

The poor can teach us many things. When we priests minister to them, the power and presence of Jesus work miracles. I had many other experiences during this time, but I would need an entire book to tell them all.

My missionary career in Nigeria ended on New Year's Day 1970 when I was medevacked out of the country with several different tropical diseases. The war ended, and Nigeria was reunited.

One of the things about being a missionary was that I experienced aspects of the Church's work of which most people are unaware. My admiration for the priests, brothers, and my own Vincentian confrères who worked in Africa during this turbulent time is unbounded. It is surpassed only by my admiration of what the missionary sisters accomplished. What these great women did there and in so many places throughout the world is a wonderful story. It is a chapter in the Church's life that has yet to be written.

My missionary career was interrupted in 1968 when I was asked to complete postgraduate studies at the Catholic University of America. The contrast between missionary life in Africa and the academic world of Catholic University could not have been greater. I arrived in July of 1968, just a week before the publication of *Humanae Vitae*. The reaction on campus to this document was negative, to say the least.

I attended a now-famous meeting of theologians held to protest Pope Blessed Paul VI's historic encyclical. Many of the "big name" theologians were in attendance, all of them unanimous in their opposition to Pope Paul VI and *Humanae Vitae*. One of the speakers berated Pope Paul for daring to suggest that significant abuses would follow the free availability of artificial contraception.

I wonder what he would say today. Even Pope Paul in his most depressed moments could never have imagined what was to come and what bitter fruits the sexual revolution would produce. If ever a man was a prophet, and if ever a papal encyclical turned out to be a prophetic statement, it was Pope Blessed Paul VI and his much reviled *Humanae Vitae*.

The next phase of my ministry took me to All Hallows Seminary, Dublin, where I was appointed the spiritual director to the seminarians. I remained at that post all during the seventies, which was a time of great change—not all of it for the better. I was glad to be involved in the work of seminary training, even though I found the transition difficult to make. But I could see how important this work was to the Church, and I was delighted to see so many fine young men go through and be ordained.

During my time in All Hallows Seminary, we kept hearing reports of priests leaving the ministry. I asked myself what could be done about this crisis. It was then that I started a program for the spiritual renewal of the priesthood. It was modeled on a movement set up in the United States by Fr. George Kosicki, C.S.B. The aim was to gather priests together to pray and intercede for the priesthood, and specifically for the spiritual renewal of priests throughout the world. Since its beginning in 1976, this program has grown in strength from year to year and is clearly meeting a need in the spiritual lives of many Irish priests, and also others from outside Ireland.

Through my involvement with this, I began to work in a full-time ministry to priests in 1985. I worked in collaboration with Sr. Briege McKenna, O.S.C., and—with the blessing of our respective superiors—we formed a team to give priests' retreats. Since 1985, our retreats to clergy have spanned every continent and in more countries than I can remember.

It appears that everything I experienced in the priesthood has been a preparation for the work that I intend to keep doing until the Lord tells me to stop. We priests are expected to minister to everyone and to give to everyone, but there are few opportunities for us to receive ministry. I thank the good Lord for the grace to be involved in such a unique ministry.

I have felt particularly blessed that so much of my priestly ministry coincided with the pontificate of Pope Saint John Paul II. I remember the great thrill everyone experienced when he was elected. I was never disappointed in this great man. He was an exceptional influence on my own life and on the life of the Church, to say nothing of his historic influence on the world stage.

I read his writings avidly and am grateful to God for giving us a man who proclaimed the Word "in season and out of season," and welcome or unwelcome, he insisted upon it. His personal holiness, his physical courage, his profound intellect, his deep sensitivity to the needs of the poor, his reaching out to the other churches, and his truly priestly heart will bear fruit for generations to come.

It is a great pity that much of what he has written, particularly his *Theology of the Body*, has been so little heeded by the church at large. I had the privilege of celebrating the Eucharist with him on one occasion, and I was immensely impressed by his deep faith and devotion. What I particularly loved about this good man was the simplicity with which he showed himself to be a devoted child of Mary. I believe that he, more than anyone else, has been instrumental in the great revival of devotion to Mary, the Mother of God.

In connection with Pope Saint John Paul II, I had a strange experience at the World Youth Day in Paris some years ago. Before going, a priest said to me, "If you see the pope, tell him to take a leaf out of the book of his brother bishops and retire." I thought at the time that it was a particularly peevish and unkind comment but forgot about it until the Mass at the World Youth Day. I was privileged to con-celebrate that day, but I was far away from the Holy Father. I could see him at a distance on the stage. I was, however, fortunate enough to be beside a large television screen on which I could plainly see him.

As he walked across the stage bent over and obviously in pain, the words of the priest came back to me. *Maybe he should retire,* I thought. *Maybe it is time for him to bow out.* But no sooner did the thought come to my mind, when an inner voice said to me, *"How can he resign from being a living image of My suffering Servant? How can he retire from being the very presence of My crucified Son? Now is the most fruitful period of his ministry."*

I was astonished by this thought. Being old and infirmed and having to suffer is part of a normal human life. When his contemporaries or other people see him in pain, yet still proclaiming the gospel, we take heart. Old age and infirmity have their own power and can bring blessing to the Church. Pope Saint John Paul II was a man and a saint, and I thank God for this great pastor and for the authority of Peter, which he exercised so courageously and prophetically in the world.

Making Jesus present in the world, acting *in persona Christi,* is something the Holy Spirit continues to teach me. I regret that so many priests seem not to value the sacraments as much anymore. I witnessed a priest deny the Eucharistic presence in a church filled with young people.

During my life, I have experienced a great love for the Eucharist and the sacrament of Reconciliation. The healing ministry, I believe, is exercised by priests in the Church through the sacrament of the Anointing of the Sick and prayer. Over the years, I witnessed countless miracles take place through this sacrament. I believe that any priest who lays his hands on a sick person and prays for healing can expect healings to take place. All the Lord wants from us is simple faith.

The controversy surrounding the priesthood today, particularly regarding the ordination of women, has caused great division and disaffection. I believe completely in the pope's teaching on this matter. I cannot help but think of what happened in the Church of England when it decided, against the advice of Saint John Paul II, to go forward with the ordination of women. It split the Anglicans and has caused a great number of clergy and laity to leave the church.

Such division among Christians is not the work of the Holy Spirit. In my experience, the greatest opponents of the ordination of women are almost all female. When I think of the contribution of women to the up-building of the Church here in the United States, and how they have initiated whole systems of education, nursing, and healthcare, I am convinced that their most important role lies in the area of giving life and nurturing love in the world.

There is also the controversy surrounding clerical celibacy. I remember what Fr. Cantalamessa wrote in his little book on chastity: "The question is not why are Catholic priests celibate; but more rather, why are all ministers of the gospel not celibate?"

After all, it was Jesus Himself who *invented* celibacy, as we read in Matthew 19:10–12. Celibacy has been a source of great fruitfulness in the priestly ministry. One has only to think of men like St. Francis Xavier, St. Vincent de Paul, and many others to realize what a blessing this charism of celibacy has brought to the Church and to the lives and ministry of those who embrace it joyfully.

The shortage of priestly vocations is temporary. It is God who gives vocations. We need to pray: "The Lord of the harvest please send laborers into the harvest." I am sure that vocations have been affected by past scandals. I also know that most people realize the truth about this; namely, it is the fault of a very few, and the priests they know are good and faithful men whom they respect and love.

I am convinced of the importance of daily interior prayer. If I can, I like to pray in the presence of the Blessed Sacrament. I love to pray the Rosary and have a great devotion to our Blessed Lady, who has helped me so much in the course of my life, especially since I made the St. Louis de Montfort Consecration as a seminarian. She has been a real mother to me, a great friend and a powerful protector.

I have received many graces through the intercession of St. Joseph, St. Vincent, St. Edith Stein, and many other saints who have inspired me by their wonderful and dedicated lives. I love them all. After all these years of being a priest, I can say that I have cherished every moment. The priestly ministry was by far the best way for me to spend my life. If I had to do it all again, I would do it freely and joyfully.

Bio–

Fr. Kevin Scallon is the international Spiritual Advisor for Magnificat, A Ministry to Catholic Women. He was ordained in the Vincentian order in 1961. A native of Northern Ireland, he has served as a parish priest in England, as a missionary in Africa for five years, as seminary spiritual director, and director of retreats and missions. In 1976, he began Intercession for Priests, which has developed into a worldwide, full-time ministry to priests. His great love for Jesus is evident in his Eucharistic healing services. He is the author of *I Will Come Myself* and *Is Anyone Sick Among You?*

Rev. Fr. Raymond Skonezny, S.T.L., S.S.L.

————⊶◇◇⊷————

A s I share this testimony I approach my eighty-first year. I have many stories to share, especially certain incidences in my life. In so doing, I see that nothing has happened by chance. Divine Providence guides, directs, and helps us in all our lives.

I was born in the small coal-mining town of Connellsville, Pennsylvania, on May 11, 1929. One of my grandparents came from Poland; the other from Germany. When they migrated to the United States back in the 1880s and 1890s, they required sponsors. That was the only way an immigrant could enter. In the cases for both sides of my family, the sponsors came from a huge coal-mining area in Pennsylvania.

Growing up in 1938, I attended a public school close to my grandparents' home. I recall my grandfather Ignatius Zimmerman's comments after listening to Hitler speaking on the shortwave radio. "That is a terrible man," he told his son Edward. "He has a lot of charism in what he says and how he says it, but he is going to cause a great amount of harm!"

I didn't realize what he was talking about, of course. In 1938, Hitler marched into Czechoslovakia; in 1939 he invaded Poland. On September 1, 1939, England declared war on Germany—the Second World War.

The Zimmerman family on my mother's side had six sons and six daughters. The sons went to war, and one of them was killed in New Guinea. One son fought in all the wars in the Pacific Ocean and managed to survive. Another was a tank commander in Fort Knox. They all went to war and fought bravely, and I have a recollection of this time.

Peddling papers during the war, I remember one newspaper's headlines: "Forty-five B17 planes were shot down going to Trieste." Every B17 bomber had ten men in it, and therefore 450 men were killed. They had awakened that morning in England, gone to war over Germany, and were killed. It was a common event at the time, but it made a profound impact on me and really stuck in my mind.

Fortunately, I was too young to get drafted into that war, and Dad was too old. He tried to sign up for the Army, but they did not accept him. He had seven children to support. My family ended up with nine children, although the last baby died at about six months, so eight children remained.

I recall passing the coal mine and watching the men coming out of the mines with their faces black as black can be from coal dust. Dad worked in the mines too, but I never saw him that way. My father's best boyhood friend, a single man who was also my godfather, was killed in the mine about five feet away from my father. The roof collapsed, and he was crushed.

I was deeply impacted by this event as a youth. I was also edified to see how my mother greatly supported her husband over the death of his childhood friend. She strengthened him when Dad pondered why he hadn't died. My mother reminded him that God had probably spared him for the sake of his treasure—his eight children.

There was fear when we heard the whistle blow because we knew something had happened at the mine. The wives and other townsfolk would head to the mine to learn what had happened. Had somebody been killed? It was a dangerous place to work. My father was eventually transferred to the coal-pumping room and took care of the pumps. When the mine shut down after the war, my family moved to California.

I graduated from high school in 1946 and enlisted in the Navy, with the promise of receiving a four-year college education afterward. My mother—with tears in her eyes—said, "So soon, Ray, so soon. You are leaving so soon."

I was seventeen years old and wanted to see the world.

My mother and father were faithful religious parents. We said the Rosary often—practically every night. My mother made sure we kids were always dressed up to go to church. I became an altar server, so I was part of the church in that sense. My mother worked in the church, especially when they had strawberry festivals and things of that nature. She also took care of and cleaned the church every week.

The church was a reality in my life. I think Dad was there more from the influence of his wife, but ultimately he became active in the church.

One of the primary influences on my life in regards to religion was my mother's great love for Mary. I think my love for Mary stemmed from my mother's influence. I always had the sense that the Virgin Mary is my mother. On our kitchen wall beside the sink, Mother hung a picture of Our Lady of La Salette, who originates in southern France. Mary is sitting down with her hands over her face, crying over the sins of the people.

"Who is that?" I asked my mother.

She said, "That is your mother."

"What is she doing?

"She is crying."

"Why is she crying?

"She is crying over your sins."

Well, I was a young kid in high school, so I said, "She doesn't have to cry over my sins. I don't have any to begin with!"

My early years were formed by the influence of my Catholic family. I was the oldest child, so I had responsibility in taking care of my brothers and sisters. I worked hard. We were a working-class family, but we had everything we needed. We had a home and a garden. We always had enough food. I marveled at how my mother planned the menus for such a large family on a small budget.

I joined the Navy because I dreamed of becoming a Navy pilot and going to Annapolis. As it turned out, I never took the test to enter Annapolis. I wasn't happy in Navy boot camp, but afterward I enjoyed attending the two radio (Morse code) schools. One dealt with Russian codes and the other in English codes. I worked in naval intelligence and spent two years in Yokosuka, Japan.

My last year in the Navy was 1950. I was stationed on the large naval base south of Yokohama, Tokyo Bay. One evening when I was headed out on liberty, it began to rain, so I ducked into the library. On the front desk, I noticed a book. The cover jacket caught my attention. The picture revealed a monk with a cowl hood over his head and his hands folded in prayer.

"Who is that?" I asked.

"A Catholic monk," the librarian replied.

"I thought they all died in the Middle Ages."

"No, they haven't," she said.

Curious, I picked up the book and started looking through the pictures of these monks working out in the field. They were in big Quonset huts in a monastery with their hands folded in prayer. Thomas Merton, a Trappist monk from Gethsemane Abbey, had written the book.

Later, I checked out the book and started reading it. Halfway through, however, I returned the book to the library. It was stirring me in a direction I did not want to go. It bothered me in the deep recesses of my heart—the idea of a man turning all of himself toward God alone.

I had plans for my life—to go according to my plans. With the GI bill following my years in the Navy, I planned to attend Notre Dame University. I hoped to get into the aeronautical engineering program.

I had all of these ideas and goals mapped out, but this book by Thomas Merton disrupted my future plans.

Even after returning the book to the library, I kept thinking about what it had presented—prayer and the gift of self to serve God. At that time my spiritual life consisted of going to Mass on Sundays, saying prayers, and saying the Rosary. That was it.

Thomas Merton's book depicted a way of life that was totally "consumed" by God. It was a life where monks gave themselves willingly and completely to God. They served Him in a quiet, hidden manner far removed from the world, but praying for the world. I had never thought about that.

I found myself going to the top of the barracks in the Yokosuka naval base, looking out at the star-filled sky. *What am I going to do with my life?* The end of my tour of duty was fast approaching. *Should I re-enlist? Do I really want to go to Notre Dame?*

"Yes, I do," I told myself.

Well then, what was gnawing at my mind and heart concerning God and the Trappist monastery? What was that all about?

Something else occurred around this time that deeply impacted me. It was Christmas Eve in Japan, and I was going to Mass alone. On my way, I heard discussions among the others that four chief petty officers had too much to drink at the club. They'd driven in the wrong direction and ended up driving their Jeep off a pier. They drowned.

This shocked me. I thought about these men on my way to Mass. *Is that how I'm going to end up someday? Is that what it is all about? Who are you, Raymond, and where are you going in your life?*

I went back to the library, checked out Thomas Merton's *Seven Story Mountain*, and finished reading it. The end of the book showed pictures of monasteries. I wrote to the monastery's abbot in Utah asking if I could visit, but I received no response. In a way I was relieved. I would be discharged from San Francisco and planned to take the train home to Pennsylvania.

The day I was leaving Japan on the bus to board the ship that would take me to San Francisco, we had a mail call. What do you know? There in my mail was a letter from the monastery! "Yes, we would be very happy to see you," the letter read. "Please stop by and see us on your way home."

There was some consternation, not knowing exactly what I should do. Well, I decided I might as well check it out. I visited the Trappist monastery outside Ogden, Utah. Then I resumed the train ride, passing by Notre Dame in South Bend, Indiana, on my way to my parents' home in Pennsylvania. I longingly looked at the golden dome of Notre Dame.

I was highly impressed by the men in the monastery in Utah. It was like a big farm with about 2,000 acres. The monks worked in the fields cutting alfalfa and making bales of hay, picking them up, and putting them in the barn. Then I watched them go into the church and pray.

They rose at 2:15 a.m., starting the Divine Office at 2:30 a.m.. It was a silent life. The monks didn't speak. They used sign language. That really took me aback. I don't know why. I had never been attracted to the diocesan priesthood. As a matter of fact, I was never attracted to the priesthood at all.

But this shook me up! It really disturbed me. So I talked to the abbot. "You know I have the GI bill. Do you think I could come back and check this place out?"

"Why don't you go to the delayed vocation school at St. Mary's College in Kentucky?" he suggested. "It's not far from a Trappist monastery there called Gethsemane."

I followed the abbot's suggestion. I applied and was accepted at St. Mary's. I took five years of Latin in one year—thirteen classes a week. I also took Greek, physics, and Shakespeare. I found the studies to be intense but I loved to study, so I enjoyed these classes. I went there for two years.

But I knew I had to go back to the monastery in Utah. If I didn't, it would always be in the back of my mind that somehow I didn't answer this call that I felt was coming from God. I stayed home for the summer and went back to school in the fall. At the end of that school year, I called the abbey and told them I was coming that fall.

"Please come," they said. "You're welcome here. Try it out and see if you want to stay."

After a period of thirty days at the monastery, I became a postulant and then spent two years as a novice. We had simple profession for three years, and it was a beautiful life!

There was a certain pattern to my life. I woke up at 2:15 a.m., went down to the church at 2:30, and we sang the Divine Office. At that time they had what was called Matins, and they had Lauds, and they had a half hour of mental prayer. Then we went to Prime, Tierce, Sext, None, Vespers, and Evening Prayer. Seven times a day (at least) we were praying in church. In between times—for at least two hours in the morning and two hours in the afternoon—we worked outside in the fields.

I was a student at the monastery and took philosophy for three years. I also had four years of theology. We studied in the morning and worked on the farm in the afternoon. I didn't mind the work. I was young. If I had a nickel for every bale of hay I picked up and put on the wagon, I would probably be a millionaire today.

As it happened, Rome sent a letter to all of the monasteries and churches, stating that anyone who planned to teach students who would ultimately be ordained must have an official license and credentials to teach. The abbot decided to send five of us to Rome. I was one of those chosen.

I could have gone to Ecole Biblique in Jerusalem, the Louvain in Belgium, or to the Angelicum or Biblicum in Rome. It was 1961, and I decided to go to Rome.

This was an incredible time for me. I had thought I would never leave the monastery. The only other time I left that monastery was when I went to the hospital. I'd caught my little finger in the metal grinder while working on bolts for a farm building, and I needed stitches.

Going to Rome was exciting, and I enjoyed everything about being there. The studies at the Angelicum and then the Biblicum were intense in order to receive a degree of "licentiate." A licentiate is something between a master's and a doctorate degree. The men at the Biblicum were mostly in their early twenties. I was thirty-six.

I found myself studying in Rome during the Second Vatican Council (1962 to 1965). We went to the Vatican, to St. Peter's Square, and watched the bishops, cardinals, and the pope as they went to St. Peter's for the conclave. For the first time in my life I grasped what it meant to belong to the Catholic Church.

It was incredible to see. I had come from a small coal-mining town, where my local parish Church was all I knew. Then after four years in the Navy, I entered monastic life in Utah. Now I was at the center of the Catholic Church during a historical council.

This had all started with Jesus and His eleven disciples in Galilee. "Go, therefore, and make disciples of all nations, baptizing them in the name of the Father, and of the Son, and of the Holy Spirit, teaching them to observe all that I have commanded you" (Matthew 28:19). That was 2,000 years ago. I marvel at the mystery of it all. The Church is beautiful. The Church is perfect in as far as it comes from God.

But we are not perfect. We have many flaws—ambition, greed, lust, anger, and all kinds of things that happen to people in the Church. It can happen to priests, to bishops, and even to cardinals. There are periods of time when the Church struggled. There is always a metanoia, the process of continual renewal in the Church.

My experience in Rome was mind-bending. It was enriching—the beauty and wonder and awe of the Catholic Church. I could talk to any other priest, even if I had to talk to them in Latin when I didn't know their language. The bishops had sent these men to learn and study in Rome to become teachers in their diocese.

It was an exciting time. A lot of things were happening, especially in the Biblical schools run by the Jesuits. As I listened to the Jesuit professors talking, I wondered what was going on. There were all kinds of ideas floating around in the Church at that time.

After I graduated and received my degrees, I went back to the monastery in Utah. The result was that I had lost my customary sequence of a monastic life. I found it difficult to return to the quiet, contemplative life after the busyness of Rome. Somehow, I lost my peace about monastic life.

I talked to the abbot and said, "I would like to go out into the world and maybe become a parish priest."

I also wrote to the Navy asking whether I could be a navy chaplain. The Navy responded positively. They asked me to get some parish experience and then call them. I went to the Los Angeles Archdiocese because my parents lived there. Shortly afterward, through the workings of the abbot and the bishop, I became a priest in the Orange Diocese. I became involved in parish life, different parish movements, and was invited to attend a Cursillo retreat weekend.

A Catholic couple asked me to go, but I said, "I don't need to go to that retreat. I was a monk for all those years."

"Well, Father, people in your parish are going. Maybe it would be a good idea if you knew what was going on there. Perhaps you could understand them better."

I considered their point and decided to go for their benefit.

Cursillos in Christianity is an apostolic movement of the Roman Catholic Church. It was founded in Majorca, Spain, by a group of laymen in 1944. The Cursillo focuses on showing Christian lay people how to become effective Christian leaders over the course of a three-day weekend.

The weekend includes fifteen talks, some given by priests and some by lay people. These talks are called "rollos." The major emphasis of the weekend is to ask participants to take what they have learned back into the world on what is known as the "fourth day." The method stresses personal spiritual development, as accelerated by weekly group reunions (after the weekend).

On my Cursillo weekend, I was completely taken aback. For the first time in my life I met a group of men—lay people—who humbled me. I surprised myself by this thought. Some of the men were truck drivers. Others worked in different fields. I met professors, lawyers, and doctors. They were ordinary lay Catholics, and all were very good, holy men.

I was impressed. The Lord touched me, and it affected my life profoundly. As a result of attending the retreat, I was asked by the person in charge if I would return to give some talks. I agreed. So, I gave some of the talks on the weekends following.

Shortly afterward, Bishop Johnson asked if I would be the priest director of the Cursillo movement in the Diocese of Orange. Rather reluctantly, I said I would. I remained the director for about twenty-four years—the best of my life. My priesthood was confirmed and influenced by the witness of committed lay leaders in the Church. As a priest, I was humbled by hearing the talk of lay leaders. Many recounted their sufferings, challenges, and commitment to live the faith, no matter how difficult their situations.

I became great friends with many of the lay leaders, and we developed into a family of brothers and sisters. I know their wives and children. Twenty-five years later I am still "grouping" with many of the same men once a week, every Thursday. I call it a "geriatric club." During the meetings, we discuss our interior life, what we read, and how we strive to improve our spiritual life. In a certain sense I have become responsible to these men, and they become responsible to each other to live the Catholic faith.

In 1992, a group of ladies contacted me to share about Magnificat, a Ministry to Catholic Women. I learned it had started in New Orleans. The goal was women helping one another live the spirituality of Mary and Elizabeth at the visitation scene (cf. Luke's Gospel).

I approved and said, "That sounds like a good idea." I had five sisters and felt one of the things lacking in the Church was a strong women's movement. Magnificat was both Marian and Charismatic.

Shortly afterward, I served on the board of directors for the Lestonnac free medical clinic begun by Sister Marie Therese Solomon. Sister asked another board member, Kathleen Beckman, to help arrange a spiritual pilgrimage to Lourdes. On the pilgrimage, I spoke to Kathleen about starting Magnificat in the Diocese of Orange.

Kathleen was reluctant to commit. She was a young mother with two grade-school children and was also helping her husband start a business. I invited her to a Magnificat prayer breakfast in the Los Angeles Archdiocese, and she agreed to attend.

Once we had the experience of attending a Magnificat breakfast, we met with four other ladies who desired to start a chapter, and a team was formed. I went to Bishop Norman McFarland and asked permission to begin Magnificat in the Orange Diocese. He asked me to be the Spiritual Advisor and gave permission for the start of the chapter in 1992.

In the process of being in Magnificat, I became acquainted with Charismatic spirituality for the first time. I was hesitant in the beginning. This was a new experience for my priesthood. It took me a while to learn about the spirituality behind some of the Charismatic manifestations such as the raising of hands in praise and worship, resting in the Spirit, and praying with the gift of tongues. But I realize that these are charisms of the

Holy Spirit given for the good of the Church.

Magnificat has become very important to me. When I retired from Cursillo, Magnificat became a central part of my priestly life. It seemed that every time I turned on EWTN, I saw one of our Magnificat speakers— Johnnette Benkovic, Archbishop Cordileone, Bishop Cirilo Flores, and Archbishop Cordileone's mother, Mary Cordileone.

We were excited when Bishop Cordileone's mother, Mary, agreed to speak at our Orange Magnificat Chapter following the bishop's testimony. I was impressed by Mrs. Mary Cordileone. Her simplicity, authenticity, and deep faith were evident as she told her story of an Italian Catholic mother of a priest—a bishop now. Her husband was a fisherman and frequently away on the ocean fishing. When they brought in the fish, they had money. When they didn't bring in the fish, they had difficulty. They had to borrow money, but they always paid it back.

Mary Cordileone lived a Catholic life: simple, authentic, and real. There was nothing flashy or extraordinary. She was much like my own mother, who lived a quiet, Catholic life with a great love for Mary, the Lord, the sacraments, and prayer—especially the Rosary. To my way of thinking, women like this, ordinary mothers, are the heart of the Church.

What is the beauty of Magnificat? It brings out the beauty of feminine dignity, a purpose, and a destiny that belongs to women. No one can take it away. Simply, that you who come to Magnificat would always pick up the spirit of Magnificat—the dignity and value you have as woman—and that you would use this to touch other women in your life.

This is not meant to be something you hide within yourself. You should give it away by lifting up and encouraging other women, and by helping them discover the dignity they possess. You can teach them to open their hearts to God. You can teach them to love our Blessed Mother.

I encourage you not only to come to a Magnificat meal, but also to have a sense of your dignity as women, the sense of your value, and the role you play in today's world, which is very important. Without your maternal help, without your prayers for the priests and the bishops, they will lose the gentleness and love they need to be true shepherds.

Look at Jesus holding a lamb. We are all His lambs. Priests must have that image in their own minds that they are gentle with the lambs of the Church, and with the lambs in the world.

I will pray for you. Please pray not only for me but also for all priests, bishops, and the cardinals. Pray for our Church. The world does not like us. The Church is meant to have gentleness, humility, obedience, and above all—love for God, and to love that Mother who always says, "Do whatever

He tells you" (John 2:5).

Another ministry the Lord called me into was deliverance and exorcism. Having trained with other priest exorcists and their teams, I served on the diocesan healing, deliverance, and exorcism team for years. I witnessed several major rites of exorcism. I mention this because a great spiritual battle is presently waging. I ardently encourage you to wear the armor of God (Ephesians 6). Keep praying. Keep living a sacramental life. Call on St. Michael, the angels, and the saints to help you in the fight against evil.

This ministry has intensified my awareness of the power of the chief exorcist working through the ministerial priesthood. But the priest never works alone in this battle. We are grateful for our lay teams who work alongside us. We must continue to proclaim the victory of Christ.

In June 2015, years after I gave my testimony at a Magnificat prayer breakfast, I entered the hospital to undergo open-heart surgery. I planned on being in the hospital for seven to ten days and told my friends I would be up and walking the day after surgery.

As it turned out, I spent three months post-op in the cardiac intensive care unit of Hoag Hospital in Newport Beach. I don't recall all I underwent during that time, but I do recall several key lessons—both spiritual and physical.

I was tormented by evil spirits one night, who tempted me in this manner: "Your God doesn't care. You're a fool for believing. You are alone, and your God doesn't care about your suffering." It was difficult to fight the good fight in my physical weakness. It was a spiritual battle that went on all night long. Ultimately, though, I gathered up all my strength and said, "This is what I believe." I recited the Apostles' Creed, and the devil left.

On another occasion, I experienced the image and presence of Jesus, the Divine Mercy. This was a time when I was almost ready to give up. Jesus of Mercy—the promises given to Saint Faustina in her diary—flooded my soul to strengthen me in the course of recovery.

One time I went into a coma for several days. Close friends and the Norbertine Fathers gathered at the foot of my hospital bed to offer the Holy Sacrifice of the Mass. Once, during the actual consecration of the Holy Mass, I awoke from the coma, repeating the words of consecration—words that were so familiar to me over the course of my fifty-five years of priesthood. I opened my eyes to the amazement of all who were in the room who thought I was dying. God's mercy is truly amazing.

There were many spiritual experiences, lessons of love and mercy that I learned during my three months in the intensive care unit. I was finally discharged to a nursing home for a time of rehabilitation. Then God's providence arranged for the Norbertine Fathers of St. Michael's Abbey to invite me to live with them. They would provide the medical and spiritual help I now need at the age of eighty-seven.

I have come full circle and once again live as a monk at an abbey. My life has been and still is one of prayer, silence, solitude, reading, and contemplation. Besides the Norbertine Fathers of St. Michael's Abbey, my Cursillo and Magnificat friends continue to bless me with the gift of holy companionship and intercessory prayer.

For that I am thankful.

Bio –

Father Skonezny, the eldest of nine children, grew up in a Catholic family in Connellsville, Pennsylvania. After serving in the U.S. Navy for four years, he discerned the call to become a Trappist monk. He entered Holy Trinity Trappist Monastery in Huntsville, Utah, in 1952. In 1961, he was ordained a priest. The abbot then sent him to Rome, where Father Skonezny studied at the Angelicum and the Biblicum, and received licentiates in Sacred Theology and in Sacred Scripture. After seventeen years in the Trappist monastery, the Lord called him to the diocesan priesthood in the Diocese of Orange, close to where his aging parents lived. He was assigned as the director of the Cursillo movement, where he served for twenty-five years. From 1992 to 2012, he served as the Spiritual Advisor for the Orange Diocese Magnificat.

Rev. Fr. John Struzzo, C.S.C.

I believe that beginning with our experience in the womb, we develop attitudes, values, and beliefs that help us survive childhood traumas, abuses, and wounds. These also influence our future religiosity and spirituality. Before I was born, my mother's first three pregnancies were miscarriages. The next three were boys who died within the first year of their births.

Pregnancy number seven was my older sister, who was thought to have Down syndrome. She had the mentality of a four-year-old. My older brother was the first normal birth, and I was number eleven, born five years after another sister.

My mother had coughing episodes, sometimes lasting three to four hours every day, and suffered from a severe infection in her lungs most of her life. When she carried me she coughed quite a bit, which I believe led me to become an anxious child. In spite of her illness, my father expected my mother to do very hard work on our farm, as well as all the housework. We had no indoor plumbing or running water while she was alive.

When I was four years old, my older sister taught me how to read and write. She often read me stories. She continued to tutor me until I was eleven, when she left home for nursing school. By the time I was in the third grade, I was reading at a high school level, and I was doing algebra and advanced math.

My mother died when I was eight years old. She was in the hospital for four months, but since I was under fourteen years of age, I was not allowed to visit her. Not permitted to attend the funeral, I never really grieved over her death. Nor did I really know her because she was always sick or busy with chores.

My mother made everything—including my clothes and curtains in the house—from flour sacks, which she bleached and then dyed. Although she had eleven brothers and sisters, they never visited, since they disliked my father so much. My father was a jealous man. He did not encourage my mother to make friends with our neighbors, nor did he allow her to go to church. He went to Mass on Christmas, Easter, and St. Joseph's Day, the only time the entire family went to Mass together. We attended the Holy Rosary Church where most of the parishioners were Italian immigrants, about fifteen miles away in Kansas City, Missouri.

When I was nine, an Irish Catholic family moved nearby, a half mile away. They had eleven children who became my friends. I frequently stayed overnight and ate meals with them. They were materially very poor, but generous and loving. They became my substitute family with whom I attended Mass on a regular basis. The youngest, who was three years old at the time, remains one of my best friends. I visit him annually, even though he lives in Kentucky. I performed the marriage for his three boys, and I baptized all his grandchildren.

My father cursed frequently and was very abusive, angry, and often violent. Consequently, I never knew him personally and avoided him as much as possible. I remember him using the horsewhip to beat my older brothers until they bled. Since I was the youngest in an Italian family, I was not abused. But seeing my brothers and sisters being abused affected me greatly—as if it had been done to me.

My father remarried when I was twelve. He had met the woman only once, and the marriage was arranged. She had four children, was German, very poor, and a fundamentalist Protestant. I didn't get along with her or with her children. There was little common ground between us: the difference of faith, nationality, and her children, who received mostly D's and F's. When I received all A's, this made her angry.

Before this time, when I was eight, I had begun working in the fields at nearby farms, where I picked various fruits and vegetables. This allowed me to pay most of my own expenses from the little money I made. My new stepbrothers stole my money, which I kept in a dresser in my bedroom. When I complained, my stepmother blamed me for not being more careful. She was not kind. One time I overheard her telling her children, "We can have our dessert now. John is asleep."

I recall asking my stepmother a sensitive question about sex, but her response was laughter. After this, I never asked her anything more. I also realized that my father and stepmother did not seem to care if I was home or not. Thus, I spent many overnights with the kids I tutored or with my Irish neighbors. I was in the fourth grade and attending public school when my teacher first asked me to tutor the slower students in my class. This practice continued during the rest of my grade school and high school years as well as during college. I realized that I learned much more when I could teach others.

In the sixth grade, I attended a Catholic school. My father would not pay my tuition, so I had to work for it myself. My pastor provided me with odd jobs to make it possible. As an altar boy, I served most of the weddings and funerals and received one- or two-dollar stipends. Other jobs included counting the collection money and doing janitorial work for the pastor. One of the main benefits of going to a Catholic school was attending daily Mass and learning about the faith. This sustained me in many ways until entering the seminary.

After completing grade school, I wanted to go to the Catholic high school, which was in the city seven miles from where I lived. I often hitchhiked to get to school. My father was not supportive. When school ended at three o'clock, I walked to my job, which was next door to the canteen in the hospital. It was a mini-drugstore and sold food such as milkshakes, chili, and sandwiches. We also sold over-the-counter medicines and gift items for the patients.

Work ended at 9:30 p.m.. I returned the keys to the owner and walked to the bus station a mile away to catch the eleven o'clock Greyhound bus home. My stop was along the highway, another mile from my house. I arrived home about midnight and studied until five o'clock in the morning. I would sleep about an hour. Then I got up and—skipping breakfast— milked the cows and hitchhiked to school. By this time, my brothers and sisters had all left home, so I had to cook for myself if I wanted to eat. I would spend a quarter for lunch at school, and I could eat what I wanted at the canteen in the evening.

I worked like this about four nights a week. On weekends, I did janitorial work for the hospital and the school of nursing, which was next door. This was my schedule during my first three years of high school. My teachers encouraged me to try for a scholarship at Notre Dame but said I needed to get involved in more extracurricular activities. I soon became student manager of baseball and basketball; joined the glee club; and joined the National Honor Society. I still worked on weekends, but I had to quit my job during the week to fit in these activities.

During my junior year, my pastor told me that I should consider becoming a priest. We had a Holy Cross priest from Notre Dame at our parish during our annual mission. I came to know him personally, and I liked the Notre Dame football team, so that seemed like a good place to start. My freshman-year counselor told me I would never make it at Notre Dame. My SAT scores were not comparable to most students at Notre Dame.

But God is good, and I received a scholarship from Notre Dame. I had considered being a priest since my altar boy days. Since I was ten years old until I was about eighteen, I served Mass regularly. So, while I was there, I joined the Congregation of Holy Cross.

For the first time in my life, I felt part of a family. I found Notre Dame to be strict and theologically orthodox. I graduated in the top two percent of the university and was told I was an overachiever (after being told previously that I would not get into the university). Sometimes you just can't win!

I enjoyed my time at Notre Dame, and I enjoyed being in the seminary after my first year. The seminary was located across the lake from the university, although we had total access to the campus.

The seminary was very rigorous. We got up at six o'clock in the morning, said morning prayers, went to Mass, and had time for meditation and thanksgiving after Mass. Breakfast was served at eight o'clock, then a time of silence for inner reflection most of the day, except when at the university.

In the evening, we were not allowed to visit the university without special permission from the rector of the seminary. Because of my experience with my father, I became fearful and mistrustful of authority figures. I had learned at home that I could not trust anyone to be there for me, so I had better do things myself. Although I didn't realize it at the time, I didn't even trust God.

I wouldn't ask for help unless I had no choice. I was somewhat paranoid, anxious, and scrupulous during my seminary years. During my training, I spent one year at our novitiate in Minnesota. This is like a religious boot camp, where seminarians are weeded out.

We began the day at 4:45 a.m., sang the Divine Office, and had one hour of meditation. Then we celebrated a High Mass and had thanksgiving afterward. Breakfast was at 8:30 a.m., and then we would study the spirituality of the Holy Cross and Gregorian chant.

The examination of conscience took place before lunch. After the meal, we worked hard doing manual labor in the afternoon. At 5:00 p.m., we had another hour of meditation and evening prayer. After supper a nightly prayer, then bedtime was 9:00 p.m.

We had silence during the week except for two hours on Sunday and Wednesday afternoons. At this time, we could talk at meals and on feast days. It was a time of rigorous spiritual training. We were never allowed to leave the grounds except in an extreme emergency. We could not take naps or drink coffee during the day. We had no access to the media. No newspapers, television, or radio.

In hindsight, the weakness of the program was the fact that it ignored human psychological and psycho-sexual development, and much of the spiritual teaching was beyond most of us. Grace builds upon nature. Instead of integrating our emotions and passions into our total personality, we tended to repress them.

After graduating from Notre Dame, I went to Washington D.C. to begin my theological training. Holy Cross had its own graduate school in theology near Catholic University. I was there for four years and enjoyed it. Washington is a great city.

We had one free day a week. Some of us would go to the Congress, the Supreme Court, or visit the White House, as well as the museums. I learned much about the way our government works. It was while I was in Washington that President Kennedy was assassinated in Dallas. I stood outside the cathedral and witnessed the dignitaries as they attended his funeral Mass.

Since the theology school was in the process of becoming re-accredited by the Mid-Atlantic States Association for the graduate program, the theologians were encouraged to complete a thorough investigation of every aspect of seminary life and curriculum. The theology program consisted of four years, after which—if approved—there was ordination to the priesthood. The class before ours had developed a one-hundred-page questionnaire for all theology seminarians to fill out.

Just before my deacon year, my last year of theology, the questionnaire was tabulated. I was elected chairman of the theology school to implement the results of the questionnaire. The first thing I did was abolish every other committee, which was agreed upon by the faculty and fellow theologians. We had 120 theologians and approximately thirty professors at the seminary, mostly Holy Cross priests. As chairman, I felt the most important change needed was to make theology more pastoral. Our committee met once a month and I decided that in the third month we would tackle the issue of pastoral theology.

I began the meeting with a discussion of the meaning of pastoral theology. This gathering included the faculty and eight of us who represented the seminarians, although all the other seminarians were present too. After an hour-long explanation, I said, "Now we agree on what it means to be pastoral," even though I realized that we did not all agree.

I then launched into a discussion about the practical implications for reforming our curriculum, beginning by suggesting that an obvious change would be to reduce canon law from four years to one year of study. The canon law professor, who was also our seminary assistant superior, asked what aspects we thought should be changed. I explained that we spent an entire year discussing penalties in the church: excommunication, suspension, and interdict. For all its practical value, the nuances could be discussed in one week.

Our canon law professor said, "John, you don't understand how much of this you need to know as a priest."

"Father," I replied, "you have been a priest for twenty-five years. On weekends, you have heard confessions and celebrated Mass at our co-cathedral in downtown Washington. How many cases of excommunication have you heard in these past years?"

"One," he said.

I then asked the same question of each member of the faculty. No one could give me one case. I said, "I rest my case," adding that if there was any place in the country where people would confess behavior that deserved penalties in the church, the co-cathedral would be an obvious location. It saw numerous visitors in that area, and the fact that it was anonymous.

The canon lawyer said, "John, don't you think the Vatican would tell me not to teach all these things if they were not necessary?"

"No, they would expect you to use your common sense," I replied.

The superior interrupted the meeting. "Let's end now before we come to blows."

In retrospect, I really respect Holy Cross for allowing such discussions, which were rare in most seminaries. Most of us in Washington D.C. had been through Notre Dame and had been taught to think for ourselves. My class included men with graduate degrees, and one had a doctorate in law. We could back up everything we asserted, and all were well respected academically. Yet, I was concerned as to whether my assertiveness and constant questioning would hinder my acceptance to the priesthood.

I had been kicked out of class twice by one professor, whom I judged to be incompetent. The dean of the college was my spiritual director and a friend. He immediately put me back in the class and gave me more ammunition to question the professor because he wanted to remove him from the faculty. This priest refused to teach our class again, but was reassigned to us during our deacon year. He made his class a total self-directed study, where we simply took tests and assembled but rarely discussed what we learned. In my estimation, it was one of the better classes we had. This priest was eventually made a bishop in Rome.

At the end of my deacon year, I was approved for final vows and was ordained a priest in 1965, toward the end of Vatican II. After the council ended I—like many other priests—was confused about the teachings of the Church and its practices. Many priests at that time were simply telling their people to follow their conscience, without understanding what conscience meant and how to form one's conscience. This was especially true on the topic of birth control and issues related to sexuality. In retrospect, I realize I too was rebellious against the Church's authority, an extension of my relationship with my father.

After ordination, I was assigned to a large parish in South Bend, Indiana, for four months. When I arrived at the parish, I walked in on the pastor hugging and kissing the cook. He looked at me and asked, "Who are you?" I introduced myself, and all he said to me was, "Don't trust anyone, not even me."

This reinforced my feelings of self-reliance. He then left for a three month summer sabbatical to celebrate his twenty-fifth anniversary of ordination. The assistant pastor, who I was to replace, was packing to leave the priesthood for marriage. I was left—fresh out of seminary and ordination—with an older priest to run the parish.

This illustrates the kind of confusion much of the Church was going through at that time. Because there were only two of us, I was very busy the whole summer. I was left with many marriage cases to resolve, and with much counseling. I enjoyed the work and got along well with the older priest, who was acting as pastor.

The pastor had received many gifts of wine for his twenty-fifth anniversary, so we had many visitors for dinner throughout the summer. The cook was renowned for her skill, and the pastor insisted that dinner would be a special time for the priests to be together without phone interruptions. He insisted that every dinner would include a tablecloth and good wine.

At the end of my tenure at this parish, I returned to the University of Notre Dame to continue my graduate work in sociology and became the chaplain to the freshman class. I lived in a dorm with the freshman and found it enjoyable. In that dorm, we had a special chapel that allowed me to say Mass daily and hear confessions regularly.

The rector of the dorm spent most of his time in the laboratory doing experiments in botany. He had just received a PhD in botany. Consequently, I was the rector in effect. Every Tuesday I had a special Mass for those who had made a Cursillo, which was a weekend retreat. In that group were people like Ralph Martin, Steve Clark, and others who later became leaders of the Charismatic movement.

After one year at Notre Dame, I completed my Master's Degree in Sociology. I asked my superiors' permission to continue studying psychology and religion at Columbia University and Union Theological Seminary. No Catholic priest had ever studied religion at a secular university or a Protestant seminary.

My superiors said no. They told me I was needed at a high school in Chicago. I went to Chicago and taught at Notre Dame High School. The principal asked me what I was doing there. I told him that I was supposedly needed. He said that was not true, but since I was there, he asked me to start a new department in social studies. I spent a year teaching four classes in sociology. Two of the classes were senior honor students, and two others were comprised mostly of the seniors who were on disciplinary probation.

I did well with both groups. Instead of immediately disciplining the latter group, I called them in one by one to talk. I listened to their problems and developed a positive rapport. The most difficult of these students told me that when he was a young child, his father would take him to a house of prostitution. While his father was visiting the prostitutes, his son sat on the steps outside the house, waiting.

The boy loved his mother very much and was confused about his father's behavior. This student later became involved with drugs and sexual promiscuity. I had empathy for him and gave him assignments to study drugs and sexual behavior among youth, as well as other social problems. He found these assignments very interesting and did well with them.

After finishing one year of teaching at the high school, I decided to complete my Doctorate in Sociology. Even though my religious Community desired that I attend the best schools in the country, I went to Florida State University. I felt inadequate going to an Ivy League university, even though I had an A average at Notre Dame. I completed my doctorate at Florida State in three years, while most students take much longer. My dissertation focused on the clergy in Washington D.C. who had publicly dissented on birth control. This was just after Pope Paul VI had issued his encyclical, *Humane Vitae.*

I discovered that those who dissented publicly did so out of great compassion for families that already had many children. They did not consider the encyclical infallible, and their dissent was a result of much discussion and prayer. A common thread was a specific course the priests attended on moral theology at the Catholic University with Fr. Charles Curran, a leader of the dissent movement.

I then compared those fifty-four priests with the remainder of the diocese, priests who did not publicly dissent. However, I found that many of them privately dissented and were telling people in the confessional to follow their conscience. They were doing the same with parishioners who had remarried outside the church without an annulment. The finding was the same when it came to the practice regarding artificial birth control.

I developed strong friendships with my colleagues during graduate school. This was also the time of the sexual revolution in America and rebellion against all authority. I became more and more liberal in my theological thinking and pastoral practice.

After I completed my doctorate, I applied to many universities for a teaching position. Even though I was groomed to teach at Notre Dame, in 1967 the university became private, no longer governed by the Congregation of Holy Cross. Consequently, the order could no longer appoint people to university positions. Priests had to compete like any other professor. The sociology and psychology departments at Notre Dame were anti-clerical. Thus, they did not want a priest in their departments. I eventually received offers at Northern Illinois University and Sacramento State University. I accepted the offer at Northern Illinois. The salary was significantly higher than that offered by California.

I was the first priest the university had ever hired. They began by asking if I was going to teach sociology or Catholicism. I shared with them an experience I'd had at Florida State when I was teaching as a doctoral student. A student in my class asked me if I was an atheist. This question came about because I explored all points of view in a discussion. Therefore, the student surmised it was obvious that I was an atheist. I told the student I was a Roman Catholic.

He said, "You can't be by the way you teach."

I explained that not only was I a Roman Catholic, but I was also a Catholic priest. However, I was not allowed to wear a collar in the classroom but had to dress in a coat and tie like the other professors.

I began to realize that teaching was a great gift from God. After four years at Northern Illinois University, I was nominated teacher of the year by the school of liberal arts. However, after four years of teaching not only sociology but also social psychology, marriage and family relations, and psychology, I became burned out. I was also involved in counseling with students and some faculty members. I was so successful that I decided to go back to school and earn a Post-Doctorate in Psychotherapy.

At that time, psychology was in its heyday. For every opening at the best schools, there were about 300 applicants. I was rejected by several top-ranked schools. A friend suggested that I should take a clinical pastoral education (CPE) course instead, which I did at the Worcester State Hospital in Massachusetts. CPE is a requirement for chaplain work in the military or in hospitals or prisons. Not only did I complete CPE in residence for one full year, but I also completed a psychiatric residency and studied clinical psychology and marriage and family psychotherapy at the same time. This entailed a ninety-hour week. Once again, I felt burned out after that year.

When I finished the year, I went to the Institutes of Religion and Health in New York City to complete a Post-Doctorate in Marriage and Family Therapy and Individual Psychotherapy. I took classes in the morning from eight o'clock until noon. Then from one o'clock in the afternoon until ten o'clock at night, I worked at a psychiatric clinic in Manhattan four days a week.

On the other day, I counseled at a marriage and family clinic on Long Island. While I was engaged in therapy, I was also required to go through therapy myself. Thus, I had individual and group therapy twice a week. This process began while I was in Worcester. Since I had basically grown up without a mother, I looked for a Jewish mother as my therapist. I thought the stereotype of a Jewish mother being a caring, involved, protective person was just what I needed.

The woman I found was cold, insensitive, and distant emotionally. At the end of our year together, she told me to tell my next therapist how difficult I was, and she was considered one of the better psychologists in New York.

The next year I found my "Jewish mother" in a man who had been trained in the same program that I was currently taking. He was a pastoral counselor. I found him to be understanding and sensitive to my needs and issues. I completed a three-year program in two years. I became close friends to several of my colleagues and mentors. Besides having supervision twice a week, I was also made a supervisor for the newer students.

Another dissertation was needed for my post doctorate. This time I selected a couple whom I counseled for a year and a half. I was also assisting at a parish on the upper West side of Manhattan on weekends, where I also resided. It was a rough section of Manhattan. I had to take the subway home late at night and then walk five blocks through a crime-ridden area. The rectory was robbed about every six weeks. However, it had the reputation of having some of the best preachers in New York. I felt honored to replace one of them.

After I completed the program at the Institutes of Religion and Health, I was offered a grant to start my own counseling center. I did this at my alma mater, Notre Dame University, for the general community of South Bend. It became quite successful, and I hired two associates to work with me to handle all the clients that requested treatment. I lived at a house in South Bend with two other Holy Cross religious. I enjoyed the work but disliked South Bend, Indiana. To me, it had one of the worst climates in the country.

After two years, I received an invitation to San Francisco to work as a therapist in a residential treatment center for priests and nuns. It was called the House of Affirmation. My role was individual therapy, group therapy, and psychodrama. I was also their main retreat presenter and lecturer throughout the country. While I was engaged there, I was involved in private psychotherapy at my home in San Francisco.

After five years at the House of Affirmation, I was once again burned out. I called my provincial, and he asked me what I would like to do next. I told him I wanted to stay in San Francisco and do private psychotherapy. Usually it takes about three or four years to develop a private practice, but I was able to do so in one year. I was already engaged in AIDS counseling in the region.

I found San Francisco an exciting city, with many opportunities for the theater, opera, dance, and excellent restaurants. As a result, I was becoming more secular and materialistic. Many of my friends were involved in the New Age movement and the occult. In fact, there was a popular New Age church in the area that I occasionally attended with my friends. I decided to study New Age philosophy and practices at the Berkeley Psychic School, where I engaged in those practices in a limited way for about seven years.

I believed that the future of theology was integration with Eastern religions. I became a disciple of Yogananda. He was one of the first gurus from India to visit the United States in the 1920s. His direct disciple was in San Francisco, with a large group of disciples and a house in San Francisco and in the Sierra Nevada about two hours away. I made retreats with them about twice a year and used their guru as a spiritual advisor.

I found it difficult to find parish work in San Francisco. Many priests were sent there by their bishops and provincials to find themselves. They therefore took up most of the weekend supply in the parish. I did assist in the mission area at St. James Parish, where thirty-eight different languages were spoken. I spent six years assisting on weekends at this parish, as well as with Mother Teresa's sisters nearby as a part-time chaplain for seven years. I had the privilege of meeting Mother Teresa twice a year, when she came during her sisters' profession of vows.

When I first met Mother Teresa, I disliked her because she preached blind obedience. This is something we in Holy Cross were trying to reject. We believed that it was good for religious to question authority and to have an enlightened obedience. Soon I came to appreciate the great holiness of Mother Teresa.

My life began to change radically in 1987. One of my great concerns was where to celebrate major holidays. When I was young, I made sure I worked on those days so I wouldn't be alone at home. I had a close friend, who used to be a Holy Cross seminarian, and who invited me to spend Christmas with his family. I spent a week with him in Florida. At the end of the week, his mother asked me if I would like to go to Medjugorje. This is where the Blessed Mother was thought to be appearing daily to six children since 1981.

I was not interested.

She said, "I've been trying to sponsor a priest. If you want to go, I will pay your way."

I asked her to give me time to consider the offer.

After three months of reflection and prayer, I decided to go to Medjugorje. My decision revolved around the free trip to a communist country—a first for me—and the thought that perhaps the occurrences in Medjugorje might be real. In May, I signed up with Yugo tours, operated by Yugoslavian Airlines and considered one of the worst airlines in the world at that time. We were supposed to stop at Split, Yugoslavia, and take a bus from there to Medjugorje.

The plane landed in Belgrade instead. We were stuck at the airport over twelve hours. Since it was a communist country, they gave us no information about how to get to Medjugorje from there. I finally learned there would be a flight to Dubrovnik late at night. I called our hosts in Medjugorje and explained our circumstances. They advised me to take the flight and then take a bus from Dubrovnik to Medjugorje, which they would arrange. We were supposed to arrive in Medjugorje at two o'clock in the afternoon, but instead got there at three o'clock the next morning. However, our host was waiting for us with dinner and a warm welcome.

I decided that since this was a spiritual place, I should have a spiritual intention for being there. I told the Blessed Mother that my intention was about my priesthood. Priesthood had become very secondary to me in San Francisco, and my role as a psychotherapist was primary. When I got to the house in Medjugorje, I learned that the group staying at the same house would not let me be just another pilgrim. I had to be their chaplain. We were staying four nights, and at the time, there were 152 priests and two bishops visiting.

I learned that priests used to be in attendance during the time of the apparitions, so I went to the rectory and asked permission. The associate pastor told me that was no longer the case since it was now too crowded. Priests could go to the choir loft at apparition time, which only held a few people. He didn't sound hopeful.

That evening I went to the rectory and asked the pastor if I could attend the apparition. Surprisingly, the pastor granted permission for the next day as the secretary to the bishop. I went to the apparition and saw three flashes of light on the wall in front of me.

I thought they were reflections of cars passing by. However, there were no windows in the choir loft. I discovered later it was Mary's calling card, by which she began all her apparitions.

The apparition lasted about six minutes. During that time, I cried uncontrollably but silently—not with sadness but with a joyful release. There were four visionaries present.

The next day I asked permission to say Mass in the original apparition room, which now is a sacristy. I was granted permission for my group. I also heard confessions each day and experienced miraculous conversions. On my last day, we were once again in the airport over ten hours, this time because of a plane malfunction. We waited for another plane to come from Ontario, Canada.

Yugo Airlines only had five planes in their fleet for international travel. While we were waiting at the airport, a young woman came over to me and said, "I don't know about the rest of your group, but I know you're coming back. When you do, you will stay with my family. I'm the cousin of Vicka, one of the visionaries, and my name is Anna." I realized that all of these experiences were signs that my priesthood was important to God, and the Blessed Mother interceded for me. It must become the center of my life.

At that time, I had no intention of returning, but a year and a half later, I did return at Christmas time and stayed two weeks with Anna's family. This time many life-changing events began to occur. The second day, a young man from Belgium with AIDS came to me. I had been counseling AIDS patients for ten years, so it made perfect sense that God would send me such a person. I spent half an hour counseling him and hearing his confession.

That evening at the Croatian Mass, the pastor told me to go to the far left corner of the church to distribute Communion. While there, this young man was the first person I saw, and he asked if he could see me again. I told him I was available after the English Mass the next morning. After that Mass, he told me his long story, and I replied as a good psychotherapist as well as a priest.

After talking for two hours, he told me, "I know you are struggling with your priesthood."

I was shocked. I had never told him!

"The Blessed Mother wants you to meditate on two passages in Scripture," he said. "It's very important that you remain a priest, but you are trying to have it both ways." One of the scriptures he gave me was from Matthew 6:24, "You cannot serve both God and mammon."

God used both of us to help each other. After this, we visited all the visionaries together and spent another two hours praying. The next day, I made the Stations of the Cross up the hillside. I had done this before, but this time I got lost and found myself on the backside of the mountain at the third station.

There were large stations positioned up the mountain. I decided to make the rest of the stations in my imagination. I knew there was a cross at the top of the mountain, but to get there, I had to walk through thorns and brambles. When I reached the top of the mountain at the cross, I asked the Lord for clarification, and prayed, *What is this supposed to mean?*

I heard in my heart God saying to me, *"Your life will be different from most priests. You will not have the external markers to guide you, but only the marker of faith. But you will reach the same place."*

I told my spiritual director this later, and he agreed that this was the story of my life. Much of the rest of my time in Medjugorje was spent hearing confessions, con-celebrating Masses, and much personal reflection.

My last day was Christmas Eve. After Midnight Mass, it was totally dark outside, with no stars or moon. My host, who could not speak English, pointed to Apparition Hill, where Mary was reported to have first appeared. The whole hillside was covered with blazing lights. I looked at it from a distance and thought it was interesting but then went to bed. I still had a lot of personal conversion to go through to appreciate such happenings.

After I returned to San Francisco, I realized I had to leave the Bay area. If I wanted to be saved, I needed to put my priesthood in first place. However, it took me three more years before I accomplished this goal. My life after Medjugorje gradually changed for the better. I began to pray the Rosary daily, which I used to do before ordination.

However, we were taught in the seminary there is too much Marian devotion in the Catholic Church, and we should focus more on the Mass, the Divine Office, and exercising social justice, especially for the poor. After my first visit to Medjugorje, a woman from Philadelphia asked me if I knew Eileen George.

"No," I told her.

She asked me if I would like to meet her.

I answered, "Not really."

She urged me and insisted that I meet her. One year later, she sent me an ad for a retreat for priests led by Eileen George. She wouldn't take no for an answer. Out of politeness, I called her secretary, inquired about the retreat, and was informed there was only one more opening. The retreat was in the middle of nowhere in Putnam, Connecticut. I asked her how I could obtain transportation. The next day she called and explained that two women would meet me at the airport in Providence, Rhode Island, and drive me to Connecticut. Then on Friday, when the retreat was over, they would drive me wherever I wanted to go.

I signed up.

I arrived at noon, and Eileen arrived at four o'clock. When I met her, she looked at me and said, "Father, I have been waiting for you and praying for you." Then she said, "All the priests talk to me personally, and I want you to be the first one."

I was going to psych her out at first, but I signed up on her list for the next morning. That evening she gave an introduction. Afterward she grabbed me. "Let's go talk now." For an hour and a half, I told her my long story. "Father, I knew this about you," she responded. "God the Father has revealed your life to me. The important thing is that you were truthful. Not all the priests are truthful. But here is what God the Father wants you to hear."

I did not want to hear from God the Father, and she relayed some difficult things. However, I felt peace and love as I listened to the words. I felt this must be how God chastises us. Eileen gave me eight hours of her time that week. On the third day, she talked about the priesthood and the detriment of the New Age movement.

"Eileen," I said. "You just explained much of my life."

"I know, but don't worry about it. Just fall in love with Jesus. He will take care of all that for you."

Many people feel Eileen had the gift of reading souls, like Saint Padre Pio. She also had many other mystical gifts that were visible to others.

She'd had terminal cancer for the past twenty-five years, a brain tumor, and frequently was unable to sleep. At the time that I met her, she had not slept in three weeks. Yet, through all her suffering, she smiled and was very warm and friendly to everyone.

She recounted that she once had a fever of 106 degrees and felt like she was dying. Because she was in such pain, she was crying. She said God the Father appeared to her, and He was also crying and said, *"Eileen, when I see you hurt like this, I hurt with you."*

Eileen asked Him, "If it hurts You so much, why don't You cure me?"

God the Father replied, *"I could, but let Me show you something."* He showed her hundreds of faces, mostly priests, who had been saved because of her prayers and suffering. I believe I was one of those faces. Afterward, He told Eileen, *"If you want Me to cure you, I will do so right now."*

She declined, as she now understood the value of her suffering.

I met with Eileen several times after this initial meeting. She more than anyone else was influential in bringing me back to orthodoxy and appreciating the importance of my priesthood. Prior to meeting Eileen, I did not have a personal relationship with Christ. Like my father, I kept God at a distance, fearful of Him, as if He was waiting to catch me off guard and send me to hell. I never truly trusted Him. After several retreats with Eileen, and after attending healing Masses with her, I gradually developed an intimate relationship with Christ and the Blessed Mother.

The second time I made a retreat with Eileen, she said St. Thomas Aquinas appeared to her while we were talking. She calls him "Tomasito," which means little Thomas, because he is so fat. Thomas told Eileen to remind Father John that he learned much more from the tabernacle then he ever learned in books or manuscripts. "Tell Father John that one of his greatest gifts is his curiosity, but that also is one of his curses. Tell him he reads too much. Tell him to go before the Blessed Sacrament with a pen and notebook because Jesus now wants to teach him directly."

I did not do this for five years. I'm not sure why, but I had never learned how to journal and was fearful Jesus would say, "You better shape up or ship out." I still had a lot of guilt about my former life.

Besides Eileen, God sent many holy people into my life, who inspired and guided me in my search for holiness. I became personally acquainted with all of the visionaries at Medjugorje and with people like Sister Briege McKenna and Maria Esperanza and her family. Maria was a visionary approved by the Catholic Church in Betania, Venezuela.

Another influential person in my life is a grandmother in central California. One day she was listening to my CDs on spiritual warfare. As she was listening, her whole car started shaking. She wanted to meet this priest who was causing her car to react this way. She eventually finished the CDs and prayed about the supernatural happening. She heard Jesus tell her in her heart that from now on she must pray and sacrifice for me every day. I met her a year later at a conference in Southern California, where I was speaking.

Since then we have become close friends, and she continues to be an important prayer warrior for me. She also has many Charismatic gifts, like the word of knowledge, visions, and words of Scripture she receives when she is praying. We pray over the phone together, and she has been a great help to me in my spiritual journey.

Another important influence has been the Intercessors of the Lamb, a religious Community who are now defunct. I spent two years living with them in Omaha, Nebraska. They helped me understand the Ignatian spiritual exercises, spiritual warfare, and deliverance ministry. They also helped me realize that God speaks to us constantly. They taught me journaling as a way of hearing God's voice.

As I reflect on Medjugorje and the people the Lord has brought into my life, I realize the pivotal role they each had in causing a change in my life. During my years after Vatican II, and especially during my training in psychotherapy, I was depressed much of the time. I was living a secular life, which was legalistic and without an intimate relationship with Christ. Much of my life was lived in my head rather than in my heart. I experienced confusion regarding the teaching and practices of the Church. I was counseling people to follow their consciences even when they disagreed with the Church's teaching. I was following the same principle in my own life, as well.

I had a major issue in trusting God. I also suffered from childhood wounds of abandonment, rejection, emotional abuse, and suffering vicariously from the physical abuse of my brothers and sisters. My whole life had been focused on self-reliance, raw courage, and using my own resources rather than God. I had a strong ego, but feelings of inferiority and lack of trust in myself often conflicted. I was self-centered yet thought of myself as a victim.

After Medjugorje, I gradually realized what a great gift the priesthood is, and it became central to my life. I feel more like a priest today than ever before. Also, as a result of the years I've been involved in marriage counseling, I realize that when spouses have a good relationship over many years, it's because they know each other's minds. That's why they frequently finish each other's statements. When we develop an intimate relationship with Christ, we get to know His mind. Thus, much of my confusion about morality and dogma was cleared up from knowing Christ personally.

My prayer life became much more from the heart, rather than just the head, with both becoming integrated. I understood that it's not what we do that's important, but what God does in us, through us, and with us. Our most important act in our spiritual life is total self-surrender to God of all that we are, and all that we have. The more we do this, the more God takes over our lives and continues His mission on earth through us.

We are the hands, feet, and heart of Christ. Christ is Lord of our life, and of all things. He always brings good out of evil. Like the father of the prodigal son in the parable, Christ is always merciful and loving. He is not so much concerned about our failures and sins as he is about our heart. He wants us to get up again after we fall and entrust everything to Him. When we return to God through the sacrament of Confession, we are stronger than before.

God blessed me with many gifts when hearing confession, especially in helping people get to the root of their sins and to guide them to total conversion of heart and mind. He strengthened my gifts of healing and allowed me to pray for those with spiritual issues such as in the deliverance ministry, where the Lord frequently brings people in need to me.

The more God gives us by way of gifts, the more we are attacked by the evil one, and the more crosses we encounter. I believe this is God's way of keeping us humble. That means we must pray more and have others praying for us. I try to make a holy hour every day, which is necessary for me to persevere in my ministry.

I still have a lot of distractions and dryness in my prayer life, but the important thing is to show up in humility. What God wants most of all is our heart and saying yes to His will and plan. Discernment of God's will is now an important part of my spiritual journey. Instead of deciding for myself what I feel like doing, I ask God what He wants. My role is to bring others to Christ.

I was at the airport in Salt Lake City, Utah, one day waiting for my next flight. As I was sitting there reading, praying, and meditating, I heard Christ's voice in my heart. *"Father John, I wanted you to minister to the woman sitting next to you on the plane, but you would not let Me do so. You ignored her. I can only minister to her through you, because you are My hands and My feet and My heart. I want you to understand that every person in your life is an opportunity for ministry, even if you do not speak to that person. Sometimes, all you should do is smile, or just acknowledge that person."*

In receiving that message, I felt no criticism but peace and love from Christ.

I now understand there are no accidents in life. Since I have totally consecrated my life to Christ through the heart of Mary, every person in my life and every consequence has been sent to me by Christ and the Blessed Mother. My job is to accept God's permissive will. This is the way God often intervenes in my life. All these interventions are opportunities to grow in holiness.

I am thankful to the Blessed Mother for appearing in Medjugorje, and for all the subsequent people and circumstances God has sent into my life. I have a long way to go on my journey toward holiness, but now I can trust in God's love and mercy.

Without God, nothing is possible, but with Him, everything is possible.

Bio–

Fr. John Struzzo, C.S.C., answered God's call to be His priest in the Congregation of the Holy Cross fifty-one years ago. He received his calling with great zeal, obtaining a Doctorate in Sociology and a Post-Doctorate in Marriage and Family Therapy and Individual Psychotherapy. Besides being a university professor, Fr. John has served on the clinical staff of the House of Affirmation, a residential treatment center for priests and nuns with severe emotional problems. Highly educated, he truly believed he could better serve the Church with a more liberal curve in his walk of faith. "You were doing so well; who diverted you from the path of truth?" (Galatians 5:7). It is often difficult to understand why or how we sometimes end up on the wrong path when our intentions come from our heart. Unexpectedly, through the mantle of love and protection of our Blessed Mother and prayers of the faithful praying for our priests, Fr. Struzzo experienced "the heart of reconversion." He more clearly perceived God's call to boldly preach the truth in love and to return to the basics of the Catholic faith. One of Fr. John's passions is evangelization and catechesis. He has done extensive research on New Age movements, Eastern religions, spiritual warfare, and modern-day issues in the Church. He has been active in evangelization and the healing ministry throughout the world and—most recently—involved in inner healing and deliverance ministry.

Rev. Fr. Bao Thai, S.T.L.

I grew up in a family of five children, of which I'm the youngest and the only one to become a priest. I was born into a non-baptized family in July 29, 1970, in Saigon (identified with the present-day Ho Chi Minh City), Vietnam. Nine years later on August 15, 1979—through an incredible series of events including the intercession of Our Blessed Virgin Mary—my mother, my four older siblings, and I converted to Catholicism. This was on the feast day of the Solemnity of Our Lady's Assumption. On December 22, 1985, on the special occasion of my father's baptism, our Lord stirred within my heart a deep desire to become a priest. As an energized teenager I was unstoppable, holding firm God's calling in my heart.

To celebrate the gift of my priesthood more fully, it helps to understand what it was like being born into a non-Christian faith. I grew up with the indigenous practice called the "veneration of our ancestors," respecting and venerating those who have gone before us. There is a distant similarity in this to the Catholic doctrine of the Communion of Saints.

The Vietnamese people who practice the veneration of their ancestors believe in God, Who is the Creator of heaven, earth, and the whole universe. However, they have no concept of God the holy Trinity, and they believe that after death the souls of their ancestors enter heaven. The living have a filial duty to pray for the dead, for the repose of a soul. They believe that with prayers, spiritual offerings, and good practices, the souls will soon enter heaven and be with God. Both my parents' families were born into this practice, and many of my extended family still devoutly honor this practice.

I consider it a special blessing to have been born on July 29, the day our Catholic Church annually celebrates the feast of St. Martha and St. Mary as an obligated memorial. I believe that with God's grace I have been given both gifts of serving and listening. After much prayer and meditation upon God's healing and personal love in my life, I humbly share this miraculous story, which took place almost forty years ago through the care, the protection, and the intercession of the Blessed Virgin Mary.

"My soul exalts the Lord, and my spirit has rejoiced in God my Savior" (Luke 1:46–47).

Before the end of the Vietnam War, Dad and Mom were involved in the military services of the former republic of Vietnam. My parents' boss at the time was Mr. Nguyen Thach Van. He was an executive assistant of Mr. Tran Van Huong, the vice president of the former republic of Vietnam. Mr. Nguyen was a devout Catholic, whose hobby was pottery. He loved my dad and mom as his own children. Every time he met my parents, he sang the Prayer of Saint Francis of Assisi hymn. My parents called him their spiritual father. He was my Catholic grandpa.

One inspirational day he formed and painted a colorful statue out of clay of Mary, Our Lady of Fatima, and gave it to Dad and Mom. My father at the time was very fortunate to hold a high-ranking status in the military as an officer and a major. We had a beautiful home with large front and back yards. Even though we were not Catholic, we opened our home—both the front yard and the living room—so the Catholics in the neighborhood could come together to pray the Rosary before that same statue of Mary, Our Lady of Fatima.

What a miracle! Catholics united and praying a Rosary in a non-Catholic family's home. I still vividly remember that image. I also remember the many people who gathered in my house, and Mary standing on a high altar in the living room. While praying a Rosary and singing Mary's hymns, the people also carried her around the yard and crossed through the neighborhood and around it as a sign of heavenly blessing to each family. The "Hail Mary" prayer and Marian procession have been implanted in my soul since I was younger than five.

On April 30, 1975, the Vietnam War ended. The Fall of Saigon, aka the fall of the former Republic of Vietnam into the communist regime, has been commemorated as "Black April" among the people of the former republic. At that time, my home was located right in the center of the military unit's headquarters. My dad, Thái Văn Minh—a paratrooper and a major in the airborne forces—was captured and placed in the communist prison just a few days before the war ended.

Because of the invasion of Saigon, my mom, Nguyễn Thi Kim Anh, my four siblings, and I quickly left our home behind and escaped into another area next to the surrounding wall of the unit. We lost everything and became poor, starting over from scratch. We were alone and without the presence and support from our father. Mother did her best, working two and sometimes three jobs per day to provide food for her five children. I was four years old. My older sister Tuyền was ten, and my other siblings Tuyến, Huy, and Diễm were nine, eight, and seven years of age.

Being affected by the war's aftermath, we moved into a poor area, where most of our new neighbors were Catholic. Our home's roof and walls were made of corrugated aluminum. Because of the thinness of the material, we could hear everything—every single movement—from the Catholic family who lived next door. The beautiful words we overheard were the recitation of the Rosary led by the lady of the house, Bác Sơn. She and her family prayed the Rosary three times a day. They prayed in the morning, in the early evening, and at night.

After 1975, Mom became a grammar school teacher. Whenever it was time for the neighbors to pray and we were being playful, Mom would say, "Shhh. Be quiet. Let them pray." The silence and the recitation of the "Hail Mary" gradually entered my soul.

"Hail Mary, full of grace, the Lord be with you …" That was indeed a grace from God that we did not recognize at the time. Even now I am grateful to God, to Mary, to my parents, and to the lady next door, Bác Sơn, who became my first Catholic contact. She made such an impact on my life as a young child. Her daily prayer life through the Rosary became the first step of faith evangelization to our family.

Don't hesitate to pray the Rosary out loud!

Four years later during the summer of 1979, the city was hit by malaria. This disease contracted from mosquitos can cause comas, seizures, yellow skin, and even death. Recent reports show that even today, 300–600 million people get malaria each year and one million die because of this disease. Thankfully, only my sister closest in age and I contracted malaria.

During my illness I witnessed the deaths of my schoolmates, classmates, and friends in our neighborhood. They died one by one, day after day, one after another. "Your friend across the street just died" or "your friend from school just died," Mom said. "A boy next door died as well." In the meantime, my sister was getting better. However, I became worse.

While lying in bed one day, I remember being terribly sweaty due to a high fever. Feeling hungry, I asked Mom for a small bowl of hot rice soup. She went to the kitchen, but upon returning, she panicked when she saw me in an epileptic state. She prepared to rush me to the hospital.

Three images remain with me from that journey. As I opened my eyes, each time the event—while ordinary—became sacred in that I would never forget the traumatic experience.

In my first image, I was confused. Instead of seeing the bowl of soup I craved, I was in my mother's arms and she was running down the street. Facing upward, I saw the huge trunk of an oak tree, its branches moving up and down, and the sky.

Second, I was inside a taxi heading to the hospital with Mom and the Catholic lady from next door, Bác Sơn. Cradled in her arms, I felt an itchiness on my chest. When I attempted to scratch at it, my mother—always a loving, tender, and *firm* mother—tried to stop me. She pulled off a green-colored, wool scapular from my chest. It was the scapular of Our Lady of Fatima, given to us by my Catholic grandpa. Mom had put it on me as soon as I became so sick.

We were not yet Catholic, yet we had the Marian scapular!

My third image was arriving at the hospital. The doctor claimed there was no treatment. I had an incurable disease. He offered his advice. "Take him home, allow him to eat and drink whatever he can, and let nature take its course."

My mother was overcome with grief and began to cry uncontrollably, sobbing like a child. This was the third image I remembered before becoming unconscious. While my mother was sobbing, the doctor unexpectedly returned and asked, "Where is your son?"

"Here," replied my mother.

The doctor and several nurses whisked me into the emergency room. Surrounding the hospital bed, they turned me over. That was the last image my mother saw through the glass window before they took me away. The receptionist instructed my mother and the neighbor lady to sit in the waiting room. Mom felt desperation and hopelessness as time stood still for her.

But God's grace shone upon us. I came out of surgery and was transferred to a regular recovery room that evening. My mother was with me, beside herself with joy. "He is alive! My son is healed. Thanks be to God! Thanks to the Virgin!" Tears of happiness and gratitude coursed down her bony face. To this day, my entire family—even my mother and I—have no idea what happened or what the doctors did to me. All we know for sure is that God's intervention took place that day.

When we were younger, we had the statue of Mary in our home. Later on, we had the scapulars. Though we fled to another home because of the ending of Vietnam War, the original statue traveled with us to our new, poor home. However, the statue broke from us running around and moving. During the time when I was sick, my mother and siblings used Scotch tape to keep Mary together. They placed her at my bedside and prayed to her for me.

We've all asked my mother, "What did you do besides cry after the doctor denied treatment? What made the doctor return to ask for Bao?" My mother admitted that during that moment of hopelessness, when she had no one to turn to but God alone, she prayed to the Virgin Mary, Our Lady of Fatima. In her despair, my mom threw herself onto God's throne and asked for the intercession of the tender and loving Blessed Mother.

"Mom, what did you pray?" I asked.

"I asked Mary to intercede to help my youngest son to live, and I promised … "

People often think that my mother offered God and Mary her youngest son, allowing him to become a priest. While that is a good guess, it didn't happen. We were not yet Catholics and were only converted after I was healed from malaria.

Mom said, "I promised Mary that as soon as Bao became better, I would take myself and my five children to be baptized into the Catholic Church."

I am humbled at the knowledge that if Mom had not kept that promise, I would not be a Catholic priest and a living testimony of faith.

I learned many virtues from my mom. The first one is fidelity—to be faithful to a promise after making it. Mom was faithful to her promise to God and Mary. When I first entered Mount Angel Seminary, this same virtue was emphasized in my priesthood formation, the virtue I had learned from Mother since childhood. To this day I have kept it, thanks to my mom.

When we moved, we were fortunate to learn that most of our new neighbors were Catholics. They were very friendly and often invited us to go with them to church and attend Mass. They also gently told us, "Don't get in line to receive Holy Communion. Just be seated and pray." We were not Catholics at the time.

In those days, the custom of folding your arms across your chest to indicate the sign for a blessing instead of communion did not exist. As a little boy, I wondered what the people were eating. What were they receiving on their tongues? What was Holy Communion? The more questions I had, the more I wanted to receive the Eucharist, and the stronger my desire to attend church often.

I'll always remember the first three churches we attended with my neighbors.

The first was Nha Tho Ba Chuong (the Three Bells Church), governed by the religious order of preachers known as the Dominicans. This order was instrumental in spreading the Rosary and emphasizing the Catholic belief in the power of praying the Rosary. The history of the Holy Rosary has attributed its origin to Saint Dominic, the order's founder, through the Blessed Virgin Mary. Our Lady of the Rosary is the title received by the Marian apparition to Saint Dominic in 1208 in the church of Prouille, in which Mary gave the Rosary to him.

Pope Pius XI said, "The Rosary of Mary is the principle and foundation on which the very order of Saint Dominic rests for making perfect the life of its members and obtaining the salvation of others."

As a child I attended the Three Bells church, joining with the group of people coming from all corners of the city to gather before the statue of Mary located in the beautiful alcove, to recite the Rosary for her intercession to God. There was another alcove of St. Martin de Porres. I also went to visit him, although I had no idea about anything involving the black saint's life. Since I witnessed many people praying to him, I stood and prayed to him too.

The second church was Nha Tho Ky Dong (the Our Lady of Perpetual Help Church), governed by the religious order of the Congregation of the Most Holy Redeemer. They are Catholic priests and consecrated religious brothers known as Redemptorists. They have a sacred picture of Our Lady of Perpetual Help. Every first Saturday in the early afternoon around two o'clock they dedicate an hour to pray to the Blessed Virgin Mary through a Novena litany and Rosary. I joined the sacred hour monthly. The church also has a beautiful grotto of Our Lady of Lourdes. I never missed joining the people before and after Mass to stand there and pray.

The third and last church I attended with our neighbors was named after Our Lady of Fatima, Nha Tho Binh Trieu. Every time Dad and Mom got through a difficult situation during the Vietnam War, they went to that church to thank God and to pray to Our Lady of Fatima. They made three special plaques engraved with words "Thanks to Mary."

Mom often rode her humble bicycle—with me in tow—to this shrine to offer Mary a beautiful bouquet and ask for her guidance and intercession. Before my family left Vietnam permanently for Orange County in July 1993, we went back to Our Lady of Fatima to give thanks to God for the many blessings He had bestowed on us during our life through the intercessions of Blessed Virgin Mary and all the saints.

All three churches are engraved in my childhood memories as unforgettable images before I became a Catholic.

While my mother was looking for a Catholic church for us to attend, she met another teacher at the grammar school where she taught, a nun, Sister Nguyen Tien Tu. The nun recommended the Dac Lo Church in the Tan Binh district and the pastor, Father John Baptist Nguyen Duc Han.

"I'd be happy to introduce you to the priest," the nun offered. "He will teach a CCD class for you and your five children, and he will baptize all of you."

We enrolled ourselves in the church and began to study faith formation immediately after I was healed from malaria and felt well. On the Solemnity of the Assumption of Mary on August 15, 1979, Father John received all of us into the Catholic Church with the three sacraments of Christian initiation—Baptism, Confirmation, and Holy Eucharist.

I was only nine years old on that joyful day when my family celebrated their entrance into the Catholic Church. Later, Father John told me that I kept singing a refrain from the song about Mary's assumption into heaven— not only on that special baptism day, but also every single time I returned to his church for the process of mystagogy.

The lyrics of the song's refrain are: "Mother, when you return to heaven, please take me to go with you. Passing through the earth to the paradise, how blissful it is. Mother, when you return to heaven, how joyful it is. Pray for us to be with you, everlasting in heaven."

Then began our devotion to Mary and all the saints.

A miraculous returning home happened after I became a Catholic in 1979. It was a few years later that my dad was freed from the North Vietnam communist prison and returned home safely. This was a day of tears and of joy! What a day of gratitude to God and Mary!

A few years afterward he went to the Dac Lo Church and studied in the RCIA program with Father John Baptist Nguyen Duc Han. On December 22, 1985, my father was received into the Catholic Church with the three sacraments of Baptism, Confirmation, and the Holy Eucharist.

From 1979 to 1985 we received so many blessings that we called them miracles from God. Some of the miracles included the fact that Dad was still alive, that he had not died in prison, and that he could make his way back home safely from the communist prison and became a Catholic. So many people had died during the war. They had died in prison or in the ocean when they attempted to flee the communist country. We were so blessed that Dad was still alive and had become a Catholic.

Now my whole family is Catholic. Now we are God's children.

The first time God called me to be a priest was at the moment of my Dad's baptism. I was fifteen years old and a sophomore. Together with my mother and siblings, I sat in the front pew praying for Dad and giving thanks to God for his first day into the Catholic Church. We all encountered the heavenly blessing.

The blissful feeling led me to utter to God, "I want to be like that priest, Father John, to perform a baptism." Father John had baptized all seven members of my family. I wanted to be like him, to be sent out to baptize God's children. It was the very first time I truly believed I heard God calling me to be a priest through that glorious event. I have never forgotten that sacred day, December 22, 1985.

Three years after receiving my first calling, I received my second calling to a priestly vocation. This time it was much stronger. On June 19, 1988, at the Vatican, Pope Saint John Paul II canonized 117 holy martyrs who had died in Vietnam in the 18th and 19th centuries. The canonization deeply impacted the entire country of Vietnam, and especially the Vietnamese Catholic Church.

The canonization hit home with me. Many young people, including myself, asked the question, "Who were these 117 holy martyrs?" I unceasingly asked my Catholic friends, including Father John, about these martyrs. Curious, I obtained an old, worn-out book with dark-brown pages.

Among the 117 martyrs persecuted between 1745 and 1862, ninety-six were Vietnamese. Twenty-one were bishops and priests from Spain and France: eleven Spanish Dominicans and ten French members of the Paris Foreign Missions Society (aka MEP – *Missions Etrangères de Paris*).

Much gratitude should be given to the foreign missionaries who entered Vietnam to begin the evangelization of Catholicism. Being brought up in the indigenous practice of ancestor veneration, and through the canonization of these 117 holy martyrs, I was once again connected to the ancient fathers of faith in Vietnam. I was so grateful to God for sending these men and women to my homeland. Through them, the Catholic people in Vietnam received the new culture of life—the culture of Jesus Christ.

These twenty-one holy martyrs died for the faith, along with the Vietnamese martyrs. They were foreigners who willingly left everything behind in their own European countries for the stranger Asian continent. Then they traveled to Vietnam to evangelize and finally sacrificed their lives because of their faith in God and the Catholicism they taught and preached.

Because of and through their testimony, I encountered Christ, the Savior of the world. Without their evangelization and sacrifice of life and blood, I would not have become Catholic or obtained faith in Christ. So once again, I am grateful to God. The canonization of these martyrs indeed transformed my vocation calling to a higher degree.

As a young man graduating from high school in 1988, I told God and these martyrs that I deeply yearned to be a priest. I wanted to follow the footsteps of these martyrs not only to please Mother Mary but also to give thanks to God, to render thanks to Him Who had given my family and me so many blessings in life. Becoming a priest was a humble token of praise and thanksgiving. From that day on I prayed that my vocation would become stronger and stronger.

And praise be to God, it did.

As the son of a Vietnam veteran, there was no way to enter a seminary in Vietnam. Father John, however, said to me, "Never give up. You still have a chance when you are in the USA. For now, keep your vocation calling alive by being involved at your parish in any volunteer ministry of your choosing. At the same time, try your best to get into the university, and do not give up your study. Choose computer science for a major. You are good at math."

I listened to his wise advice. My vocation calling was indeed growing stronger. I was a confirmation catechist until I left Vietnam in 1993, graduated from university with a BS degree in 1992, and taught high school from 1992–93. What a blessing it was that the school was next door to the Notre Dame Cathedral of Saigon. I always left the teacher's lounge at noon to walk to the cathedral for quiet prayer time, which I did for the entire academic year.

The land of the free and the home of the brave finally became my home and the homeland of all opportunities. My whole family—Dad, Mom, my four siblings, and I—arrived at Los Angeles International Airport (LAX) on July 16, 1993, on the feast day of Our Lady of Mount Carmel. It's Mary's day!

I am humbled to say and believe that I have been blessed by God and Mary since birth. St. Barbara Church in Santa Ana was the parish where I attended the very first Mass in my new homeland. Father Joseph Nguyen Van Luan (who is currently a pastor at Our Lady of La Vang Church in Santa Ana) presided at Mass, and I met him afterward. Father connected me immediately to church life in the USA, and without hesitation I participated in all kinds of ministry activities in Orange. I was so happy, so blessed! I could not imagine or even dream that my vocation calling was once again alive and now occurring in the USA.

Two years later, Father introduced me to the Diocese of Orange. I could not withhold my tears of praise and thanksgiving to God when I first stepped into Mount Angel Seminary, Oregon—my alma mater!

I believe the joy and strength I have comes from the celebration of the Eucharist, Our Lord Jesus Christ, through the care and intercession of His Mother and our Mother, the Blessed Virgin. All I have comes from praying the "Hail Mary," which I pray every day in good times and in bad, in sickness and in health.

The chief exorcist of Rome, Father Gabriele Amorth, recalled in *The Value of the Rosary* that one of his colleagues heard the devil say during an exorcism: "Every 'Hail Mary' sends a blow to my head. If Christians knew how powerful the Rosary was, it would be my end."

Yes, it is indeed. Even if one does not complete the entire Rosary, one can say a few decades per day. Each and every "Hail Mary" is a blow to the devil. He is afraid of—and only defeated by—her Son, Jesus Christ our Lord and Savior.

> "If you follow her, you will not go astray. If you pray to her, you will not despair.
>
> If you think of her, you will not be lost. If you cling to her, you will not fall.
>
> If she protects you, you will not fear; if she is your guide, you will not tire; if she is favorable to you, you will reach your goal."
>
> ~ St. Bernard of Clairvaux

Hail Mary, Full of Grace! Hail, Holy Queen, Mother of Mercy, our life, our sweetness and our hope! My goal is still a priest until the moment of my death and to be in heaven with you and with your Son, the High Priest forever.

Bio–

Fr. Bao Thai was born into a non-baptized family in July 1970, in Saigon, South Vietnam. Nine years later, through an incredible series of events and the intercession of Our Blessed Mother, he and his entire family converted to Catholicism on the feast day of the Solemnity of Our Lady's Assumption. In August 1985, our Lord stirred within his heart a deep desire to become a priest, and he answered God's call. Fr. Bao left Vietnam in 1993 with a degree in computer science and a new-found faith and hope.

Fr. Bao's studies led him to Mt. Angel Seminary in Oregon in 1995, followed by St. John's Seminary in Camarillo, and ultimately to Rome, where he completed his education at the Angelicum (the Pontifical University of St. Thomas Aquinas), where he received his Licentiate of Sacred Theology (S.T.L.) in spirituality. Through being grounded in his faith, learning, and hard work, Father Bao has enthusiastically served God's people since his youth. Since his ordination to the priesthood in the Diocese of Orange on June 7, 2003, he has served in four parishes and is currently the pastor at St. Cecilia Catholic Church and School in Tustin, California.

Rev. Msgr. David L. Toups, S.T.D.

My journey and my life is a witness, a testimony of what God does in us, through us, and for us. There are two scriptures that serve as a loose outline. The first is Romans 8:28. "We know that all things work together for good to those who love the Lord and have been called according to his decree." The second verse is Revelation 22:17. "The Spirit and the bride say 'come,' and let him who hears say 'come.' Whoever is thirsty, let him come and whoever wishes, let him take the free gift of the water of life."

The Spirit and the bride say "come."

I grew up in, praise be to God, a beautiful Catholic home. By that I mean it was a family striving for holiness. Ironically, my father entered the seminary as a young man, which was a great blessing for me when I felt a tug toward priesthood. I knew going to the seminary didn't mean that I had to become a priest. My dad had obviously left, so it gave me the courage to say, "Let me try. The worst thing that can happen is it will make me a better man like my father."

This faithful, prayerful home was in Houma, south Louisiana, which is a long-time stronghold of the Charismatic Renewal. I was familiar with praying in tongues and singing. It was something very natural for me from infancy. It was part of my life. When we were sick, my mom laid hands and prayed over us in tongues, and so life in the Spirit was something natural.

The initial thoughts of my vocation to the priesthood came as an altar boy. I believe every good Catholic boy who serves at the altar at some point should ask, "Am I called to do this?" There was that tug on me at a young age. I thought, *I'd like to do this.*

I told my mom I wanted to be either a Catholic priest or a lawyer.

"Oh no!" she said. "I've got a schizophrenic son."

Growing up in a faith-filled house, scripture, the Word of God, Sunday Mass, and the family Rosary were part of the fabric of our lives. My mother's favorite scripture was Romans 8:28. We started with the premise that all things work together for the good for those who are called according to His decree.

As we live our life of faith it's important to trust that even when we see the chaos around us, when we can't see God's hand, we still trust that in some way God will use everything for our greater good. I love telling the seminarians that God is the ultimate recycler. As a country we celebrate Earth Day. God was green before it was popular to be green. God uses the garbage in our lives and creates good from it. We must be patient and walk with Him, and live with Him, and claim the promise of Romans 8:28.

Honestly, that verse has always been on my family refrigerator. It has been on my lips probably since the moment I could speak. Since the Holy Spirit was so much a part of our home, it came naturally to trust the Holy Spirit's working in and through us, to trust in the spouse of the Holy Spirit, Mary—the Blessed Mother—to be a mother to all of us.

Life was good until I got into high school and college. Those who have children and grandchildren must be patient and trust in the promise of Romans 8:28. Trust like Saint Monica, who prayed for Augustine. Place your children and your grandchildren in the hands of the Father.

Thank God I didn't go completely off the rails, but I was a stereotypical college fraternity brat. I was involved in all the trappings of a pre-law student interning for the public defender's office in Pinellas County. Summers home were wonderful. I was "Mr. Resume," recording everything that would make me look good. I was class president in college, I was vice president of my fraternity, and I was working for the public defender. I had all the things the world would say are necessary to succeed.

The summer between my senior year of high school and my freshman year of college God planted a seed that would bear fruit years later. My parents decided to send me to Medjugorje and to Rome on a pilgrimage. A good friends' mom was leading the pilgrimage. Her boys and I were in high school together and played basketball. Adults and a few young people that my parents knew and trusted were on this trip, so my dad thought it would be good for me—to plant seeds.

It was a great experience. It was a great experience of fun because there's no drinking age limit in Europe. And it was a great experience of prayer because all that I received as a young person came to a culmination in the eighteen-year-old I was at the time. I experienced a taste of the essence of the spiritual life.

Medjugorje is known as a place of pilgrimage, certainly a place of special devotion to the Blessed Mother, but also a place of deep reconciliation. I believe the most important fruit of Medjugorje is as a place of conversion.

I went to Confession. This was the first time I went to Confession on my own. I wasn't in line with my class in parochial school, and I wasn't with my parents at a penance service for Advent or Lent. I *chose* to get in line. I brought my big eighteen-year-old sins, which burdened my heart, to the Lord that day. I experienced a freedom, a joy, and a taste of sonship that I had never before tasted. It was exquisite.

Then I went back to college and I forgot all about the experience. But that taste and that knowledge of God's love remained.

Years later I read my journal. My father was dying, and I was at home caring for him. When you're a caregiver, and your patient is asleep or you have some down time, you tend to do anything you can to distract yourself. During one of these times I cleaned drawers from my high school days and found an old journal. Our tour guide had urged us to keep a journal while on the pilgrimage to Medjugorje.

As I read it, I saw the classic mind and heart of an eighteen-year-old boy. On one page: "We just met these girls from Louisiana. We're going to hang out tonight at the Buffet Medjugorje and drink beer." On the next page: "I talked to Father Justin today. I think God might be calling me to be a priest."

It was amazing to read this years later. The date for this particular journal entry was June 14. Eight years later I was ordained a priest on June 14, 1997. The beauty came full circle for me.

Even in college and through all my involvement in various activities, Sunday Mass kept me grounded. I didn't want to go, but I knew that every Sunday night—even though there were no cell phones—I spoke to my parents. Sunday nights I touched base.

I loved my parents, yet I knew they would ask, "How was Mass?"

"Oh, it was good," I'd say. I wasn't going to lie to my parents, and I wasn't going to admit I didn't go to Mass. So I went. Sunday Mass was not an option to my parents. Growing up it was part of being children of the household of God. They said this by their actions of encouraging us from our earliest years, "This is who we are. This is what we do."

I am so grateful. I have missed Mass maybe once in my entire life, and I can't even remember the specifics, but it probably happened at some point during college.

While I didn't want to go to Mass, it stung my conscience not to. It was an important touchstone in my life. I cannot stress enough the importance of this, especially for those who have impressionable young children. Dad used to lovingly say, "Until you have a job and an apartment, you follow our rules."

We did not doubt his seriousness.

Now it's a different age, a different generation. It's a lot tougher, but that importance—that very simple action of encouraging us to go to Church—works. Mass was simply not an option. Some may think, "This isn't going to transform a kid's life if he decides not to go to Mass with me." Yet, I would say it *did* transform my life, that it was part of the fiber.

While home during the summer between my sophomore and junior year of college, I worked at the public defender's office. I interviewed alleged criminals the night after their arrest. I was a twenty-year-old pre-law student, and it was exciting to take the testimony that the public defender was going to use in his defense. Life was good.

I was feeling good about life until a chance event. A dear friend of mine, who went to college in Clemson, became involved in the faith. Now, unfortunately, it was outside of our Catholic tradition, but she was beautifully involved in campus ministry and on fire for the Lord.

She and I went to dinner one night, and out of the blue she said, "You know, David, I really have to say this. You're a hypocrite."

I felt like she had taken a brick and smashed it on my forehead. It hurt, but she was one-hundred percent correct. I professed to be a Catholic and a Christian. I went to church, but probably five out of seven nights a week I was drinking, carousing, and doing whatever I wanted—living the way I pleased, living for myself and not for God.

This was one of those moments in my life that hit me hard. I had plenty of excuses. I'm the youngest of three and was raised in south Louisiana. We moved when I was a junior in high school to Clearwater, Florida. It is amazing that now I am a priest in the Diocese of St. Petersburg, since that is where my family settled.

When someone close to you says you're a hypocrite, it makes you look at your life. My two older siblings had gone through college, done the same crazy young-person things. Now they were married and had lovely Catholic homes and families.

I was waiting for the same thing to happen to me. *I've got two more years, God. You can't call me yet!*

St. Augustine went through the same thing. He said, "I want to be chaste, just not yet. I want to follow you, God, just not yet." While I did feel a calling, I had been holding God off. This was my little bubble. This was my window for fun. *Don't encroach on my time, God. I'm in college.*

However, as Psalm 111:10 says, "The fear of God is the beginning of wisdom."

I asked myself, "If I died today, where would I go?" What was my destination? What was the trajectory of my life at this moment? I did not like the answer. It was not a resounding, "Heaven!" It was a big question mark.

I said, "Okay, I've got to give my life to God."

At the same time, I was reading a book by Scott Turow called *One L*. It was about the author's first year at Harvard Law School, when the students entered with great ideals and wanted to make a difference in the world. By the end of that first year of law school they began crawling on top of each other to get to the top of the class. The common consensus was, "Forget the system, forget the little guy. I want to make big money."

As I read this I saw myself, my selfishness and self-centeredness. I knew that was my path and it scared me. And so, in the middle of that summer I said, "Lord, I'm all yours. I want to be the best Catholic attorney I can be."

I started going to daily Mass on my way to the Pinellas County Jail, attending St. Cecelia's in Clearwater, my home parish. I began praying the Rosary I had prayed as a child, and I started reading the Scriptures. God was working in the heart of my twenty-year-old self, transforming my life. My parents were lovingly observing but not interfering. They said, "I think God's doing something in David's heart."

Obviously, He was not calling me to be a good Catholic attorney. Every time I read the Word of God, I felt the call of the apostles when Jesus said, "Drop everything. Drop your nets and follow Me."

However, I was not open to that line at the time. I didn't want to drop everything. Worldliness was important to me. I was the vice president of my fraternity, and this was a huge accomplishment. It seemed at the time that I had so much to give up. *Oh, my God, how can I possibly do this?*

It has now come full circle. St. Cecelia was my home parish when I was young, and the two priests I hired and currently work with me at the seminary were then my parish priests. Monsignor John Cippel was the pastor, and Father Arthur Proulx was the vocation director. In those days they observed a young Dave Toups suddenly showing up at daily Mass. I'm sure they wondered what was going on.

Father Proulx wisely invited me to a barbeque. In God's providence, goodness, and perfect plan, it turns out that when my father was in the seminary in south Louisiana, one of his classmates was the Bishop of St. Petersburg at the time. He has known my family for over sixty years.

I did attend the barbeque. While sitting on a picnic bench listening to one of the seminarians, I thought, *These guys are pretty normal*. Honestly, I had expected to meet guys that were a bunch of losers. Instead, I was surprised and walked away thinking, *These are really good guys*.

One seminarian shared the story of his calling. It impacted me, and I was deeply moved. As Luke 24:32 states of the road to Emmaus—my heart was burning within me.

The bishop walked by. Knowing my family as he had for years, he paused and gave me one of those nice little Italian slaps on the cheek like in *The Godfather*. He looked at me and said, "Jesus told the apostles, 'Drop your nets and follow Me.'" Then he walked off.

In hindsight that is a great vocation line. The Holy Spirit had been saying this to me already in a deep and profound way. But to now have a successor of the apostles calling me out was life changing. I looked at the seminarian next to me and felt myself turn white as a ghost.

The seminarian saw my discomfort. "Let's go get a coffee and continue this conversation," he said.

We did, and I confided later that night, "Man, if I could do it right now, I would drop everything and go to the seminary."

"Really?" he said.

"Yeah, but I can't."

That was my excuse. I seemingly and superficially had so much going on. The Lord, however, was pounding. The Hound of Heaven was chasing after me. The bishop "happened" to know my family for sixty years, the vocation director "happened" to be living in the parish I attended, and he also knew my family. He'd known me since high school.

This took place in the middle of June. At the beginning of July I arrived at the parish and said, "I want to give the seminary a shot." My dad had done the same thing, and I felt assured that this didn't mean I was signing in blood. I needed a time of discernment. I told Father Proulx, "I'll give it six months."

"Whoa," he replied. "You've got to give it at least a year."

I played it cool. "I'll give it six months."

My fraternity brothers were skeptical about my decision. "Toups? He'll be back. This is like self-induced rehab. He'll be back." My girlfriend was less than enthusiastic when we broke up. It was not a good day.

I immediately transferred into the college seminary. On August 4, 1991, the Feast of St. John Vianney, I was sitting at the St. John Vianney College Seminary in Miami. The Lord had worked, I had responded, and I knew I was not strong enough to go back to Florida Southern and back into my fraternity life. I was willing to live a Christian life. I knew this was right and thought, *The window is open. If I'm going to give God a fair shot, I've got to go now.*

Obviously, I stayed longer than six months. A number of things took place to make this happen, praise be to God. Amen! Thank you, Jesus.

I was raised in a Charismatic home, and since the life in the Spirit was very much a part of the expression of the Catholic faith as I knew it,

Baptism in the Spirit came at the same time as conversion and vocation.

Roberto, now rector of St. John Vianney College Seminary where I was sent to study, was then the seminarian across the hall from me. He is now Monsignor Robert Garza. Roberto and I became good friends. Ironically in God's providence, we are both in charge of different seminaries in Florida, our college and our theologate, which is our graduate school. He was a parishioner at San Isidro in Pompano Beach, and we attended the English Mass on Saturday. The pastor always invited us up front afterwards to pray over people.

From my first seminary days, praying in tongues, praying over people, and seeing the faithful rest in the Spirit came naturally. This is what I had been raised to believe, so for me it was awesome to see how God was working in my life, understanding how to use the gifts of the Spirit.

After spending two years at St. John Vianney, I went to Rome for five years to finish my graduate studies. When a young man is in the seminary it is called "formation." It's as if God crushes areas of your life that need change and forms you—like a ball of clay molded by the Creator into whatever He desires. While this is a lifelong process, many healings in my heart and in my life happened during that time.

One of the most magnificent things God did for me was His healing me to stop drinking. Imagine spending five years—actually seven years altogether—in Rome and never having a glass of wine. It's unheard of, yet God put that desire in my heart. I have not had a drink since 1994, and I count that as a healing and a grace of God.

Another miracle was a healing of memories from those crazy things I did in my youth. I needed to let go and allow God to heal me. I received a strengthening of my faith. In those years when I was a seminarian in Rome, I was privileged to encounter two saints of the twentieth century: Saint John Paul II and Saint Teresa of Calcutta.

Pope John Paul II was the pontiff during my years in Rome. Once a year, we seminarians had a one-to-one with him. We shook his hand, and he would give us one of those nice little slaps on the cheek and say, "Good, good, grow in holiness."

The other person who frequently came in and out of Rome was Mother Teresa. I worked with her sisters, the Missionaries of Charity, so I had the privilege of meeting Mother Teresa five or six times. On one of those times she spoke to me and another seminarian after Mass. Mother Teresa was tiny, something like four-feet-eleven. She looked up at us and touched us with her hands. Her hands were like baseball mitts because she worked hard, loved, and touched and healed so many people. They were amazing hands. She said, "If you don't want to be a holy priest, get out now."

I looked at Father Ken Malley, my classmate and said, "Is she reading our souls? Should we leave? I don't know."

However, her point was well taken. Whatever we do with our lives we must give it our all. We are to grow in holiness. Mother Teresa would say the gospel is on one hand. She'd take your hand and play with your five fingers. Then she would say, "Jesus said, 'Whatever you did to the least of My brothers *you did it to Me.*' These five fingers will remind you that every time you touch someone, every time you help someone, realize you are touching Christ. Realize you are doing His will as Matthew 25 tells us."

It was remarkable. I was surrounded by so much holiness. Rome is also the human face of the Church. A dear friend of mine says, "The only thing that happened in Rome was the Romans exchanged togas for cassocks." It's obviously a joke.

But there is the human side of this divine institution that Jesus gave us, so we should not be discouraged. When we look at the original twelve, Judas sells Christ out, Peter denies Him, and the rest all run from the cross except for John, the beloved. Why should we be surprised? Why should we be scandalized? Jesus has continued to call clay pots, cracked pots, and vessels of clay. That's why priests constantly need your prayers. While priests need to strive for holiness, we see the humanity of it all. Jesus came to save us.

So, Rome gave me this incredible, well-rounded image of the Church, the saints, and the sinners. The good, the bad, and the ugly. When I espoused myself to my bride, the Church, on June 14, 1997, I knew my bride. I knew her and I loved her, warts and all. I know her good side. I know her bad side. I know when she makes me crazy. I know when I'm enamored by her.

That's marriage, isn't it? That's what priesthood is. When a young man comes to me and says, "Father, I think I'm called to be a priest, but I also feel this call to marriage," I say, "Great!" That's what priesthood is. The discernment you must make is, "Am I called to be a spouse and a father to one person and one family, or am I called to be a spouse and a father to the Bride of Christ, to the whole family of faith?"

Those same virtues that make you a good husband and father are also priestly virtues. The Lord does not want to suppress those manly callings or yearnings of your heart.

I became a priest on June 14, 1997—Flag Day. I jokingly remind people to raise the flag and remember me on that special day. As a priest, I continue to hear the Spirit and the bride say "come," calling me.

I spent four years as an associate pastor at St. Francis Cabrini with that same priest who is now at St. Vincent de Paul. Monsignor John Cippel was at another parish, and I was sent to him. He is the same priest who was my pastor growing up. It's fascinating to witness how the Lord worked to put me in contact with this holy shepherd and priest, who helped form my young, priestly heart. Afterward, I was sent back to Rome for two more years to finish my doctoral studies.

After that time, I came to St. Vincent de Paul Regional Seminary as a professor and dean of students, where I met people such as Dr. Carol Razza. She and I prayed every Tuesday afternoon before our formation meetings when we discussed the growth of our seminarians. It is a tradition that we still carry on to this day.

Whenever you're in an institution like a seminary or a church, the constant need for "weeding" becomes necessary. We prayed for the Lord to either transform or remove anyone who needed to be transformed or removed. God was doing marvelous things, working through our ministry in the seminary that was forming our future priests. Little did we know that I was the one who was going to be removed, when my bishop sent me to work for the United States Conference of Catholic Bishops (USCCB).

That made Carol angry. "God, what are you doing?" she asked. "How can you take him away from us?" She received an answer in prayer, yet she didn't tell me until five years later when I returned as rector.

Carol explained it to me this way: "It was important because you were the only priest that we could connect to spiritually, who knew the spiritual heartbeat of the seminary. So I was angry and said, 'Lord, I can't believe You removed him. Of all people here, You remove *him*.'" And profoundly, Carol heard the Lord say, "I had to remove him so that I could bring him back to do My very best work."

I had to remove him so I could bring him back to do My very best work.

Little did either of us know when I left the seminary that my bishop would ask me to go to Washington, D.C. to work at the USCCB. It is our national headquarters. It was a great experience but not one I felt called to lead for the rest of my life. After a three-year term, I called my bishop and said, "Do you have a parish in the Diocese of St. Petersburg? You've got a pastor who is ready to come home."

Bishops enjoy hearing a priest say, "I'm ready to fill a spot." He said, "I have just the parish for you—Christ the King, South Tampa, South Dale Mabry, downtown." It was a vibrant, loving, and active parish. I loved it. It was a wonderful experience.

After a year, I received a call from my bishop. "The bishops of the board of trustees just met at Saint Vincent de Paul Regional Seminary. They want you to be the next rector." I knew, simply because of my previous experience and my degree, that at some point I would be called back. I expected to have about five or six years in the parish to really enjoy the people of God, but that wasn't to be the case.

I said, "Bishop, please hold off on announcing this news. Please do not allow the good that we're doing here to go to waste, making me a lame duck for my second year at this church." I was permitted to love the people of God, to be a pastor, and to be a shepherd. In 2012, I was called back to St. Vincent de Paul.

Through God's goodness and God's plan—Romans 8:28—there were many lessons I learned along the way after many years of priesthood and in the years since I entered the seminary. Everything in our lives culminates to this point. Everything we have ever learned prepares us to live for today.

As the dean of men my first three years, I knew I was doing God's work. I knew the importance of forming our future generation of priests. When I was called out of the seminary, I was scratching my head. "Whatever, Lord, whatever Your call."

The Spirit and the bride say "come." We do what is asked of us.

While in Washington, D.C., I worked for a committee of bishops. It's like a staffer on Capitol Hill in Washington, except we're staffers for cardinals and bishops. Cardinal Sean O'Malley was the chairman of the committee I served. Being the rector of a regional seminary is essentially serving a committee of bishops because it's owned by the seven dioceses of the state of Florida.

Everything I did at the seminary, the first go-around, was laying the foundation for my later appointment as the rector. Everything I did in Washington, D.C.—serving a committee, knowing how to work with a group of important men, my superiors, learning ways to relate to them as a peer but at the same time I was not their peer—was a calling to serve them.

Learning that delicate dance and balance, then later translating that knowledge to being a pastor in Tampa, was probably the most important event that formed my heart to return to be rector of our seminary. Now I knew—through first-hand experience—what it was like to be a pastor, both the joys and the struggles.

As I now prepare these men for priestly ministry, I'm able to share not from book knowledge but from the heart. I give thanks to God for what He has done in my life. I am also grateful for the opportunity the Lord has given me to serve as rector of our seminary since 2012.

How did I became a monsignor? At the end of Pope Benedict's pontificate, someone was made a monsignor for decades of meritorious service, and it's an honor. In my case it was bestowed because I was called at a young age to be rector at our regional seminary. It's not because of me but because of the office I hold that I was made a monsignor.

The *Tampa Tribune,* a local newspaper, ran a story because I was a "local boy." The sidebar showed a picture of me, the local priest, named Chaplain of his Holiness, Monsignor David Toups. The main headline? "Pope Benedict XVI Resigns."

Pope Francis stopped designating the title of "monsignor" to those under sixty-five, so I'm the end of the line. I jokingly say my autobiography should read, *The Last of the Monsignors,* similar to *The Last of the Mohicans.*

More important than any title is the gift and privilege to be a priest, to stand at the altar *in persona Christi*—in the person of Christ. When our priests say the words of consecration, "This is My Body, this is My Blood," it is Christ operating through us. When we absolve sins and say, "I absolve you from all of your sins," the *I* is Christ. The gift the priest receives in ordination is to stand in the person of Christ, to be a disciple, a full-time disciple. I get paid to follow Jesus.

Most people have jobs and families and various ministries. When I was a parish priest, people would often say, "Oh gosh, Father, you are young." They were excited to have a young, dynamic priest. I tried to be active, attending all the events possible. People said, "Father, I see you at everything, and we are so happy that you come." And I said, "Well, wait a minute. If you see me at everything that means you are at everything too. I get paid to do this. You are doing this on your free time. You're the real heroes."

How beautiful it is to be a disciple of our Lord Jesus Christ, to serve the laity, the lay faithful, the baptized. I heard a permanent deacon and wonderful friend of mine, Deacon Jim Keating from Omaha say, "As much as we focus on the importance of knowing who we are and a unique priestly spirituality, we have to love the spirituality of laity even more because that's our bride. I have to love my bride. I have to know everything about her. I have to be prepared to give my life for her." The Spirit and the bride say "come."

Along my life's journey I have experienced four life lessons. The first is Romans 8:28, the good, the bad, and the ugly. The Lord is with us—all things work together for good. He will make manifest His goodness. Think of the most difficult moments in your life. For me I can say on a familial level that it was the death of my parents. My father died in 2006 and my mother in 2014.

As one journeys with loved ones through cancer and through sickness, caring and suffering with them—there is so much beauty in the midst of trial. In my case, as the priest of the family, it felt like everything fell on me.

"You're not married. You take care of Mom. You take care of Dad." My siblings—to the extent they could—tried to help.

Both of my parents' extended sicknesses happened during summertime, and I am a seminary professor. God's timing, God's plan.

My bishop called me the first time when my dad was diagnosed. "Cancel all of your summer plans." I was supposed to teach in Omaha and give retreats. This is typical of what seminary priests do during the summer. We are not assigned to a parish, and the seminaries close.

The bishop said, "Cancel everything. Your family needs you. Go and care for your dad." I was both my dad's chaplain and his hospice nurse. It made a man out of me. As a son to care for his father—to be a father to my father—was extremely special.

I was worried. *What's going to happen? I've got to go back to the seminary.* In God's timing, though, He worked it all out. All the burdens and all the worries were in His timing.

My mother's situation was identical but eight years later. She was diagnosed when I was still a pastor in Tampa. It was terrific timing. I could be with her on my days off and journey alongside her. I could take the time that I needed. When I was sent back to the seminary four and a half hours away, I came home once a month. I talked to her daily when I could.

There was a burden, as there always is when you have a sick loved one. My prayer was, *God, what are you going to do? Who is going to care for her when it's the end?* She didn't start to fail until Memorial Day weekend. As a seminary rector, I was headed home that weekend, and I didn't go back for another two weeks. I was able to stay and care for Mom, be with her, and journey with her.

My siblings came, and Mom died at 8:28 p.m. on June 7—the official time of sunset as recorded in the paper. It was also the vigil of Pentecost, my mom's favorite feast. It was exquisite. Romans 8:28, "We know that all things work for good for those who love God," was the scripture of my mother's life. She lived by it. We lived by it, and we continue to live by it. We trust God in these painful moments. When we are anguished, when we don't know what to do, we trust that God is with us—Jesus, Emmanuel, God is with us. So trust!

Trust is the first life lesson. The second life lesson is prayer. Stay grounded daily in your prayer life. I was blessed from my first week in the seminary at St. John Vianney in Miami. I listened to an old cassette tape by Archbishop Fulton Sheen, and he discussed his daily holy hour. I thought, *Okay, I'll do it.*

This has been part of my prayer life ever since the Lord convicted my heart.

Go to Mass as often as you can make it. Certainly go every Sunday, and when you can go daily, make the time. The Eucharist is the source and the summit of a Catholic's life. We need these beautiful Marys and Marthas and Blessed Mothers, and Mary the wife of Cleopas, and the other Mary. We need the Marys at daily Mass praying for the church, praying for the children. Make the time. Make time for regular confession. Be healed so that you can be a healer in your home.

Pray the Rosary. We just celebrated the 100th anniversary of Our Lady's apparition in Fatima on May 13, 2017. On that day, we ordained the largest class for the Archdiocese of Miami in its history. Nine men were ordained priests. Praise be to God! I want to encourage you pray the Rosary. Turn to Our Lady.

Trust, prayer, and the third life lesson—Marian receptivity. Be open. Be a Marian presence. Annually I make a retreat—and once I had the privilege of making a thirty-day retreat. Before I went on this thirty-day retreat, which was an amazing experience, my spiritual director, Father John Horn, a Jesuit (who now also works at St. Vincent de Paul), began to prepare me for the spiritual exercises of St. Ignatius. In a phone conversation before I left for Omaha for this retreat, I asked Father Horn, "What should I be praying for?"

He said, "Pray for Marian receptivity."

"Really? Can you give me something a little more concrete?" I didn't get it until I started on the retreat. When it's just you and God for thirty days, it may sound wonderful—and it is. But it isn't easy. You're stuck with yourself the whole time. Imagine being stuck with yourself alone for thirty days. You had better be open to the Holy Spirit.

The Spirit and the bride say "come," and so this Marian receptivity in our lives. What does this mean? It is Mary's example. "Be it done unto me according to your will. Behold the handmaid of the Lord." *Magnificat anima mea dominum.* "My soul proclaims the greatness of the Lord." Follow Mary's example. Always be receptive to the prompting of the Holy Spirit, to the will of the Father, and to being a disciple of the Lord Jesus.

Trust, prayer, Marian receptivity, and the fourth life lesson: allow the Holy Spirit to lead. Everything I do that turns out "good" is simply His work—when I get out of the way and allow the Holy Spirit to work in my life. God does phenomenal things at our seminary. I can say this without boasting because I know it is completely and totally the work of the Holy Spirit. I get a lot of credit from people on the outside. I should get no credit. It is truly the Holy Spirit who does the work.

Institutes like a seminary do not change overnight. We are an old church with our roots back to Christ. To accomplish anything within an institution—such as the Catholic Church—is slow work. Since 2012, I've been at the seminary. Since that time, ninety percent of our faculty is new, renovated, renewed, and restored. We are seriously focused on training our men to be devoted in total holiness, desiring radical service, and giving their lives to God. That does not just happen. It takes a tremendous amount of prayer.

We completely renovated the old campus and built two new dorms, and by the grace of God we've doubled in size in the last ten years. At a time when most people think the priesthood is dying out and no one is responding to God's call, we have doubled our size. We are in no way finished. We need to keep up the good work of prayer and encouragement.

Please pray. Do whatever you can to promote the priesthood in this diocese and those around the world. We need good and holy priests. Call them out. Call out the holy men you see or know. Say something like, "I see in you the qualities that would make a good priest."

Do the little slap like the bishop did on the cheek: "Jesus said, 'Drop your nets and follow Me.'" Call them. We need them.

Look at what God has accomplished in this short window of time. It is all the work of the Holy Spirit. We trust the Holy Spirit to work in and through us. Believe in the power of the living God. Get out of the way. Let Him work. The Spirit and the bride say "come."

Come, Holy Spirit, come!

Bio–

Monsignor David Toups was ordained in 1997 for the Diocese of St. Petersburg in Florida. Since 2012 he has served as the rector/president of St. Vincent de Paul Regional Seminary in Boynton Beach. He attended Florida Southern College before transferring and graduating from St. John Vianney College Seminary in Miami, Florida. His theological studies were pursued at the Pontifical North American College in Rome while attending both the Gregorian and Angelicum Universities, receiving his Doctorate in Dogmatic Theology. He previously served in parish ministry as both parochial vicar and pastor in his home diocese. From 2004–2007 he was a professor and dean of students at the seminary where he now serves, and from 2007–2010 he served the United States Conference of Catholic Bishops in Washington, D.C. in the Secretariat of Clergy, Consecrated Life and Vocations. Monsignor Toups is responsible for numerous articles and is the author of the book *Reclaiming Our Priestly Character.*

BAPTIZED IN THE HOLY SPIRIT

by Rev. Harold F. Cohen, S.J.
In Loving Memory

[Father Cohen was the first Spiritual Advisor to the Magnificat Central Service Team—his explanation of the Baptism in the Holy Spirit is timeless.]

Prior to His ascension, Jesus told His apostles, "Before many days you shall be baptized with the Holy Spirit." He added, "You shall receive power when the Holy Spirit has come upon you; and you shall be My witnesses" (Acts 1:5,8).

The apostles prayed for the coming of the Spirit with Mary, the mother of Jesus, and a group of about one hundred and twenty. On Pentecost, they were "baptized with the Holy Spirit" and were transformed into new creatures, bold witnesses for Christ.

Pentecost comes to each of us in the Sacraments of Initiation: Baptism, Confirmation, and Eucharist. In **Baptism**, we receive the Holy Spirit and become God's children and members of the Body of Christ. In **Confirmation**, we receive a new fullness of the Spirit and are empowered to serve the Church and bear witness to Jesus. In the **Eucharist**, we receive the risen Jesus Who fulfills His role of communicating the Spirit to His friends.

Often, we do not allow the Spirit we have received to be as active in us as He wants to be. To use an analogy, He is like chocolate syrup poured into a glass of milk: it goes to the bottom of the glass until stirred up. But when it is stirred up, it permeates the milk and transforms it into something new.

We can learn how to "stir up" the Spirit (and how to receive more of Him) from Jesus in the Gospels:

"If anyone thirsts, let him come to Me, and let him drink whoever believes in Me. As the scripture has said, 'Out of His heart shall flow rivers of living water.' Now He said this about the Spirit which those who believed in Him were to receive" (John 7:37–39). "If you then, who are evil, know how to give good gifts to your children, how much more will the heavenly Father give the Holy Spirit to those who ask Him!" (Luke 11:13).

The Lord teaches us that first we must **thirst** for God, we must desire more and more of His Spirit. Then, we must **believe** that Jesus is faithful to His promises and will indeed give us His Holy Spirit. Finally, we must **ask** God for the Holy Spirit. We must pray with perseverance, asking, seeking, knocking, believing that "everyone who asks receives, and he who seeks finds, and to him who knocks it will be opened" (Luke 11:10). We can follow the example of the early Church by praying for the Spirit, in union with Mary and the apostles, as they did at the first Pentecost (see Acts 1:12–14).

What can we expect when we are "baptized with the Holy Spirit"? We can expect an immediate or gradual experience of deeper union with God, our loving Father, and with Jesus, our Lord and Friend; a fresh appreciation of Scripture; a greater love for others and a desire for Christian fellowship; the fuller presence in our lives of the fruit of the Spirit: love, joy, peace, patience, and more (see Galatians 5:22–23); the reception of one or more of the charismatic gifts of the Spirit such as discernment, service, prophecy, praying in tongues, healing (see 1 Corinthians 12–14).

This gift of a new fullness of the Holy Spirit is, I believe, **the** grace of our age. "Ask and it will be given to you!"

Questions for Reflection/Discussion

The Lord will speak to your heart as you read these very diverse journeys. We encourage you to go deeper than what is on the surface with further reflection as to what the Lord is saying to you. You will gain valuable insight, which will shed light on your particular life story.

We suggest you ask yourself some or all of the following questions (or create your own) when you have finished reading either a chapter or the entire book. This can be done in a number of ways such as individually, with family or friends, in a book study, or a small faith-sharing group.

1. How does this testimony speak to you?

2. Do you recall a time in your life when the Lord was trying to get your attention?

3. Is there a person in your life who has been key in your walk with the Lord? Why?

4. What do you consider your biggest challenge in your journey with Christ?

5. Reflect/share on God's presence in your everyday life.

6. How do you think you could improve your communication/prayer life with God?

7. How has this chapter/book made you more aware of your need for God?

8. Is God asking you to change something in your life?

9. What are the obstacles holding you back from giving a total "yes" to His call?

10. Since we are called to give thanks in all circumstances, what would you like to specifically thank God for today?

We encourage you to journal your conversations with the Lord. No matter where you are in your journey, the Lord always calls us to go deeper. He loves us and wants us to choose to love Him! As the cliché goes, *to know someone is to love them.* Allow yourself to know Him more intimately and accept His grace to do so.

"Not only that, but we even boast of our afflictions, knowing that affliction produces endurance, and endurance, proven character, and proven character, hope, and hope does not disappoint, because the love of God has been poured out into our hearts through the holy Spirit that has been given to us" (Romans 5: 3–5).

Contributor's Contact Info

All contributors retain their individual rights to copyright, use, and licensing of their individual testimonies, and have granted Magnificat® Central Service Team, Inc. copyright permission to use their testimonies in this collective work. For reprint or re-use rights to individual testimonies, please contact the appropriate contributor(s). For reprint or re-use rights to the collective work, please contact Magnificat® Central Service Team, Inc., 1629 Metairie Road—Suite 3, Metairie, LA 70005-3926.

Bishop Michael C. Barber, S.J.
Diocese of Oakland
2121 Harrison Street, Suite 100
Oakland, CA 94612-3788
Phone: 510-893-4711
www.oakdiocese.org

Fr. Michael Barry, SS.CC.
Mary's Mercy Center, Inc.
P.O. Box 7563
San Bernardino, CA 92411
Phone 909-889-2558
Email: mmcinc@msn.com
www.marysmercy-center.org

Fr. Donald Calloway, MIC
Marians of the Immaculate Conception
515 Belleview Blvd.
Steubenville, OH 43952
(877) 261-8806
Email: vocations@marian.org
www.fathercalloway.com

Fr. Raniero Cantalamessa, O.F.M. Cap.
www.cantalamessa.org

Fr. Lou Cerulli
Email: frlou@frlou.com
www.fatherlou.com

Fr. Harold Cohen, S.J. †
c/o Magnificat Central Office
Email: magnificatcst@aol.com
www.magnificat-ministry.org

Archbishop Salvatore Cordileone
Archdiocese of San Francisco
One Peter Yorke Way
San Francisco, CA 94109
415-614-5605
www.sfarchdiocese.org

Fr. Patrick Crowley, SS.CC.
Sacred Hearts Community
32481 Sage Rd.
Hemet, CA, 92544
Phone 951-767-9303
Email: crowleysscc@gmail.com

Msgr. Stephen Doktorczyk
Diocese of Orange
13280 Chapman Avenue
Garden Grove, CA 92840
Phone: 714.282.3080
Email: sdoktorczyk@rcbo.org

Fr. John Hampsch, C.M.F.
Claretian Teaching Ministry
20610 Manhattan Pl #120
Torrance, CA 90501-1863
Phone: (310) 782-6408
www.catholicbooks.net

Bishop Emeritus Sam Jacobs
www.spiritaflame.org.

Deacon Alex Jones †
c/o Joseph Jones, Sr.
Email: visionsconsultants1914@gmail.com

Fr. George Montague, S.M.
Phone: 210-667-6751
Email: montague@stmarytx.edu

Fr. Sy Nguyen
Email: syn@smdpyl.org

Fr. Kevin Scallon, C.M.
Email: retreats@intercessionforpriests.org
www.intercessionforpriests.org

Fr. Raymond Skonezny
St. Michael's Abbey
19292 El Toro Road
Silverado, CA 92676
(949) 858-0222
Info about the Norbertines, go to
www.St.MichaelsAbbey.com

Fr. John Struzzo, C.S.C.
Email: jstruzzo@gmail.com

Fr. Bao Thai
Email: padrebao@yahoo.com
www.stcecilia.org

Msgr. David Toups
St. Vincent de Paul Regional Seminary
10701 South Military Trail
Boynton Beach, FL 33436-4899
Phone: 561-732-4424
www.svdp.edu

PROCLAIMS

HOLY ORDERS
A Collection of Inspiring Clergy Testimonies

For ordering information, visit our website at
www.magnificat-ministry.org.

OTHER PUBLICATIONS BY MAGNIFICAT CENTRAL SERVICE TEAM

Magnificat Proclaims

Our first book in the Magnificat Proclaims series is a collection of nineteen powerful and inspiring testimonies given at Magnificat Meals around the world. The contributing authors are Annette Baber, Diane Bates, Kathleen Beckman, Johnnette Benkovic, Babsie Bleasdell, Dorinda Bordlee, Kitty Cleveland, Sharon Lee Giganti, Marilyn Heap, Elizabeth Kim, Kathy MacInnis, Sr. Briege Mckenna, O.S.C., Patti Mansfield, Rosalind Moss, Marilyn Quirk, Elyse O'Kane, Carol Razza, Jan Tate, and Maria Vadia.

Woman, Called By Name—For Such A Time As This

This Bible study consists of a facilitator and participant workbook and has received the Nihil Obstat and Imprimatur. The facilitator workbook includes twenty lessons (ten Old Testament women and ten New Testament women) with questions and answers, seven CDs with the twenty audio teachings, and one Music CD with songs and printed lyrics to complement each lesson. The participant workbook includes the same twenty lessons (ten Old Testament Women and ten New Testament Women) with questions for reflection and printed song lyrics to complement each lesson. The ten Old Testament lessons feature: the Creation of Woman, Sarah, Rebekah, Rachel and Leah, Deborah and Jael, Hannah, Judith and The Worthy Wife. The ten women featured in the New Testament are Elizabeth, The Samaritan Woman, The Woman Caught in Adultery, Mary Magdalene, Martha and Mary, Mary of Bethany, Herodias and Her Daughter, Women Touched by Jesus, Salome, Mother of James and John, and Mary, Mother of Jesus.

Woman, Called By Name

This journal opens wide the door to personal prayer through Scripture-based meditations of women in the Bible from both the Old and New Testaments.

Journey with Mary

This journal opens wide the door to personal prayer through Scripture-based meditations that help us to contemplate the life of our Blessed Mother, who is the role model for all Christians.

A Guide to Presenting Life in the Spirit for Youth

One of the greatest things a parent (or grandparent) can give a child is the gift of the knowledge of God's love and the power and anointing of the Holy Spirit. This booklet is a simple guide on how to conduct a Life in the Spirit (LIS) for Youth. It is designed to take place in a home setting, in small groups with the parents as teachers. The lessons are designed for youth (with some minor adjustments for age differences) from ages four through sixteen. They are offered in one to four sessions depending on the time available and the attention and maturity level of the participants.

For more information or to order, visit our website at magnificat-ministry.org.

Notes